D1000863

THE MAGICAL PINE RING

Grateful acknowledgment is made to the
A.G.B.U. Alex Manoogian Cultural Fund
for financial assistance in the publication of this book.

Margaret Bedrosian

WAYNE STATE UNIVERSITY PRESS DETROIT

Manufactured in the
United States of America.
95 94 93 92 91 5 4 3 2 1

LIBRARY OF CONGRESS
CATALOGING-IN-
PUBLICATION DATA

Bedrosian, Margaret.
The magical pine ring : culture and the imagination in Armenian-American literature / Margaret Bedrosian.
p. cm.
Includes bibliographical references and index.
ISBN 0-8143-2339-1 (alk. paper)
1. American literature—Armenian American authors—History and criticism. 2. Armenian Americans—Intellectual life. 3. Armenian Americans in literature. 4. Armenia in literature. I. Title.
PS153.A75B43 1991
810.9'891992—dc20 91-17264
CIP

Design by Selma Tenenbaum

◆

"The Two Worlds of William Saroyan" appeared in somewhat different form as "William Saroyan and the Family Matter" in *Melus* 9, no. 4(1982); 13–24.

"Arshile Gorky: The Implications of Culture" appeared in somewhat different form as "Gorky's Letters and the Armenian Ethos" in *Journal of the Society for Armenian Studies,* no. 3 (1987): 147–57.

"Reweaving the Rug: Symmetry and Rebirth in the Poetry of Peter Balakian" appeared in *Ararat,* no. 122 (Spring 1990), pp. 26–32.

Selections from "Dear Mrs. McKinney of the Sixth Grade," "S.G.," "Jack Taktakian," and "Melkon" are reprinted by permission from *I Remember Root River* by David Kherdian. Copyright © 1978 by David Kherdian. Published by the Overlook Press, Lewis Hollow Road, Woodstock, New York 12498.

Selections from "In the Tradition" and "From the Window" are reprinted by permission from *Any Day of Your Life* by David Kherdian. Copyright © 1975 by David Kherdian. Published by the Overlook Press, Lewis Hollow Road, Woodstock, New York 12498.

Selections from *Wine for the Living* by Richard Hagopian are reprinted with permission of Charles Scribner's Sons, an imprint of Macmillan Publishing Company. Copyright © 1956 Richard Hagopian; copyright renewed.

CONTENTS

INTRODUCTION

> I dream of it always and it is as if some ancient Armenian spirit within me moves my hand to create so far from our homeland the shapes of nature we loved in the gardens, wheatfields and orchards of our Adoian family in Khorkom. Our beautiful Armenia which we lost and which I will repossess in my art.[1]

Exiled from their homeland like the Armenian-American artist Arshile Gorky, captive to images of massacre and loss in the American dynamo, transplanted Armenians of the earlier twentieth century held memories of the Old Country to their hearts like talismans. They clutched at sanity and selfhood by telling their children the same stories that had been passed on to them, adding to this wealth accounts of their youth in the *yergir* (Old Country) and their escape from the Turkish inferno. Inflected with Old World dialects that would mold the accents of American-born children, only to disappear after this brief rebirth, these tales were packed with the earthy particulars of geography, agriculture, and domestic life. Even the slightest anecdote was nubbed with detail, planting seeds in the child's imagination that might one day sprout with hybrid meanings. Thus my father sowed my fantasy life early on with sprays of offhand genealogy such as this:

> My mother's maiden name was Ajemian—"of Ajem"—which meant that her family traced itself to the Achaemid dynasty in

> Persia thousands of years ago. My father's family could trace its history back four hundred years, when we first came to this village. Before that we had lived in Dersum, a Kurdish stronghold ringed by mountains.[2]

I was off and running; these simple words unlocked a world as enticing as an Arabian night's tale, archaic and sensual like a Babylonian garden, charged with mystery like a Zoroastrian fire. It did not matter that I would never see this realm as my family and our friends had; distance in time and space only sharpened its mystique, imbuing it with the lure of a lost Brigadoon. Each story cast the mountains and ravines, the springs and rocks of the Armenian terrain in high relief, and over time I would sound like a typical diasporan, adept at flourishing textbook facts like a magician's scarves; each wave loosened folds of details about historical Armenia, a name once spread across eastern Anatolia and the southern Caucasus. Succeeding waves freed images of fortresses and monasteries jutting out of the rocks, abandoned pagan temples and huge earthen mounds leeching artifacts as old as human inhabitation, rich deposits of ores that had sparked advances in metallurgy before the Armenians arrived, and early irrigation canals that still flowed with water. My name dropping reached a climax as I listed sophisticated Near Eastern civilizations—Hittite, Median, Assyrian, Urardian—that had once lived in the same neighborhood. The roll call ended with a smug Armenian smile: only we had survived to count the names. With time, though, these facts would take on a personal point that burst through the blithe recitative; the obsidian of this fire-worn turf would push through my psyche with less charm and more urgency, each shard a reminder of a legacy that lived not only in Pa's stories but in the dilemmas of my everyday life, on the other side of the world.

In an article called "The Stories We Live By," Sam Keen offers a definition of myth that speaks insightfully to anyone trying to unravel the knots of a cultural inheritance:

> "Myth" refers to interlocking stories, rituals, rites, customs and beliefs that give a pivotal sense of meaning and direction to a person, a family, a community or a culture. The dominant myth that informs a person or a culture is like the "information" contained in the DNA of a cell, or the program in the systems disk of a computer. Myth is the cultural DNA, the software, the unconscious information, the program that governs the way we see "reality" and behave.[3]

For about three millennia, Armenians have told themselves and the rest of the world stories about who they are. Like every other culture, they have sifted through the vicissitudes they have suffered and settled on the beliefs and images that best reflect their feelings of destiny and uniqueness as a people. As with the individual, the history of the Armenians has been determined by their myth, the grand story that works as curse and prophecy, nightmare and vision. "Armenologists," specialists who sort through the facts, mining deep into the minutiae of the past and painstakingly piecing together historical "actualities," may well wince at the persistence of the myth; similarly, those eager to get on with the present may start sneezing at the incense swirling through timeworn litanies. But these "interlocking" stories and beliefs have held the Armenians "in place"—some might add "locked in granite"—for a long, long time. Only by remembering the story, conscious of the wavering, deceptive line that divides truth from fiction, is it possible to revise it so that it reflects the reality of who they are in the present. What follows are some of the highlights of this story, which Armenians in America and elsewhere have used as a conserving charm.

I begin with the most basic of all Armenian images, the rock. The most famous rock in historical Armenia is Mt. Ararat, a once active volcano that used to spew curses at the barren earth, fertilizing the rugged land with her molten caress. Rising seventeen thousand feet out of the Araxes Valley in the Armenian Plateau, this mountain speaks in paradoxes: it does not move, yet mobilizes the deepest yearnings of the Armenians. Now temptingly close to the Soviet Armenian frontier, but under Turkish domain, her dreamy profile teases those in exile from her. As one contemporary Armenian poet writes, "I curse my own immobility. / Is it for nothing / this is Ararat, I am an Armenian / and we are apart."[4] But though Ararat is the preeminent rock in the Armenian myth, its symbolic power reaches through its numberless progeny, as suggested in the popular saying *Hayastan, Karastan* (land of Armenians, land of rocks). The intimate relationship between the two is elaborated by poets according to their need; one writes,

> Our rocks
> the fossilized fury
> the fossilized sigh
> the fossilized roar
> of the Armenian world.[5]

This voice of pent-up rage, sadness, and raw power echoes frequently in the myth; if there was little room to grow politically and little hope of sympathy from the outside, Armenia would meet a hardened world with an even harder resolve:

> Yes, we are small
> the smallest pebble
> in a field of stones.
> But have you felt the hurtle
> of pebbles pitched
> from a mountain top?
> Small, yes,
> you have compressed us world,
> into a diamond.[6]

Compressed, fossilized, yet radiant with the primal energy of the will, the Armenian world mates geography to psyche. Inhabited for at least 750,000 years, the land of Armenia bears traces of successive archeological periods—Paleolithic, Neolithic, and Bronze Age. Basic to the growth of many cultures, the interplay of water and stone has been especially stark here. Though it is one of the earliest homes of the vine and cereal grains, the "crop" most cherished is inedible. Enriched by volcanic floods immemorial, her subsoils are stashed with a cornucopia of metal ores and high grade stones—copper, zinc, marble, gold, tufa, arsenic.

Armenia's early inhabitants were as resourceful as her turf. Pioneers in metallurgy, they are credited by some researchers as the first producers of bronze, an alloy harder and stronger than copper. Center to a sophisticated civilization in the third millennium B.C., with an influence that spread as far south as Palestine and north to the Caucasian plain, the Early Bronze Age culture was equal in stature to her contemporaries in Iran and Mesopotamia. As the Sumerians were well aware, it was from the lands of Ararat that the Tigris and Euphrates made their civilizing descent.[7]

As suggested by megaliths scattered throughout the country, water culture was prized before the people ethnically related to the present-day Armenians arrived. Because they appear in hills close to the sources of lakes or streams, these fish- and dragon-shaped stones denote ancient water cults. Some of them, hallowed out to conduct water through channels, were probably part of a highly developed irrigation system. Not surprisingly, the next group of inhabitants, the Urartians, excelled in large public works, particularly those associated with water and agriculture. These gifted people, who evolved from the consolidation of minor kingdoms and emerged as a distinct ethnic group about the nineteenth century B.C., had to guard against Assyrian encroachment. Nevertheless, inscriptions attest that the Urartians engineered the development of the Araxes valley, constructing channels to draw water from the river, planting gardens, vineyards, and fields on the irrigated land.[8] One such inscription, by King Rusa (about 700 B.C.) is representative:

> Rusa, son of Argishti, says: "In the valley of the land of Kuturlini the soil had never been worked. Then on command of Haldi [supreme deity of the Urartians] I planted this vineyard, and laid out sown fields all round, encircling the cities with them. I led a water channel from the River Ildaruni: its name is Umeshini."[9]

After twenty-six hundred years this water channel, a titanic *vishap* (dragon) gouged out of the heart of andesite and basalt rock, still carries water—a tribute to the creative will of a culture that wed beauty and function long ago in "antiquity's high fashion."

Veined with hidden ores and waterways that spawned a rich agriculture, this land was reputed home to the Garden of Eden, a speculation essential to the Armenian myth. But just as the location of the lost paradise remains vague, so too the origins of the people who inherited it. Perhaps it is just as well: too literal an image of our sources may rob them of generative power, an axiom that Japhet, son of Noah and great grandsire of the legendary Hayk, respected by averting his eyes from Noah's nakedness. Progenitor Hayk was a more venturesome rebel: after revolting against the Babylonian titan Bel, he advanced northward to Ararat with his family. Here he finally defeated the pursuing Bel with an expertly shot arrow and went on to propagate the Armenian people.[10]

A more factual account traces the entry of the Armenians from Europe into Asia Minor to the eighth century B.C. Like other Aryan tribes, the Armens were feisty enough to dominate the superior Urartian culture. They settled in the region of Mt. Ararat, and by 400 B.C., when Xenophon marched through this country with Cyrus's Ten Thousand, a large area of the western Tigris was Armenian. Xenophon reports that the territory was "rich and large" and that the horses (many of them offered as tributes to the Persians) were smaller than those of the Persians, "but much more spirited."[11]

Through the ages many other nations would demand tribute from them; yet in surrendering their spirited booty, the Armenians did not lose their fire. Led by the lava flows that seeped into underground pockets, clotting into secret ores and gems, the Armenians also found a private space to forge what they cherished as an impermeable identity. Overseeing this alchemy were the elemental powers that ruled pre-Christian Armenia. Though much of Armenian history is wed to Christianity, the power of these older deities has bubbled up when other resources have run dry. The pre-Christian Armenians worshiped nature deities sacred to other contemporary cultures as well, especially those of Persia. Of these, Vahakn the fire-clad god of war, and Anahid, the earth mother, were among the most popular. Even with the advent of the New Word, they lived in the Armenian unconscious, reminding revolutionaries of the late nineteenth and early twentieth centuries to stop turning the other cheek and strike out with all they had.

The advent of Christianity was a revolutionary movement in its own right, one of the most melodramatic components of the Armenian myth. According to legend, the apostles Thaddeus and Bartholemew were the first to bring the Good News into the pagan country. After two centuries of slowly gaining adherents, the religion transformed the nation's future through an iron-willed evangelist, Grigor Partev (Gregory the Parthian). According to tradition, a fantastic episode involving the missionary Gregory and the pagan king, Trdat III, triggered the conversion. For refusing to participate in thanksgiving celebrations at Anahid's temple upon Trdat's assumption of the crown, Gregory was thrown into a dungeon for thirteen years. During this period, as if by divine hand, the king was struck by "a loathsome disease" that changed his features into those of a pig. Meanwhile, the king's sister had a vision directing her to Gregory's healing powers. Finally yielding to these powers, Trdat was healed; in 301, "touched by gratitude and the unshakable faith of the preacher," Trdat and his court adopted the new religion, making Armenia the first Christian nation.[12] The ironic cost of this "first" was Trdat's zealous persecution of those who refused to convert to a faith that had so recently repelled him and a continuing split in political loyalties among the princes.

Nevertheless, with Gregory averting the nation's gaze from pagan fires, committing its future to the newly risen Son, all that was needed to constellate the national myth was a resounding victory over the forces of darkness. If Avarayr had not happened of itself, the Armenians would have had to write it into the historical script. To the extent that Yeghishé, the historian of Avarayr, shaped his account to reflect the boons of Christian martyrdom, the battle was the Armenians' symbolic escape from constrictions of size and history.[13] As dispersed Armenians are reminded every February when the hero Vartan's death is observed, this event etched the Armenians' national will into history and set a standard of transcending rebellion that Armenians would cling to for the next fifteen hundred years. It matters little that some Armenians view Vartan's leadership as inept, as a willful sacrifice of life. It is Vartan's "faith," not his military aptitude, that sanctifies him.

As recounted by Yeghishé, the story surrounding Avarayr draws the eye with lustrous, soul-stirring dualities. In the middle of the fifth century, threatened by their embrace of Christianity and fearing it would strengthen their ties with the Greeks, the Persian monarch Yazdegert II began to persecute the Armenians. The most damning ultimatum was that the Armenians revert to Zoroastrianism with its practices of incest and polygamy. The demand repulsed a country that had refined itself morally and aesthetically through Christianity. In 449 Armenian nobles and clergy met and drafted a careful, adamant reply to the Persians: before conversion they would "die for the love of Christ."[14] Like avenging angels, the common people enforced this reply. Led by the fiery priest Ghevond, their clubs and slings put the trespassing Persians to rout and forced the chief magi of the Persians to ask: "Who can withstand men like these, who are neither afraid of chains, nor frightened by tortures, nor allured by wealth?"[15]

Though Vartan's early guerrilla defense of the country was heartening, division among the Armenian princes and no access to Greek aid led to a crisis in 451. In the focal battle that took place on the broad plain of Avarayr, a Persian army of 300,000 (40,000 of them pro-Persian Armenians), complete with trained elephants carrying iron towers filled with bowmen, met 66,000 Armenians. Yeghishé's account dramatizes the dark pageantry on the eve of battle. Vartan read of the resistance of the Maccabees and extolled martyrdom, and Ghevond gave mass baptism and communion to the troops.[16] But on the next day, the battle was lost, Vartan killed, and the troops fled to high mountain strongholds. Nevertheless, Vartan's death knit the nation so closely that even as the Persian columns penetrated the country, the people were entering an exalted self-exile in the remote mountains. The following passage from Yeghishé idealizes the spiritual self-sufficiency that echoes through so much Armenian history:

> Without murmuring, they lived upon herbs and forgot their accustomed meats. The caves they considered as the apartments of their lofy dwellings, and subterranean abodes were as frescoed halls. The songs they sang were psalms, and they read the Scriptures with a holy joy. Each was to himself a church, each a priest;

> their bodies served them for the sacred altars, and their souls were the offering.[17]

Through continued resistance to their presence, the Persians eventually left. At the cost of losing most of her youth, learned priests, wealth and commerce, Armenia was allowed her religion. She also gained a lasting emblem: land, people, and belief had united to defend spiritual autonomy and a self-image that rose above circumstance by "re-defining victory." As a grand legend, Avarayr shines through the cynicism of a more secular age with a light that "cannot be broken down, put out, or consumed." And yet in the end, as with any cultural myth, its shadow side would emerge, forcing some to ask: for a small, strategically vulnerable people, when does conviction lead to self-annihilation?

If the cross defended in the battle of Avarayr brought the national will into focus, one of its variants, the *khatchk'ar* (literally "cross stone"; sometimes used as a tombstone), provides an apt symbol of Armenian history in general. Its lacy, infinitely varied designs—both geometric and floral—entwine the cross, each line cut with such precision that the stark white of the surface is a brilliant foil to the shadowy grooves. The patient admirer can follow each thread as it interlaces its way, symmetrically and deliberately, from one end of the design to the other. These lovely stones epitomize not only the embrace of rock by lacework, but the tension of the cross itself—a form torn by extremes that give it integrity, an emblem of aspiration as well as suffering.

In a sense, Armenian history—particularly post-Christian—is the temporal counterpart of the cross stone, the story of a culture crossed and double-crossed because of her Christianity and her idealistic expectations of other Christian powers; of a people sometimes broken by willfulness, yet host to a pliant spirit that seizes the inventive moment; of a country crisscrossed by the cultures of the East and West, each imprinting the past with its intricate passage. Despite their tenacious self-image, Armenian forays into politics have often proved disastrous. In earlier times, the divisiveness of her feudal princes aggravated the betrayals of geography. Diverse in origin, opposed in interest, the aristocracy fragmented national unity as early as the time when the Armens encroached on Urartu.

A list of powers who have coveted, fought for, invaded, and despoiled the country reads like a who's who of world civilizations for the last three millennia. During the Urartian period, Assyria and Babylon were main rivals of the kingdom. Though the Urartians weathered these threats, the following inscription from an Assyrian campaign into Urartu in the middle of the ninth century B.C. prefigures later history:

> Aramu the Urartean [*sic*], being struck with fear by the terror of my mighty army and my mighty battle, withdrew from his city and went up into the mountains of Adduri. Then I went up after him and fought a mighty battle in the mountains. With my arms I overthrew 3,400 warriors; like Adad, I brought a great rain-cloud upon them, with the blood of the enemy I dyed the mountain as if it had been wool.[18]

In succeeding centuries, there would be few periods clear of such "rain-clouds." Though the Armenians maintained a precarious national independence till 642 and the Arab invasions, even extending their territories under the kingship of Tigran II in the first century B.C., geography involved them in power squabbles between Romans and Persians, and later Arabs and Byzantine Greeks. Periods of peace, such as during the ninth century when Ashod Bagratuni ruled with the blessing of the caliphate, the Armenian nobility, and the Catholicos, were rare respites that showed how quickly the country could blossom given the chance. But by the eleventh century, a new cycle of invasion began, when Turkish hordes from the east entered Armenian history and the national myth. In 1064, the depravities of Alp-Arslan and his horde hurled the Armenians into another cycle of ruin. Climbing over the undefended walls of Ani, the city known for the "thousand and one" churches built under Bagratuni, they cast a shadow over the land that would remain for centuries. As described by the contemporary historian Aristakes of Lastivert:

> Men were slaughtered in the streets, women carried away, infants crushed on the pavements; the comely faces of the young were disfigured, virgins were violated in public, young boys murdered before the eyes of the aged, whose venerable white hairs became bloody and whose corpses rolled on the earth.[19]

Ani retains the scars of trauma: "arid and barren. The rocks are of rosy, brown and yellow hues; the earth a dull red. The hills seem still to bear the scars of the flames which destroyed the city, and of the volcanic tremors which completed the obliteration."[20]

Invited by the Byzantine Greeks to settle in southeastern Asia Minor, Armenians eventually achieved some independence and managed to develop culturally and economically. Merchants established an enviable commercial network between East and West, and Cilician Armenia became an international trade nexus, collecting customs from Venetian and Genoese merchants. Cilician rulers also supplied aid crucial to the Crusaders, including men, horses, arms, food, and guides into the East. But nearby Moslem princes, Latin Crusader states, and Egyptian Mamluks encroached, and factionalism within the Armenian state weakened from within.

Colophons to fourteenth- and fifteenth-century manuscripts give first-person testimony as to the hardships suffered. Political unrest forced scribes to wander with their writing tools. Sometimes they escaped to foreign lands, where their status as "garib" weighed heavily on their spirits.[21] Though the colophons are usually encased in stylistic conventions and exaggerations—replete with confessions of unworthiness and attempts to parallel Armenian woes with biblical models—they amply record the social chaos that was the norm. The following excerpt from a manuscript copied in 1389 describes the advent of Tamerlane:

> [S]tretching for a distance of eight days, they filled the country with starstudded and red-painted tents, and carefully spun their ropes and masts. And if anyone in impregnable fortresses resisted them, they forthwith came upon them like a multitude of locusts; they surrounded them and squalled, bellowed, howled, lowed, barked, groaned, neighed, roared.[22]

Transformed into a chamber of horrors, the country had little strength to note the demise of the last Armenian dynasty in 1375. Immediately, Armenia fell prey to succeeding Turkish and Persian overlords, who coveted their industry and loyalty. During this period the wavering frontier dividing Eastern from Western Armenia formed. Ripped by religious tussles of the neighboring Islamic powers, deprived of a strong ruling class, Armenia once more collapsed into political limbo. The only significant shift in fortunes came from the "patronage" of the Persian Shah Abbas; in 1605, for strategic reasons, he relocated thousands of Armenians from Eastern Armenia in New Julfa, where they came to monopolize the silk trade and were treated with relative tolerance by the Persians. After yet another century of unrest and bloodshed in their native land, with many Armenians looking toward Russia for moral and material support, the eighteenth century closed with surges of Armenian nationalism spurring talk of a transcaucasian alliance with Georgia. Though the proposal never materialized, these rumblings hinted of earthquakes to come.[23]

Amid a chronology chaotic with "bellows, howls, and groans," the image of Cilician Armenia refreshes with its luminous art and full-blown commerce. Defying the odds, it forged East and West during the Middle Ages and briefly turned Armenia's cross into a flowering tree. But the bulk of Armenian history up to the pivotal nineteenth century bears a more lifeless load. Skimming the catalog of convulsions, one returns to the image of the cross and a question central to the Armenian myth as I see it: hosting the crossings and political crises of other nations, perpetually nailed to geographical and social necessities, what role was Armenia allowed in the drama of historical choice? Or more significantly, what choices did she discover she could make while still bearing her cross? A brief overview of her creative evolution suggests that in responding to the latter challenge, she grew beyond the limits of circumstance.

To begin with, the evolution of Armenian letters was as dramatic as the history and myths it would clothe and protect. In the early fourth century, though the church was well organized, its growth was stunted because the Armenians did not have an alphabet. Worship was conducted in Greek and Syriac, tongues alien to most of the people. As a result, proseletyzers had even more difficulty freeing the masses from the grip of the "elemental spirits."

But through the fortuitous collaboration of three men, the New Word also gave birth to Armenian letters. Encouraged by the support of the Catholicos Sahak, Mesrob Mashtots, a scholar and secretary at the Royal Court, submitted his proposal to create an Armenian alphabet to the king, Vramshapouh. With the king's generous backing, Mesrob traveled to neighboring centers of learning to consult with scholars and by 404 had invented an alphabet whose thirty-six letters phonetically reproduced the sounds of spoken Armenian.[24] These letters are as singular and elegant as the Armenian language itself, which is an independent offshoot of Indo-European. Anyone familiar with its rich resources cannot help admiring the simplicity of Mesrob's invention, a system that allows one to learn reading and writing with minimum effort. More than any other factor, this accessibility sparked an immediate cultural awakening.

Armed with the newly minted script, young men traveled abroad to translate the major texts of the Christian church. They returned to Armenia laden with copies of the Gospels, biblical commentaries, homilies, and lives of the saints. In a short time they had not only made much literature available in translation, but had begun a tradition of original Armenian letters.[25] In the golden century that followed, the Armenians created a literature that was Christian in worldview and informed by a classical interest in history.[26] Their translations of Greek texts—many no longer extant—were especially pleasing as works of art, combining accuracy with a sensitivity to the nuances of the original.[27]

The ties between religion and literature were so close that for many centuries most Armenian writers, poets, and historians were monastics. One of the foremost monasteries, Tat'ev, was lauded by the medieval historian Stephen Orbelian for its five hundred priests and monastics, "philosophers, profound as the sea . . . , its college . . . rich in scholars and doctors, skillful painters, incomparable scribes."[28] Even during those grimmer periods of invasion, pillage, and social chaos, education continued as teacher and pupils traveled from place to place.[29] Scribes guarded their manuscripts as dearly as life, hiding them at the worst of times in caves and the crevices of inaccessible mountains.[30] Tender of their future welfare, they enjoined unborn generations to ransom any recovered copies, urged owners to not create obstacles for any who wished to copy them, and advised the utmost care in their handling. Cherished and strengthened by such vigorous intellectual centers, the Armenian language became the most supple of instruments, beloved companion of poets and storytellers. The twentieth century Soviet-Armenian poet Eghishé Charents speaks for many when he evokes the aged, sensuous texture of spoken Armenian in the first two stanzas of a poem whose images replicate the sounds of the language:

> I love the sun-baked taste of Armenian words,
> their lament like ancient lutes, the bend
> of blood-red flowering roses in the accents,
> the lilt of Naiyirian steps still danced by girls.
>
> I love the arch of skies, the faceted waters
> running through its syllables; the mountain
> weather, the meanest hut that bred this tongue.
> I love the thousand-year-old city stones.[31]

Even in translation, these images feed the senses and unite the word with what it signifies. Like a massive rock, the language receives and empowers the meanings that cascade through the millennia. And as the encoder of this faceted language, Mesrob remains one of the great liberators of Armenian history. In "The Glory of Invention," the poet Siamanto, eager to shake the Armenians from their torpor under Ottoman rule during the early part of the twentieth century, pays homage to the far-sighted gift that allowed the Armenians to emerge as a distinct people:

> you, who with vision, invention and ardor,
> freed the Armenian offspring
> from the clever Greeks and
> fire-worshipping Persians.
> And from the world-conquering Romans.
> You kept them intact with the ruby
> cornerstone of your language.[32]

Aloof like a gem afire with its own beauty, the language has been a proud consort to the land and the people. Lit by its flashing cadences, the poet ends by reforging Mesrob's supreme legacy, cultural unity and continuity through the written word. In these lines, Mesrob becomes one with the written language he invented, the proto-poet whose adamant vision would focus and refine the will of a nation:

> Mesrob! you stand an unshatterable
> diamond rock against time,
> against the Armenian centuries.[33]

Through these centuries, the religious and literary would often work in union. The poetry of the monk Nareg (951–1003) is a case in point. Nareg's prayer book (a penitent's lamentations in ninety-five chapters) revitalized Armenian literature by not only probing into the cracks and crevices of sin, but paradoxically drawing on lavish new coinages to express spiritual unworthiness. In time the common folk came to believe Nareg's prayers could heal or guard against evil. For a modern Armenian, though, the prayers only compound the ironies of the recent past, as suggested in the following passage from one:

> We are lost, and not terrified.
> We are forgiven and do not accept it humbly,
> We are buried and do not struggle.
> We are deported and do not panic.
> We are falsified and do not protest.
> We are worn out and do not try to understand.
> We are diminished and do not replenish.
> We walk and do not look where we go.
> We are enslaved and do not feel put upon.[34]

Branded with visions of deportations and massacres to come, a modern Armenian must wonder what solace the common people found in lines that were less metaphor than actual descriptions of social realities faced daily. One wonders if listeners retreated into passivity, expanded into immortality, or heard the call to militant action. "Martyrdom," "endurance," "rebirth": these watchwords of the Armenian myth highlight the boons and the curses of the Christian legacy; they suspend us in a limbo where self-betrayals, meek and mild, grope toward the light. Nareg ultimately teaches that the most desperate plight, human existence, may be lightened through acceptance: "Oh Lord Jesus Christ, God of all . . . your name will always be on the lips of my soul and I live protected like those who call on you from their heart unendingly, Lord."[35]

Two other distinctive features of Armenia's classical culture, her churches and miniatures, flesh out her myth. Like the exquisite Akhtamar church, which Armenian-American artist Arshile Gorky called "that jewel placed in our crown of beauty,"[36] most of these churches would easily fill the larger galleries of modern museums, in marked contrast to the Gothic cathedrals whose evolution they arguably furthered.[37] In harmony with the land and people, these small structures were set like gems into the terrain, and upon entering, one still feels the intimacy of the compact shape warming with light from the outside. Built mainly of stone, both the inner and outer walls are often covered with sculpture, characteristic of the architecture of the classical Near East. Sometimes, as in the church of St. Stephen the Protomartyr, the sculpturing becomes a miniature commentary on the origin of the edifice; here, the Armenian king Gakik is sculpted out of the wall, holding a replica of the church he has sponsored. Other times, like reproductions of oriental carpets, carvings flaunt unquenched pagan energies; tangled with a riot of lions, rams, eagles, bulls, serpents, angels, promegranates and grapes, they celebrate nature before the Fall. So great was the vitality and creativity of the architects that even when the patron princes retreated to the mountains during the Arabic invasions of the eighth and ninth centuries, building continued. Here in this new field, out of the rocks, they constructed more churches and convents to honor the memories of their ancestors, sacred chambers where the Divine Sacrifice brought peace to the exiled and the souls of the departed.[38]

Illuminated manuscripts also brought peace, especially to the souls of the wealthy patrons who commissioned them in the Middle Ages. Like the churches, the most memorable—especially those of the Cilician school of the thirteenth century—were stimulated by contact with other sources, particularly the Byzantines. But reflecting other areas of their cultural growth, the Armenian painters stayed true to their own temperament, attentive to the actual and dramatic in their illustrations of the Gospels.[39] The usual result is that these manuscript illuminations free the Armenian propensity to weave together motifs derived from many sources, with sometimes astonishing results. In one set of miniatures of the sixteenth century, the artist Hakop of Julfa depicts a Christian God whose garments enfold a body in the meditation pose of Buddhism, and whose hand seems to point beyond the Christian heaven toward Nirvana. On the opposite page is the Gate to a Paradise only He can open: in the center of the miniature, over the gate, peers half of a face—the stylized image of a Creator coyly drawing the devotee closer, His huge, close-set eyes concentrated on the center of being. Such hybrids illustrate how much from both the East and West was made accessible to the Armenians from trade routes they helped pioneer.[40]

In other paintings, the artists created an ornamentation even richer that that of the Byzantine illuminators.[41] So great is this love of variety that in some Gospels even the canon tables are made lovingly distinct from one another. Often, as in the Trebizond Gospel, vivid shades of primary colors weave an elaborate design of birds and flowers that arches over the tables—the page crowned by two blue peacocks, symbols of a paradise much older than the Christian. These same tables are flanked by plants whose whimsical forms and energetic colors reassure that the Word was not born to condemn, but to delight.

The artists—especially the accomplished Toros Roslin—also portrayed dramatic events from the Gospels with imagination, focusing on episodes left out of later Gothic art. They often introduced scenes from daily Armenian life, as in the Baltimore Gospel, where the triumphant worship of the magi is signaled by the flying banners of accompanying soldiers, much like Armenian nobility returning home after a successful campaign.[42] Elsewhere, in the Gospel of Adrianople, the Virgin is depicted not as a fair and pretty young maiden, but an earthier, coarser Armenian peasant with cheeks reddened from long days harvesting wheat. Throughout these paintings, the faces and figures are unmistakably Armenian: large dark eyes gazing from under strongly arched brows, defiant noses, sturdy and compact bodies.

One manuscript in particular summarizes the cohesion between Armenian aesthetic, literary, and religious traditions. Rendered by the late-fourteenth-century artist Dzerun, it shows a teacher holding up a tablet—a *bnag*—printed with the Armenian alphabet, presenting the sacred letters to two wide-eyed students whose hands open eagerly to receive the language. Neither cynicism nor skepticism mar the miniature; with clarity and charm, it depicts the transmission of cultural traditions through the written word.

As a group, these painters had early on learned the cost of continuity; to flourish they became adept not only at assimilating but renovating. Even when Seljuk conquests interfered with artistic growth in the tenth century, treasured techniques survived repeated transplantation. As soon as Seljuk power began to weaken, the cycle of recovery resumed. The following factual account from Sirarpie Der Nersessian's discussion of Armenia and the Byzantine Empire reads like a condensed version of the Armenian myth; here, patient renewal was husbanded by artist priests whose persistence was equaled by their devotion:

> The manuscripts of the third quarter of the twelfth century are still somewhat crude, but by the end of the century the painters have recovered the old methods of preparing the parchment, the skill in mixing colors and in laying a gold background. The monks of the monastery of Haghbat played an important role in the new development; also at Horomos, near Ani . . . scribes and painters resumed once again their usual occupation of copying and illustrating the sacred books.[43]

Inspired by the subsoil of their culture, where nature had driven lava flows and pressurized out of fire and rock a kaleidoscope of color and shape, these artists did more than copy and illustrate. Mostly unknown, their lives circumscribed by religious vows and political insecurity, they kept alive the aesthetic traditions, preparing the "golden background" for the advances sure to come. Centuries later, one of their spiritual descendants, Arshile Gorky, described the dynamic effect of Toros Roslin's art on his own, and then lamented the monk's obscure place in the history of art.[44] Yet the discerning detail of Roslin's miniatures suggests that he did not seek self-recognition in fame, but through the singularly curious eye that discovered in the inimitable forms of his land and people the reflections of divinity.

Up to this point, this review has concentrated on the creative dynamics of the Armenian myth. But as Sam Keen outlines it, myth also "creates a geography of good and evil: a realm of heaven and hell."[45] Faced with the questions "Against what must I struggle? Who is my enemy?", the modern Armenian might reply "the Turk" or "world indifference" or perhaps "my inability to be heard, to get through." Such responses reflect the lasting wounds of the nineteenth and early twentieth centuries. The nineteenth century was a dramatically active time for the Armenians of the Ottoman Empire, who lived for the most part in the villages of Eastern Anatolia or in Constantinople. Having retreated for centuries into an exile of the spirit, many not having spoken the Armenian language for generations, they began to stir to a long-forgotten call. The Ottoman government, feeling the need to relax long-held restrictions on its ethnic minorities for pragmatic reasons, allowed just enough rope for the suppressed Armenian spirit to begin tugging at the knots. It was an exhilarating, yet dangerous period. Protestant missionaries from America and Europe began converting a small but important segment of the first Christian people to a "new" breed of Christianity; poets hot for liberation from Turkish rule dug beneath the bones of the Christian martyrs and found the "diamond-hard womb" of the old mother goddess a more enticing draw; Armenian newspapers began a conversation among the people, even in the villages, which united them through a network of information and opinion; and colleges founded by the Protestants in major centers of population and schools built in villages quickly transformed the self-image of the Armenians: language, historical identity, and mythic memory became one in the desire to rebirth.

Though the Armenians would never align politically around one party, some refusing to believe in any political solution to their plight, they would join in their vision of the demonic. To this day, the Turk casts a dense shadow over the Armenian psyche and the collective memory. Coming to terms with how and why is beyond the scope of this study, but as a figure in the story Armenians tell about themselves, the Turk might fill every circle in their *Inferno,* and some not yet charted. Through the centuries their offenses had been uniformly rank; as the Ottoman Empire entered decline and the split between the small Turkish upper class and massive lower class grew, it was the ethnic minorities, especially the Armenians, who did the work of the middle class, with trade, farming, and crafts commonly in their hands. Looking on, the Turkish poor might not always have remembered that many Armenians were as destitute as them. For their part, the Armenians kept to themselves as much as possible; surely many turned Moslem during the centuries, but those who did not only became firmer in their notions of *ask,* peoplehood. As they saw it, their differentness was the only line dividing light from darkness. The price of their individuality would often be paid as massacres and marauding raids on villages, *talans.* In one of the worst, in 1894–96, a massacre begun by the Red Sultan, Abdul Hamid, claimed hundreds of thousands of Armenians. Such interludes freshened the memories of old horrors with blood.

Politically and financially, the Ottoman Turks were not in an enviable position during these decades, but they were adept at pulling the strings of European powers to whom they owed money. In the words of one observer, " 'How not to do it' [was] the perfection of Turkish diplomacy."[46] Nevertheless, they unwittingly mimicked the Armenians in one respect, touting a nationalism that would return them to their roots. Pan-Turkism in the words of its chief ideologue, Zia Gökalp, would "uncover the Turkish culture which has remained in the people" and "graft Western civilization in its entirety and . . . all its living forms on to the national culture."[47] In practice, such Turkification could succeed only if the minorities within the empire were first steeped in a culture they had spent centuries resisting actively and passively. By the first decade of the twentieth century such a hope was laughable. The government shrugged off any second thoughts about reactivating the ways of the Turkish horde. Grafting a deep-seated elitism that for centuries had herded millions—including the Turkish masses—onto a Western rationalism that streamlined logistics, 1915 marked a major crossroads, not only for the Armenians but for the twentieth century. As historian Christopher Walker comments simply,"laid bare was a remorseless and unalloyed desire to kill."[48]

Technique was as streamlined as desire. Under the cover of entering World War I on the side of Germany, the Ottoman government decided to solve the "Armenian question." The genocide began officially on April 24, 1915, when Armenian leaders, intellectuals, and artists were arrested and either imprisoned or killed. Left without leaders who might organize resistance, the Armenians were left open to mass slaughter, as the following description, generic in its rhythmic ordering, shows:

> Then followed the systematic massacres in towns and villages of all young and able-bodied Armenians; the remainder, old people, women and children, were ordered to leave everything behind and march into exile. The columns started out accompanied by soldiers and by wild Kurdish horsemen who, on the way, indulged in brutality hard even to conceive, killing mercilessly and as fancy took them, and selling the women as slaves after bestially violating them. After months of horrible torture the survivors reached the Mesopotamian desert where most of them died from hunger, thirst, and the scorching sun.[49]

Aristakes of Lastikert might have written the account. "Brutality hard even to conceive" cycles through massacre narratives like an ironic recitative, for the Turks had not only conceived, but carried out, by one estimate, the murders of one-third of the Armenians in the Ottoman Empire. In their wake, the dense spray of Armenian villages in the eastern portion of Anatolia dissolved into memory. Many of the survivors ended up in parts of the Middle East, especially Syria, which was on the other side of the deserts the Armenians had been driven across in human "caravans." Others landed wherever chance brought them, each the main player in an odyssey that would never lead back home.

Detailed histories and sociopolitical analyses of the genocide abound. But what is still missing after three-quarters of a century is a full accounting of the psychological damage wrought on the Armenian people. What role did the Armenians' myth, the stories they had told themselves about who they were, play in their responses to near annihilation? In part, this study addresses this question by examining the continuing effect of Armenian history on Armenian-American writing. Yet the comprehensive treatment that this question demands has yet to appear. The most immediate response among many Armenians was a pervasive numbness to the violation. For others, the response was bitterness, heightened paranoia, and sometimes insanity; yet others suppressed their rage and sadness so deep that it could only leak by accident, mostly corroding the spirit unseen. The saving grace for the survivors was the shared will to cherish the fragments; they were bound to one another by a scarring so profound that it knit them into singular new wholes. Each piece kept the image of the lost nation alive; each bore the collective longing for home. The later Soviet-Armenian poet Barouyr Sevag captures the teasing echoes of loss drifting through the generations in his "Analysis of Yearning (Garod)." Wandering through the interiors of the psyche where time has no hold, where time can no longer heal, survivors and their progeny grope for the most intimate details of a past that has no analogue in space and time:

> I know the dark need, the yearning, that want
> in the same way the blind man knows
> the inside of his old home.
>
> I don't see my own movements
> and the objects hide.
> But without an error or stumbling
> I maneuver among them,
> live among them,

move like the self-winding clock
which even after losing its hands
keeps ticking and turning
but shows neither minute nor hour.[50]

Regular as a heartbeat, this "self-winding clock" of memory speaks only in the quiet, aloof from the public howls, the buzz of commentary; it strands us in that endless corridor where the present, weighted by nameless trauma, can no longer move us from past into future.

Yet as Keen points out in the final portion of his essay, one of the most valuable contributions of myth is the glimpse it offers into the future, "of all that remains unfulfilled within ourselves." Myth points toward "a link between memory and hope," or as Gabriel Marcel's koanlike definition sums up, "Hope is a memory of the future."[51] In the depth of their collective imagination, the Armenians have known this truth and encoded it in their great national folk epic, *David of Sassoun.* Of all the art forms and relics stamped Armenian, it most effectively unlocks the Armenian sensibility. Parts of the story go back to biblical times, and like the Armenian terrain, everything associated with the epic is richly veined; much that cannot be simply explained about the Armenian ethos and modern Armenian experience in America and elsewhere is here stowed away as myth. The characters of the epic are earthy, idealistic, pragmatic, rooted in geography, and lifted by their faith. Each is a doorway into the Armenian wing of the collective unconscious and as such can lead dispersed Armenians out of the limbo where the clock has lost its hands, back to their sources. Of these characters, it is young Meherr, the brooding hero, who first helped me grasp the spiritual plight of the modern Armenian. In many ways, Meherr's story is a paradigm of twentieth-century Armenian experience, reaching through the farthest recesses of the Diaspora with the promise of apotheosis.

Meherr's exile to Raven's Rock was a pivotal event in the folk imagination that spawned *David of Sassoun.* For centuries, Armenian bards had memorized and embellished this saga, immortalizing its daredevils and heroines in the hearts of the common folk. In the process, they had arguably done more to help the Armenians maintain a distinct identity in their native land than any other cultural force. Through the centuries, the story seeped into the popular imagination like a warm brandy, bracing the collective psyche with images of boundless courage and resourcefulness. With droll wit and wisdom, it reflected a self-image that history had reinforced for millennia. Steeped in a mystical paganism, this legendary cycle served as an inexhaustible stream of values; like tributaries, its variants strengthened the traditions of isolated villages at the same time that they intensified their national identity. For the peasants who lived in far-off pockets in the mountains, gathering for nightly retellings that ensured a sleep filled with dreams of valor, the epic *was* group tradition, it *was* national identity. During the eons when Armenia might have easily joined the parade of lost races, her dream of selfhood a delusion, when the written word lit the minds of few, the voices of her unknown bards rendered life with zest: against the golden backdrop of their epic memory they cast a future dipped in hope.

Each of the first three cycles of the epic soared on the high spirits of heroes defying limits; their libido, as figured by Colt Jalali, had power and direction. But by the time we arrive at the fourth cycle—young Meherr's—the mood has changed. Crazed by incessant fighting, cursed by his father, wandering the world and lashing out at enemies wherever he finds them, Meherr is tragically absurd. I imagine his head filled with rocks and his heart broken by disillusionment, a hero as solidly—and modernly—Armenian as the rock that shelters him. To him I now turn to find that link between the old myth and the new.

It is said that this huge warrior spends most of his time sitting deep in the interiors of Raven's Rock in the plain of Van, watching the wheel of fortune turn. For countless years he has been exiled here with his magical Colt. As he contemplates the wheel of fortune and dines on providential manna, I wonder what of the past still lives in him; does he feel himself dangling between darkness and loneliness[52] like a poet severed from his roots? Twice a year—on the Festival of Roses and on Ascension Day, two of the great feasts of the Armenians—the rock opens; at this time "Meherr springs out on his horse and rides in an hour a distance of forty days to see if the world has changed and the earth will hold him."[53]

His hour stretches before him, enough time to survey the memories locked in each outcropping. What does he see on this semiannual ritual? Does Colt Jalali speed by Mt. Ararat, hazy in the distance, a volcanic furnace now cooled of its fury? Does he spring over the Armenian highlands were ancient inhabitants once planted serpent-and fish-shaped *vishaps* (dragons) close to the sources of lakes and streams to channel water? If so, the megaliths must murmur to both Meherr and his steed of Sassoun, the native turf where they return out of lonely habit. Here Meherr's forebears founded a city for free men, a refuge for the poor, a storyteller's paradise in a landscape overpowered by mountains, undercut by gorges and ravines, alive with wild sheep and goats, stags, boars, eagles, and hawks circling overhead. At the mouth of a preordained stream that gushed out of the rocks, they made their claim. Meherr's brief return opens old wounds; everywhere he lights, he hears voices. There in the distance he sees the old woman Barav's millet field where she once chastised his father, David, for eating her turnips and letting the heathen abduct her lame daughter; the field still echoes with her timeless lament: "I cut the food from my own mouth to bring her up as a decent Christian girl and this is what happens, all because of you, you fool!" (150). And all because of you, you fool.

Meherr does not know whether to laugh or cry. These echoes always jumble his wits; they remind him of what a race of fools he had been born into—heroes like his father who took the cows to pasture, let them stray during his nap, and returned with all the wild animals of the forest! David, the Armenians' great hope against the heathen. And yet for a while, these antics had miraculously worked to their advantage; the Armenians had used all they had and it had been enough. Spurred by his own memories, Jalali leaves the field and quickly lifts Meherr to the top of the fortress where his ancestors once set a little gemlike church with a cross stone beside it: Marouta's High Mother of God. The church still stands, battered and worn, yet beautiful in the diminutive. Once a mystical green-red light burned in the form of a cross on a mountaintop; it guided Meherr's father, David, to rebuild this church after the great heathen, Misra Melik, had destroyed it. Inspired by his charge, David rebuilt the church in seven days—but only to see it fall prey to the cyclic chaos: the Arabs struck, "massacred all the monks, stripped the monastery bare and took everything they could lay their hands on" (155–156). Many times Meherr had heard the story told, of how his father then went to the ruddy-skinned Barav, who taught him the secrets of the land; she sent him to "the big rock in the narrow Twin-Ravines near the Batman river" (160). Here, David and Uncle Ohan ambushed and annihilated the Arabs. They returned to Sassoun, buried the slain monks, cleaned and repaired the monastery, brought in forty new *vardapets* (priests), forty archdeacons, forty deacons, and set Batman's Sword and the Demon of Frankistan to guard the gate again (161).

The church had always trapped the daredevils in absurdities such as this—it was hard to know where destruction ended and creation began; the Armenians only knew that one begot the other. Here, in this pitiless terrain, surrounded by heathen impieties, open to attack from east and west, fate had turned the Armenians Christian. It was exhausting. Language, literature, art, architecture—each carrier of culture was stamped with a greenish-red cross that branded the dark and held the daredevils in its grip. In times of massacre, it would signal retreat into the recesses, commanding them "store up your strength"; then, when the danger was past, it would flash without mercy: Recoup. Rebuild. Regenerate. Artists and priests, peasants and warriors, crippled women and crazed men, for centuries all had followed the unrepentant light.

And to what end? The question irritates Meherr, time enough to ponder this inside the rock. The minutes outside never stop for an answer and spur the Colt Jalali onward. Today is the Festival of Roses, a day of miracles that even permeate the rock. The fragrance of the ancient ritual is calming. Long before the apostles Thaddeus and Bartholomew brought the Good News to Armenia, before King Trdat and Gregory the Illuminator thrashed out the drama of conversion, long before the elegant cross stones bore witness to the new Word across the countryside and Vartan defended the faith against the Persians, the Festival of Roses had graced early June. Unaware that they were barred from the Kingdom of God, the common folk took their joy in the elemental powers that ruled nature—Anahid, who received the holy heifers pastured on the Euphrates and whose adamantine womb supported women in the rites of the *hieros gamos* (the sacred marriage); Tir, who invoked the rains and presided over oracles and dreams; Vahakn, of the fiery hair, flaming beard, and solar eyes, who routed the monstrous *vishaps* (dragons) at the foot of Mount Ararat, beloved of Astghik, goddess of love and beauty. Their sacraments were to the earth, to the waters and sun, to the mysteries of matter spiraling through the seasons. On the day of Astghik's Festival, *Vartavar,* men and women, young and old, gathered around the milk-fountains and springs, sprinkling rose water on one another and flying the sacred doves. The perfume of the roses filled the village, anointing the air itself, rising with the doves for the pleasure of the goddess of love. She blessed them with a shower of miracles; visions of laden vineyards and nights of dreamless sleep descended as white doves lit on the red roses.

Meherr sighs. Had it ever been this simple for his people? Or were thoughts of long ago always scented and buoyant?

His hour is up. He has traveled forty days' distance, and the world has not changed since the last time he came this way. Jalali feels the earth pulling at his hooves and with a painful neigh reverses direction for the homeward trek. As they approach the rock, Meherr notices that the walnut tree guarding the entrance swells with a new crop; its branches reach out and breathe to currents from every direction. Time has only been suspended inside the rock. Meanwhile it is comforting to come back; only Jalali had known the relief Meherr had felt when his father and mother spoke from their graves, trying to calm their orphaned child as he gazed at the shattered life around him. Powerless to help him find rest, his mother had advised:

> Stop roaming around, your journey's at end
> You are immortal, deathless on this earth
> There is no freedom from all your torment
> Save in Raven's Rock. Go to Raven's Rock
> That's the door to knock.(274)

Condemned to eternal awareness, Meherr had only entered the refuge after bitter testing. Seven mounted angels had tortured him, leaving him in despair. The ground had crumbled under Jalali's legs until it reached his knees. Finally, when it seemed as if the earth itself were closing in, the talking raven had flown above the plain of Van—a proud, fiery bird that wooed Meherr's arrow with slow mesmerizing circles over the lake. This wounded bird led Meherr to the rock, massive and aloof to entry. Yet Meherr recognized it at once, the promised sanctuary where he and his beloved horse would pause, go deep inside, and catch up with their destiny. Sobbing, Meherr had vowed, "If I can split this rock open, I am not guilty. If I cannot, I am guilty" (276). He swung his mace and the rock split wide open. As Jalali pranced in, the ground held firm.

Now reentering after his semiannual quest, Meherr once more relaxes into the spacious interiors, the nooks where spectacular ghostlike shapes whisper of grains of barley that will grow to the size of hazelnuts, of an earth able to bear the tread of superhuman heroes. Time and space are suspended in crystalline niches, and the silence is outlined by a black stream; it is Jalali's urine dripping through a crack, the only sign that anyone is inside. Looking about him once again, Meherr smiles. Without question, it is an Armenian rock, layered and veined with copper and zinc, gold, marble, tufa, metals aglint by their own light. Life inside is simple; duties and customs are suspended and nothing interrupts his meditation at the small church and monastery he has carved out for his devotions. But it is hard to say whether Meherr's faith matches that of his ancestors; after all, his needs are few, and his search for vindication ended when he first tasted the manna. Yet as he watches the wheel of fortune turn, following its slow kaleidoscopic swings, his heart still flares with old wounds. Ever since he entered, he has followed the fate of the world as it rose and fell on the wheel; constantly he has traced the fortunes of those he left behind, eager to know of their journey after his retreat.

For a while there were images of what appeared a new breed of daredevils, poets and revolutionaries who wept at the sight of soil red with wounds, soil that precipitated cries and roars, and sometimes armed first with soul.[54] Meherr the heirless one watched as they threw aside the Cross and invoked the older deities, intent on fertilizing the diamond-hard womb of Armenia so that a savior might be born. He watched in bemusement as newspapers, schools, and new Christian sects called Protestant prodded the sleepy villages awake. So much change so soon, each one raising the wheel, as if the Armenians were on the verge of rebirth right there in the heart of the Ottoman Empire! In his daydreams, Meherr even fantasized that he might be able to leave the rock with such vitality sweeping the countryside. Watching his countrymen tasting the apricots of May and drinking from the springs with hopes of freedom sprouting in the fields, he could feel the pull of future reunion. Finally, a moment came when the wheel reached its zenith; the arms and hands of old antagonists clasped and the images of new Ottoman rulers flickered on the inner walls of the rock; a new dispensation where all races would live and share rule as brothers was promised. Faintly, Meherr remembered that his father's stepmother, Ismil Khatoun, had once said, "Arabs and Armenians can be brothers" (164). Would she have said the same about Turks and Armenians?

But no sooner were the last vows spoken than the wheel teetered downward. Quickly, chaotically the images on the walls of the rock lost focus. At first Meherr could not follow it all, it happened so fast. Was he projecting the twisted shapes of a private nightmare, or were there really rocks inside his head? Or was he watching a fast replay of Armenian history with no break, no pause for water or prayer? As he felt his insides plummet with the wheel, he remembered how much in another life outside the rock he had loved to fight as earth yielded to air. Like Jalali, his spirit had been elastic and sprang to each challenge with no thought of death. Likewise, Armenians only went through cycles, outliving defeat in the crevices of the land. The axiom had been the rock bottom on which he rested—until his father cursed him. David had dreaded the power of his son; his seed would devour the world (250). And so David had caught the ear of God and the angel Gabriel drew the manly vein from Meherr's loins. It would be David's last act of will before the victory cross on his arm grew black. Now as his son watched the sun come out at midnight in a nightgown and Turkish fez,[55] he knew the land had cursed the Armenians. Whole villages were emptied across the eastern interiors; water jug and loom abandoned; lessons half finished; church bells silenced. The apricots left on the trees would not be picked by the Armenians.

Human caravans left their villages for the last time under a severe light. Caravans from different regions joined, streams that dried up in Deir-er-Zor in the deserts of northern Syria. The Euphrates, once the watering place of Anahid's heifers, was dammed and red with human sacrifice—to what deity, it was uncertain. Once Meherr noticed a burning bush—could it be that God had come to lead his kinsmen out of this inferno? But as the image came into focus, he closed his eyes; these bushes were aflame with the limbs of babies. Enough. He went to his altar, lit a candle, and stuck it in the tray of sand. He knelt until he could feel the firm coolness of the rock against his forehead. For infants burned and dismembered by daylight, he said a prayer. For children orphaned for all time, he said a prayer. For women, daughters of Barav and sisters of her lame daughter, violated under the summer sun, he said a prayer. For men, young and in their prime, whose backs had once shouldered sheaves of autumn wheat, now heaped in the nearest ravines, he said a prayer. For the old, blinded as their children melted into oblivion, he said a prayer. For all who would die crazed in far-off lands, unable to speak their grief, he said many many prayers. At his altar, the caravan of lament moved him from sadness into puzzlement. Was this what he had been sent here to witness? Suspended in time, removed from the scene like an unneeded prop, what was his role in all this? His mother had promised him freedom from torment inside the rock, but even here he could feel the earth growing more evil; even magical Jalali would trip if he tried to romp where ghosts wandered in thirst. And yet, how much he would have liked to reach through the walls of Raven's Rock and greet these kinsmen, to let them know that he, Meherr the deathless and heirless exile, had felt the sun's betrayal in his shadowed cell.

Meherr groped backward to another time, when his ancestors had founded Sassoun as a refuge for the poor and tyrannized. Of all the pleasures Sanasar and Balthasar, founding *pahlevans* (champions) of the blessed names, had looked forward to, it was the nights they loved the best. There in the well-protected town, they would join their neighbors, talk and tell stories, and never feel lonely (52). Stories carried them back to the beginnings, they were like streams that split rocks into two; stories made them alert and wise, they seeded the future and redeemed the past. They washed the heart clean, soothed frazzled nerves, and unlocked stores of courage hidden from the common hours. No true daredevil could thrive without them. Now at his vigil, Meherr still wondered: would he really outlast his people? Or had his exile been the beginning of theirs? If so, what meaning could there be in this fate? With whom would he share stories when he left the rock?

The questions led him to the confusions of his first days in this cool vault when he had paced in time to his destiny—deathless, heirless. What was the point? To mark every catastrophe that befell his people on the wheel of fortune? To listen to Jalali whimpering for lack of exercise? Deathless, heirless—a riddle for his mind to chew on as he digested the manna, a jingle to taunt his twilit days and nights. Deathless, heirless—he had become a sterile cross stone watching death scything the fields. This was the work of a monk, not a daredevil in exile! And still the wheel kept turning, mocking his vigil with more phantasms. The figures looked like shards wearing rags; only rarely did their eyes look to the distance; for the most part, they kept their vision close to the ground, intent on sifting through the piles of rubble. Not much marked them as kinsmen; the months and years had scoured them down to the basics. The hair had dulled, the eyes had a vague hollow look, the feet were rough like the earth. Like Meherr and Jalali they had been exiled to the interiors and had lost track of themselves, their destiny suspended in a void as vast as the Syrian deserts and as deep as a bottomless ravine.

Long familiar with the nothingness of an heirless immortality, Meherr viewed its reflection in time and space. Yet as he watched, he felt the riddle of his fate softening. The shapes of future generations wavered before him, a ragged caravan trickling from the expanse of wasted forms; barred from the rock, it charted its way through mortality; en route, women and young orphaned girls began to earn their living threading needles and darning the holes in wasted cloth; boys gathered wood and fetched water for stray benefactors; others lounged in graveyards, waiting for the chance feast that came after the funeral. For the most part, they would only find refuge in what could no longer be broken down. The thought was strangely consoling as Meherr felt the hardness of the rock through the shadows, cool and inviolate like the eternal; even in limbo there were moments of grace that descended dovelike on the parched heart, when one felt light toppling doubt; he picked up his prayers from where he had left off. . . . And for all those who had searched for seeds in the wastes of camels and donkeys, for those who had found niches in the cracked earth to lie low and suffer the lice, for those who would make do with the fragments left—hands and nails, bones patched with sun-scorched skin, a will set on breathing through heaps of rotted flesh—Meherr made the sign of the Victory Cross.

It is tempting to continue with Meherr as he contemplates the fortunes of the Armenians during the great dispersion, because he steadies the eye that follows the cataclysmic changes they passed through in the late nineteenth and twentieth centuries when so many left or were forced to leave their homeland of almost three millennia. These upheavals still preoccupy many Armenian writers and artists, many of whom assert the pervasive sadness as memory approaches a vacuum, though others feel the dispersion as release; it has scattered the Armenians "like stars"; they are now everywhere in the world's vision, as resilient as the small "grain of marvelous Uranium which/cannot be broken down, put out or consumed."[56] At least, this is the great hope. But the American dynamo has transmuted even the most adamant of dispersed Armenian ores, sparking new forms of literary and cultural fusion.

Way out in the farther reaches of the Armenian diaspora, also known as the American West and the Central Valley of California, the village may have shrunk but it had lost none of its imaginative appeal for my family and our Armenian circle. Though I had neither heard of these writers nor met Meherr until the wheel of fortune turned me in the direction of mining my ethnic background, they would ultimately help me weld familial relics into a genuine legacy. Meanwhile, removed though it seemed from the center of Armenian—and American—action, the farming community where I grew up was the ideal field station for an introduction to multiple forms of ethnicity, especially my own. Tucked away in vineyards and orchards that cascaded with fruit in the summer, tiny Parlier was both an outpost of the diaspora and bastion of American agribusiness. The Armenian community was entrenched in both. Yet, we did not refer to ourselves as Armenian-American. I cannot remember that we called ourselves anything except "Hay"—a label derived from our eponymous hero, Hayk, great great grandson of Noah and one of the more expert archers of the ancient myths. The language we used in the home was *Hayeren*. The foods my mother prepared were *Haigagan*. And the values my parents were intent on sustaining served *Haiutiun*. Yet throughout, the newspapers we read included the Fresno *Bee* and the Los Angeles *Times* as well as *Nor Or* (New Day) and *Yerdasart Hayastan* (Young Armenia). Over the decades, the real battles my father waged and won were not those that had once preoccupied so many of his displaced generation in the thirties and forties—no longer was he fighting the American Legion in Selma, California, for the right to show a film about "Soviet" Armenia to local Armenians who supported the new homeland. More likely, he'd be going to court against the county of Fresno for putting faulty pipes on our property. Despite the shifting orientation, though, the identification "American" appeared most prominently on the passport when we *left* the country.

I was beginning each school day, five days a week, thirty-six weeks a year, pledging allegiance to the stars and stripes. Granted, this is one of the most unprepossessing of routines in a child's life, the words slurred into indistinguishable pulp as the last morning bell rings. But standing back from it now, when I rarely have occasion to salute the flag and sometimes struggle to remember the words, I am struck by how much this routine was also an attempt at a daily initiation into assimilation. Diversity might stay, but only for the greater glory of the one nation under God. Otherwise, *Haiutiun* was best abandoned for the word *democratic,* the words *en masse,* or at least its local variant. The initiation was always imperfect, for neither I nor my ethnic classmates ever died to the old while in school. No magic words of allegiance erased the more primary loyalty to family and feeling, and beyond this to a latent self that remained in limbo with Meherr; no subjects unraveled the core ambivalence that occasionally threatened to strangulate when my closest friends—both daughters of immigrants like me, one Japanese and the other Danish—realized we lived in between. At best, we put up a good show, writing essays about California Herefords in good American English or collecting shepherd's purse and filaree for our botany class. In high school we gave speeches to the Lions Club about "Maturity: Its Privileges and Responsibilities"; we then demonstrated our maturity by hiding out in the school basement whenever pep rallies for the Parlier Panthers were held on Friday afternoons. Secure under the cover of chitchat accompanied by Puccini, we resisted the efforts of cheerleaders and football team, our screaming classmates and indulgent teachers, to exercise—and exorcise—the id for us. Life at the margins really became exciting when Mr. Goishi, aptly entitled the vice-principal, heard us giggling through the din and chased us deeper into the shadowy basement—which I now see as our own less romantic version of Raven's Rock. If we were not yet fully in touch with our instincts, we nevertheless eluded group catharsis. If we were in between, we would discover ourselves best by the most circuitous and individual of ways, succumbing to neither parents nor school.

The bulging school bus was the link between our two worlds. And midafternoon, when it deposited us in farmyards that looked like variations on a theme (Betty's had an elaborate Japanese garden in the front; Karen's a European spread of tulips and marguerites; and mine, scallions by winter and green peppers, eggplant, and okra by summer), was the great transition into another world and language. For me, one of the great symbols of this transition was the voluminous walnut tree guarding our farmhouse. It presided over the tasks of each season. In the spring my mother would lay out freshly picked grape leaves, which she would then stuff into bottles for winter meals. In the summer it would catch any stray current, especially the multistranded stories Pa was trading with Armenian neighbors; the breezes lifted the stories into higher and higher orbits under the summer skies. In fall Ma would gather the nuts, string them on strong thread, and dip them in juice made from grapes she picked after the raisins were made. Because they had stayed on the vines the longest, they were the sweetest of the fruit; the result was *rojig* and *bastegh,* Armenian delicacies that dried in the sun and tasted as wholesome and earthy as an autumn harvest. And in the winter, branches bare, the tree sometimes blackened as scarlet dusks flared with shortened days—more often, it held the fog close and held everything else away from the brooding air. There were no rocks to speak of in this landscape, nor was our house anything like the interior of Raven's Rock; the surrounding countryside was simply a glut of green most of the year and the inside of our house was perpetually veneered with dust from the fields. Nevertheless, I like to think now that the walnut tree and the rituals staged under it were signaling that Meherr was close, even if we were not aware of it. I like to think that just as this melancholy warrior had followed the fortunes of the Armenians in their native habitat, pressed against the rock as he watched individuals thieving breath, he paid no less attention to the rise and fall of our own breath halfway across the world. Surely it was his spirit that reached into our daily lives and tested the solidity of the earth under our feet.

I also like to think that when I became aware of another label for my identity—Armenian-American—and began to test its solidity, exiled Meherr was close by, as interested to see what I would make of this term as I was to see his reemergence. What began formally as an intense exploration of matters I had previously taken for granted—behaviors, motivations, attitudes, values, the great abstractions that shape culture—was quickly translated into a meditation on the daily perplexities that had shaped *my* life, a meditation that more often than not led to indigestion than equanimity. Why did my parents think I'd been kidnapped in third grade just because they weren't *absolutely* sure I got on the school bus? What had they really thought after they hopped in the car and made their way to the edges of the school yard, where they could see me on the fringes of the crowd, watching the other kids play jump rope? Why was the word *amot* (shame) such a burdensome criticism, especially if I talked too much or let my legs open just a bit while sitting on the couch listening to the grown-ups? Why were my parents always alert to the needs of surviving villagers whether they lived in Dinuba, California, or Aleppo, Syria, always on call to take Varter Baji to the doctor or Sala Bedros to the lawyer, collecting money to send to Dziadzan so far away? The questions tangled through the branches of my life like a hoary veil. In coming to terms with each, I could feel Meherr's vigilant presence, reaching beyond the rock, forcing me to replay all those encounters of grammar school and high school when the American creed—the past need not avert my attention—played second fiddle to some sanction in the Armenian ethos. Like so many others, I was consciously rediscovering what Arshile Gorky had once summed up for all of us: to be an Armenian in America is a strange fate. It was also forcing me to create a new context in which I could embrace both.

Ideally, thinking about these matters fosters a humility about what can be legitimately pidgeonholed; like the narrator of Maxine Hong Kingston's autobiographical *The Woman Warrior,* I "continue to sort out what's just my childhood, just my imagination, just my family, just the village, just movies, just living."[57] Nevertheless, there is a circle with its center in Raven's Rock where many of the images and concerns I have come to identify as "Armenian" are reflected in the imaginations of other Armenians and Armenian-Americans. Its radii extend far to wherever dispersion has landed the Armenians, pulling many into the orbit of a shared mythos. They may not agree with or like its demands, they may not even be aware of them, but for many, part of their psyche has emerged from—or stays imprisoned in—the rock. It is the effect of this heritage on Armenians living in America that I propose to explore in this study, especially as Armenian-American writers and one Armenian-American artist have "repossessed" and reinvented their ethnic identity in a milieu rich with new oppositions. Through it all, I am aware that the term *culture* remains as slippery as anthropologists insist; but as a point of entry, it seems that culture must be something like Raven's Rock—a refuge and a resource that can be mined indefinitely for veins of imaginative wealth and new stories to live by. Whatever label we use to unlock its secrets, it is "the door to knock."

TRANSPLANTATION

At times I feel as though
It is the sky on my shoulders
And not my head—
At times I feel as though
It is the sun in my mind
And not my thoughts—
At times—but time and again—
It is the universe, I say,
Become portable in me.[1]

For Meherr's kin, April 1915 had proved the cruelest of months, breeding not lilacs but severe collective trauma. As the survivors straggled out of the dead land, their baggage mainly consisted of a tightly wadded-up bundle of memories and desires—seeds of stories and regeneration to come. Within a few years they had experienced massacre, exile, and the indifference of a world too preoccupied by its own angst to give a damn. Burdened with this loss, what were the thoughts of the last Armenian immigrants of the 1920s as they stepped into the inspection rooms of Ellis Island, spoke their names for the first time in America, and gave the place of their birth? Did their tongues warm on the sun-baked syllables or stumble over the reminder that they were the last remnants of a people—now by definition—without a homeland? Did the irony hit that if there were an Armenian nation, it now existed as that abstraction, diaspora, composed of any rags and refuse salvaged from the Turkish fury? Such thoughts competed with more pressing concerns. Where would they end up in America? Would relatives and countrymen have work waiting? Would they ever understand the businesslike sounds of English well enough to get ahead? Or would words escape their meaning, "like empty shoes," or the "gestures of a blindman/In the face of a mirror"?[2]

Always, they posed for photographs, staking claim to pride, purpose, sobriety. The clothes were neat, dignified, the posture erect, the gaze focused: they had escaped hell intact. But as Virginia Tatarian's "Photograph of Five Ancestors" suggests, that "sense of heat," of passions briefly put on hold before the camera, could not be fully repressed, seeping into the pictures with the power of instinct:

> Age and the quick hands
> of American children must
> have moved upon these faces
> to fade them so. Men are caught
>
> in the usual camera stance
> of starched and formal bones, yet
> there remains a sense
> of heat, unschooled as an instinct.
>
> For one enduring moment,
> they are grand as bishops or elks
> but cannot forget that
> this is a kind of pretence,
>
> like children who play at
> not being children, serious
> in unfamiliar dress, at
> home, on rainy afternoons.[3]

For children who spent long afternoons fading those "starched and formal" images, time set a stage for improvised rituals and steady contemplation; by staring long enough, a child might unlock the secret of his Armenian origins, perhaps find her own eyes scanning the future. Here, at the moment of transition, wary of demons at the new crossroads, parents were stoic, forbidding, hinting looks that would later chastise and channel ancestry.

As children would find out on the first day of kindergarten, this code was not Western, a theme explored by Jack Danielian in "Armenian Cultural Identity: Problems of Western Definition":

> Deriving from an ancient culture long antedating Western notions of cultural progress and Western definitions of the civilized man, the Armenian is privy to a different existential reality. We need to study and identify that reality in its *intrinsic* forms and with compatible methods, not force it into *extrinsic* structures which can depersonalize and desubjectivize it.[4]

Becoming aware of the "intrinsic forms" of this reality requires an understanding of the Armenians' specific concerns as Armenians and as immigrants, the effect of their self-awareness as Armenians on their adaptation to America, the typical and stereotypical situations and personalities that emerged with time, and the key values and beliefs that endured even as names were changed and assimilation blurred physical and social demeanor. Only after such a review can we begin to explore the directions Armenian-American writers have taken in portraying group history, and the nature of their self-discovery as Armenian-Americans. Because tracing these cultural patterns involves more than citing raw sociological data, I have again taken much of my material from actual or fictionalized experience: anecdotes, stories, poems, letters, and the memories and desires that gave these form.

ENTRY

Adaptable and industrious, Armenians had prospered wherever they took their trade. India, Iran, England, France, Poland, Holland, America—Armenian communities could be found in each at the turn of the century. Those that concern us most are the American groups: their evolution, their welfare relative to the rest of the population, their importance in receiving the influx of Armenians during the first decades of the twentieth century.

Except for isolated individuals (such as the mythic "George the Armenian," a silk culture specialist asked by the Virginia colonists for advice on this industry), Armenians did not reach America until the early nineteenth century when the American Protestant mission began to promote the educational advancement of its young converts. After completing their training in mission schools, some were sent to America for further study. The life and fortunes of one such student, Khachik Oskanian, was a propitious sign of changes to come. Graduating from the College of the City of New York in the late 1830s, Oskanian became a feature writer for the *New York Herald,* where he popularized stories of Near Eastern life. Following in the steps of earlier promoters of the American paradise, Oskanian also urged the Armenians, whom he dubbed the "yankees of the Near East," to emigrate from the Ottoman Empire and take advantage of American homesteading laws. His home in New York became a transit point for many who accepted his offer.[5]

By 1870 there were about seventy Armenians in America, living mostly in New York and Boston. Chain migration was the pattern; as soon as one Armenian found work in a city, he would attract others by letter or word of mouth. Because the Protestant centers were in the Northeast, Armenians first settled here. Their numbers had reached two thousand by 1890—mostly made up of students, merchants, and professionals—when the first phase of immigration ended.

During the next phase (1890–99), twenty thousand Armenians, many of them fleeing the Turkish massacres of 1894–5, entered the country; many settled in New York, New Jersey, and Pennsylvania. By this time, the mystique of America, a land of open opportunity Armenians had not had for millennia, had penetrated even into the interior villages of the Ottoman Empire. But leaving demanded luck and sacrifice. One had to have contacts in the outside world and money to pay for transport and to bribe officials unwilling to allow passage. Transportation was another problem, for the only means out of the mountainous interiors was by horse-drawn carts straining over primitive trails.[6] However, if they did manage to leave the Old Country, the immigrants could expect the help of the Armenians already here and lenient immigration laws.

From 1900 to 1914, as the Ottoman government intensified its hostilities, most Armenians became convinced that exile was preferable to staying, particularly after the killings in Cilicia in 1908. During this period, tens of thousands more immigrated, especially extended families able to collect their money and any stray members of the family—cousins, aunts, grandparents, infants—able to make the journey.[7] But the outbreak of World War I made it almost impossible for Armenians to escape the slaughterhouse. When the war ended, another twenty-five thousand—many lone massacre survivors—managed to enter. This flow ceased in 1924 when quotas were instituted.

After World War II, the American government allowed "displaced" Armenians from countries overrun by the war to settle in America. Most of these Armenians came from southern and eastern Europe, Egypt, Greece, and once more from Turkey. During the last three decades, other Armenians have emigrated from Soviet Armenia or fled the upheavals of the Middle East, taking refuge in the United States, Canada, South America, and Australia. Although these periodic influxes have at times aggravated historic suspicions among the Armenians, they have also revitalized the Armenian-American community, leading in areas such as Los Angeles to the formation of complex social structures. Against the urban backdrop, thousands of Armenians daily exercise their native language and traditions at Armenian schools and at work. Armenian newspapers and community activities further reinforce cultural loyalties. Whether these recent immigrants argue the fate of the new Armenia, reenact stylized open-air rituals with the *toneer* (old-world oven), or dream of trekking up Mt. Ararat to fertilize its soil with their blood, their presence has invigorated the life of this region. At the quantitative level, they have helped swell the number of Armenians in America to more than half a million. More important, their arrival, with their diversifying points of view, has forced the Armenian-American community to reexamine its future. Basic questions have emerged: How many ways are there to be Armenian-American? Though the perspectives of these more recent immigrants have not yet filtered into literature, accounts of their experience will further delineate the constants and variables of Armenian life in America.

No matter when they left Turkey, the early Armenian immigrants underwent the trying transition that other ethnic groups have experienced. As outlined by Oscar Handlin in *The Uprooted,*

> The crossing in all its phases was a harsh and brutal filter. On land in Europe, in the port of embarkation, on the ocean, in the port of arrival, and on land in America, it introduced a decisive range of selective factors that operated to let through only a few of those who left the Old World.[8]

Handlin notes that the most striking shift demanded in transit was the "reversal of roles"; traits that served "good" peasants undermined the actual transition. "Neighborliness, obedience, respect, and status were valueless among the masses that struggled for space on the way."[9] Here Armenians diverged from the norm. For one thing, many of the incoming Armenians were not peasants, but merchants and craftsmen used to taking initiative and looking to make profits. By as early as the 1870s and 1880s, well over a thousand Armenian men—many of them artisans—had migrated from Kharpert.[10] In the *Harvard Encyclopedia of American Ethnic Groups,* Robert Mirak presents some of the other atypical traits of the Armenian immigrants: thirty-five percent had skills (gained as tailors, shoemakers, carpenters, or clerks); four percent had been in business in the Old Country; two percent were professionals; almost all were literate and almost half had been town dwellers.[11] Even some from an agrarian background had experience operating small "factories" or business tied to their farm commodoties. Strengthening these socioeconomic advantages was native spunk, a trait that helped many in the first stages of settlement.

Yet doubts must have surfaced even on the faces of early Armenian immigrants as they entered Ellis Island. Among the immediate trials that awaited all immigrants were quarantine and inspection. The government required assurance: "You must not have contracted for your job, also . . . you must be not likely to become a public charge."[12] External signs of disease and physical disability were scrutinized, and if trachoma—a common eye infection of the Old Country—was detected, it could mean refusal of entry. Other hitches could also delay processing:

> I stayed on Ellis Island for two weeks. I was healthy, so I wasn't worried about quarantine, but I had to be careful with questions about my birthplace and birthday. I had no papers, all I knew was what my mother used to say: "You were born when the apricots came to blossom." It was only after my cousin in Racine telegraphed his Congressman that I was allowed to enter.[13]

The anxiety of inspection at Ellis Island is depicted with grotesque humor in Raffi Arzoomanian's play, *Ellis Island 101.* An old Armenian, Anna, who has been denied entry for thirty years, advises the hopeful Peter about the best method of passing inspection:

> Whatever you do . . . don't pee in your pants . . . they'll give you an "X" for that. . . . And this business of fainting. They'll give an "X" for that, too, *and* for coughing, *and* for having a rash, and for having a limp or backache—they've no mind to investigate symptoms, back you go . . . and they'll give you an "X" if you can't read. That's why I was sent back.[14]

Though illiterate, Anna has learned that "papers in this country are longer from top to bottom than from side to side." But after Peter demonstrates his literacy, Anna is thwarted once more after turning the paper upside down. Her comic scream punctuates Peter's fainting fit and spells rejection for both. Though Peter remonstrates to the empty stage ("I'm a sensitive man, that's why I faint! Only a sensitive man could average a 94 while starving his way to a doctorate! I have it right here . . ."), Anna with feigned cheer shows her determination: "In case you're wondering—I'll live to see the Irishman again. I'll live to die in America." Meanwhile there is every chance that her sons, already in America, are loyally circling the island on the Staten Island ferry, hoping to reach her with their megaphones.

Nona Balakian's observations about another play by Arzoomanian, *The Moths,* pertain to *Ellis Island 101* as well: "Arzoomanian uses all the tools of expressionistic art—fantasy, hysteria, hallucination, brutal humor—to reveal the powerful hold which people have on each other, with no light to guide them out of their self-made traps."[15] But in this play the traps are not completely self-made. The thick walls of the inspection rooms, the ease with which the immigrant can be branded with an "X," and the unheard megaphones suggest that America cannot be penetrated. In fact, the primary values of the play have little to do with America, for as it ends, Peter says of the megaphone-wielding sons: "Forgive me, mama, but your sons . . . they sound like a couple of idiots." Anna replies, "Yes. America seems to have done them no good. No good at all." What *is* affirmed is the ethnic bond. Peter and Anna, two Armenian exiles in perpetual limbo, find in each other a support based on common heritage. This tie may bode well for their next attempt as Peter reassures the old woman: "Then it's Paris for you. I'll teach you how to read and you'll coach me off fainting. We'll come back."

HUSTLE

Despite possible setbacks at the point of entry, thousands passed inspection with little or no trouble and proceeded to stake territory in "The Land of Lucky Strike," the title of a short story by Laura Kalpakian. Here, as the immigrant protagonist, Dikran Agajanian, responds angrily to a denigrating comment he does not understand ("Dumbbell—Perhaps it was some relation to Jingle Bell"), we see one response to the frenetic pace of America:

> For the first time since he had been in America ambition gripped him, ambition alloyed with bitterness: Dikran had been a foreigner all his life, born to it; he did not want to die a foreigner too. Any Armenian who lived in a Turkish city learned quickly to say little, to tread easy, to fade inconspicuously if he could.[16]

Vowing to "strip his old self to wear the new country," Dikran commits himself to all that is American—from the habit of husbands kissing wives often and in public (*not* a traditional Armenian custom) to his job as a tobacco concessioneer on the Santa Monica beach, where with minimal English one can trek toward affluence, American style: "Cigarette? Cigar? Chewing Gum? Thank you. You are welcome. Candy Bar? Which one? Lucky Strike." Similarly, a real-life Armenian in George Mardikian's autobiography, *Song of America,* who is a flower concessioneer in San Francisco, earns a tidy living with an even more compact charm: "Lady, this flower is just like you,"[17] proving once more that in America the medium is the gimmick.

In general, the Armenians were caught by the same ambition that grips Dikran Agajanian, pouring energy into commerce and industry. When the first men arrived at the end of the nineteenth century, the available jobs were mostly in the "Satanic mills" of the Northeast, where labor stretched out over sixty-hour workweeks in harsh conditions for low pay. They along with the other immigrants from southern and eastern Europe—Italians, Poles, Russians, Syrians, and Greeks—fueled the economy. But the Armenians usually looked beyond the factory to more lucrative, independent work. Their skills, level of literacy, willingness to risk, and the post-1915 realization that there was no going home spurred them to push beyond when the chance came.[18]

Along with other laborers, the Armenians suffered periods of unemployment, a hardship many found very trying:

> For me, the hardest thing about coming to America was first finding work. Everywhere I'd go, there were long lines. They'd ask me, "What's your line?" I'd always answer "labor" and they'd point toward the door. I felt like going back to the *yergir* [Old Country] where I at least had plenty of work and some pride.[19]

The coincidence of peak immigration waves with domestic depression, floating the men "like fish to the top of the water," did not help matters.[20] Though the Armenian immigrant press befriended labor, the workers' loyalties before 1915 were not permanently with America or its labor movement. As a result, they had few scruples against strike-breaking in times of joblessness, a practice that did not enhance their local image.

One of the greatest injustices all immigrants had to suffer sprang from the "padrone system," an abuse that has long victimized our migrant workers. Forced to find their jobs through an Americanized Armenian boss, workers remained in his debt.[21] Chafing against such ills and being averse to the wage relationship, the Armenians left the factories and foundries as soon as possible. They branched out into every trade and business. Many made their living in response to their community's needs, serving as insurance or shipping agents, supplying Armenians with native foods through small grocery stores, and running the restaurants, boardinghouses, and coffeehouses that made city neighborhoods old-world enclaves.[22] Besides the businessmen who catered to the Armenian community, every large city boasted at least one Armenian engaged in the Oriental rug trade. Though the general population stereotyped many Armenians as rug dealers, the handful who did enter the trade transformed it. Through their connections with Old World merchants, the Armenian dealers helped satisfy the American fad for all that was Eastern.[23]

Occasionally, immigrants found work that drew together Armenian and American cultures, as exemplified in George Mardikian's autobiography. His exuberant Horatio Alger story about achieving economic success by wedding native intelligence to opportunity displays his Whitmanesque love of the democratic norm. "In the restaurant, I talked with bankers and writers, politicans and policemen. . . . They never made me feel that they were better than I."[24] Despite other reservations about being in America, most Armenians shared this pride in the egalitarian ideal. Mardikian's affection for the society and his desire to win a place in it lead him to envision his future vocation:

> I wanted to help Americans learn to eat better. I wanted to prepare the finest dishes and serve them to Americans. . . . They had been so busy building this great country they had forgotten all about the art of living. I would try to give America the best of Armenian and Near Eastern cooking, as I knew and remembered it.[25]

He thus manages, symbolically, to assimilate Americans into Armenian culture by feeding them.

Although most immigrants found work in the urban centers of the Northeast and mid-Atlantic, with smaller communities forming in the mid-central states, there was one important exception to this settlement pattern: the farming community of Fresno, in the San Joaquin Valley of California. Drawn by its climate, fertility, and resemblance to parts of their homeland, the Armenians gravitated en masse. Often they came as family units, having worked in the East for five to ten years, and saving to invest in land once they arrived. So attractive were the prospects of the region that until the 1930s, California had the most rapid growth rate of all the Armenian communities. The following description suggests how the valley impressed early Armenians as an ideal landscape:

> The *badvelis* [ministers] were in love with this land. "My dear friends," they wrote their parishioners back in Armenia, "you should see this valley. It is like the country around Van. Or it is like the Valley of Ararat. There are many vineyards and fine orchards. Far away are the mountains. Even now, in the heat of summer, they are white with snow, just like Little Massis and Big Massis. The farmers here are free. Their land belongs to them and their sons. No sultan or czar can hit them on the head and say, "Give your land to me."[26]

To this paradise they brought melon seeds from Dickranakert and Kharpert, the cuttings of vineyards underneath Ararat, and young fig trees from Izmir.[27] They planted the grapes with the succulent, exotic names of Spain—Malaga, Sultana, Alicante; laid out orchards of peaches, plums, nectarines; stocked their family gardens with cherries, pears, apricots, and walnuts. And as they tended the water that gushed through their irrigation pipes, they helped transform a desert into an agricultural Eden.

Rooted in a terrain where they could work and reap profit, the Armenians of Fresno County cherished capitalist dreams. Because many could not afford to buy land at first, they set about doing some of the most filthy, strenuous, and cheaply paid work in agriculture—grape picking. The grapes are harvested in late-August weeks when the hundred-plus temperatures steam the vineyards. Stooping underneath dusty, spider-infested vines, the picker has to adeptly cut the stems of bunches bulging with berries and then, pan by pan, lay these out on paper trays. Like most manual labor, it only yields pennies a tray for the picker. For the chance to do such work, the Armenians and German-Russians with whom they shared it could thank labor acts of the 1880s that weeded out Chinese laborers.[28] In time, as they bought their own farms, they would bequeath it to the Mexicans and local Indians.

Besides labor in the vineyards, packinghouse work also provided income. Here Armenian women, used to impeccable propriety between the sexes, had to endure disrespectful foremen along with the tedium and fatigue of culling and packing tree fruit. Yet for the sake of one day owning land, they bore the indignities and sacrificed domestic comforts. As true citizens of the Old Country, they understood that "no house can produce a farm, but a good farm can produce a house."[29] The houses these farms produced were generally not glossy magazine copy. Fading from the valley scene as farmers pour money into rambling ranch styles, the old farmhouses inhabit only the childhood imaginations of those who grew up in them. Squarish, small, uninsulated, they were a humble foil for the orchards and vineyards that fringed the yards. Often they needed paint, parts sagged with age, bloated in the summer heat. But they offered opulent hospitality to the friends and relatives who swarmed there on Sundays and holidays. In the summer especially, they overflowed with plenty—plums, peaches, apricots, figs, melons, vegetables from the garden—these plus milk and eggs from cows and chickens kept in the yard weighted their tables.

To really make it in the valley, a man had to master the art of hustle:

> I had fallen in love with California, but after the Depression hit my farm was foreclosed. So I found another way to make my living: I saw a lot of grapes left on the vines of big growers' farms. I could estimate how many tons there were by walking up and down a few rows and averaging the rest. Then I'd go and talk to the owner. I'd make sure he was wealthy since rich people are more generous. I wouldn't tell the owner how much I wanted to offer, but ask him how much he wanted first. If the price gave me room for a profit, I'd take it, get a crew of Armenians and Mexicans together, and pick the grapes. One day I made $5,000 off just one deal.[30]

Such enterprise earned the Armenians a reputation for being "hard bargainers and gamblers." A striking example of this willingness to take big risks for a profit is recounted by Mirak when in 1907, three hundred Armenians withheld sixteen thousand tons of Malagas and currants from an undersupplied market until they drove the prices sky high.[31]

But hustle is not for the novice. As the economic disaster of the Depression struck, many were squeezed off the farms and into the cities. Other times, the inexperience of the immigrants and the superior wile of the middleman could prove fatal, as in *Thieves' Market* (1949), a novel by

A. I. Bezzerides (whose background is Greek and Armenian). This story about a young Greek who goes in over his head when he starts a hauling business is a rare attempt to portray the economic traps valley agribusiness holds for the uninitiated. Seeing the hopelessness of winning at this game, Nick bitterly reflects on the capitalist ethos, where someone is always "after the gravy": "The less I pay out, the more there is for me. That *for me,* that thinking of *me,* all the time *me.* . . . If you've got something, they eat out of your hands, but if you haven't you're like the rotting produce in the gutters. Nobody wants you but the beggars and the dogs."[32] Unfortunately, the odds against the innocent are so great that we see naturalistic types fumbling for control over their lives rather than actual people, with the fertile valley a sinister backdrop.

Those who lived through these early decades in the farthest reaches of the West remember more than the joys of rediscovering Armenia or the struggles of the marketplace, though. Fresno was the scene of the most virulent prejudice the Armenians would experience in America, where the transplanted habits of overcompensating for old-country persecution jarred the pride of a young city new to ethnic tensions. Easily threatened by hints that the balance of power within their community might favor a group so resolutely reclaiming its inherited vocation, and offended by what they perceived as Armenians' pushiness, suspiciousness, dishonesty, and refusal to assimilate, Fresno natives divided their population into two groups, "those who are 'white' and those who are 'Armenians.' "[33] They objected to the high-profile self-confidence of the Armenians; said a hostile local, "They are the only foreigners in Fowler [a valley town close to Fresno] who think they are just as good as we are. I don't know why they aren't, but we think they aren't."[34] Aware of their effect on the rest of the population, Armenians retorted with bravado. "What," asked Aram Saroyan, "has the fact that we are a clannish, ill-dressed, noisy, argumentative, uncooperating people to do with the inability of Armenian professional men to rent office space in good Fresno buildings?"[35] Frictions between the groups left more scars than some may care to remember, and stamped these years in the "Armenian town" with bitterness.

THE BOARDINGHOUSE

During the first phases of migration in the latter part of the nineteenth century, most Armenian immigrants—eighty-seven percent—were single men between the ages of 14 and 45.[36] Their housekeeping was invariably makeshift: twenty or so men would band together, rent a house, divide it into rooms, and if they felt extravagant, hire a cook. Comfort was not a priority, because these men were primarily interested in saving fifty dollars in five or six years and then returning home.

"Ashod's Boarding House," a short story by John Barsamian, delightfully recreates immigrant male domesticity. The disheveled setting and loose sequence of events reflect improvised lives, and the men's responses to events inside and outside the boardinghouse suggest the peasant core of their existence in industrial Worcester. Like the farm families of Fresno, these men are not interested in amenities, and once past the two cast-iron lions that guard the house, one enters a world guided by old-country sensibility: aromatic church incense permeates a house filled with makeshift bedding, limp drapery, and pictures of Jesus Christ covering broken plaster.

The boarders are comic and pathetic in their naiveté. They get into trouble with local police after violently mistaking the "black tasseled red fezzes" of American Shriners for Turkish caps; for cheap—or free—amusement they go to the Armenian coffeehouse or the mental institution where they watch the cavortings of the insane; and within the womb of Ashod's domain, they resume the pastimes of the *yergir*—backgammon, clarinet playing, smoking, eating, arguing. Over this miniature transplanted village presides Ashod, who manages to create order and security for men in voluntary exile: he does have a parlor, even if the sole furnishings are spindle chairs and worn divans. He cooks wholesome Armenian food; he ministers to their illnesses—imagined and otherwise—and has even worked out a face-saving way to discharge boarders if the need arises.

The central event of the story centers on a macabre photographing session. Finding Hagop, one of the boarders, dead on the toilet, someone suggests, "Surely, all of us would like to have a photograph with Hagop as a remembrance, and so would his brothers and sisters in Armenia."[37] Wacky though it is, the episode condenses layers of pathos in Armenian immigrant experience. As Martin the photographer maneuvers the corpse for the best shot, the men are repulsed but comply. Despite their unease, they intuit that the photograph asserts the tie of the person to the homeland and to the group—a support unto death!

The end of the story reemphasizes the pull of the group. Unwilling to tolerate a two-dollar rent increase, the boarders immediately find an even cheaper house and with sweeping resolve, move everything over that night, even the stove. Only Ashod is left. Gathering his own belongings and the pan of cooked cabbage rolls, he reminds us that to survive, these men—like Peter and Anna in *Ellis Island 101*—must cocreate a space where they can share the most basic human experiences: food, language, exile, and death.

COMMUNITY INSTITUTIONS

"You know what they say—if there are two Armenians there will have to be three parties—one for A, one for B, and one to give them something to argue about."[38] Ancient church rituals and the familial bonds of benevolent groups comforted many early Armenian immigrants. Yet though these bridges became strong forces in the community, each was eventually embroiled in old-world political debates. Shaken more than most immigrant groups by surges of revolutionary passion, Armenian-Americans for decades led a bifurcated life. The hold of this relatively small group of activists was rooted in the Armenian longing for an independent homeland, and in trying to gain adherents, the parties set up clubhouses, newspapers, reading rooms, and marching societies.[39] In the eyes of party members, these would not only keep political and financial aid flowing, but also stabilize Armenian identity until repatriation became possible.

From their first appearance in America (during the 1890s and early part of the 1900s), the parties drew the suspicion of the Armenian community. At this time, Armenians were divided over how to respond to Sultan Hamid, the Ottoman ruler who had instigated massacres agains the Armenians in the 1890s: whether to appease him, or to oppose him and look toward Europe and the sanctions of the Berlin Treaty for support. After the massacres of 1894–95, many suspected the Hunchag and Tashnag political factions of precipitating the bloodbath to force European intervention, a charge that would poison community relationships and confuse historical accounting for decades.[40]

As time passed, the basic split between these and the other parties that emerged (the Ramgavars and Armenian Progressives) lay in their attitude toward an Armenian Socialist Republic. The Tashnags saw the Armenian will toward independence weakened and "perverted" under Soviet rule, with the Armenian church and the Catholicos serving as tools of the Soviet Union. On the other hand, reacting against the national exile engendered by the massacres, factions such as the Ramgavars found Soviet rule preferable to an independence subject to Turkish massacres.[41] Intensely biased, most Armenian institutions and organizations since 1914 have had a party affiliation, although in recent decades the community has warily begun to lay down its rusty arms.

During the earlier phases of settlement, factional disputes infected a united community. Some of the firebrands were caught by dilemmas they shared with exiled Armenian intellectuals, whose loyalties precluded an easy transition into American citizenship. Sonia Shiragian's description of her father's comrades during the thirties in "A Journey to Armenia" presents a vivid view of their character. Divided between two cultures, well educated and activist, they did not see themselves reflected in the gaze of a new world that had not even heard of their homeland. Immersed in the newspapers of several languages and cultures, articulate about Levantine history, they teetered between skepticism and indiscriminate pride in their culture, irreligion, and nostalgia toward the Armenian church. More seriously, their intellectual bent ill equipped them for what they saw as menial jobs as ice cream vendors, spotters, and haulers. As Shiragian comments:

> I am sure that on their jobs they were regarded as sullen, touchy foreigners who refused to wear sensible work clothes. Their daily contacts with Americans must have been hell for them, they were so conscious of the unintelligibility of their English. And yet they insisted that it would be foolish to prepare themselves for life in America. The Communists' bloody experiment, they said, was bound to fail any day, and with the collapse would come the end of the so-called Armenian Soviet Socialist Republic, the union of Russian and Turkish Armenia, and the emergence of Armenia as a free nation among free nations once more.[42]

As Shiragian depicts it, the sobriety of these men once more weds comedy to pathos against an easygoing American backdrop, showing their instinctive wariness of assimilation, a form of annihilation new to their cultural vocabulary. Yet as the older generation died off, the old sociopolitical mindset lost its hold. Their children remembered only that as they were growing up, references to Tashnag, Soviet Union, and the Tourian episode inevitably sparked tension, acidic arguments, even fistfights that only the grown-ups understood. They remembered only that all things Armenian came in two packages: Tashnag and anti-Tashnag. They remembered that weddings sometimes erupted into war because the bride and groom came from opposite sides of the political fence.

This split even ripped the Armenian church, the dominant institution of the Armenian-American community. The early years of the church in this country were particularly chaotic, a turmoil that began as soon as the first Armenian church in America—Sourp Pergich (Our Savior)—was established in Worcester, Massachusetts, in 1891.[43] Political factions who baited the church out of anticlerical prejudice and disputed the legality of its election procedure turned the pulpit into a forum for profane quarrels. In 1933 the political tensions that had divided the church reached a catastrophic peak. While conducting the Divine Liturgy in the New York church, Archbishop Levon Tourian was killed, allegedly by a group of political activists. The crime, reeking of old-world melodrama, polarized the community and the church. Everyone took a stand for or against the Tashnags, and even though the Tashnags denied any official part in the murder, nine party members were convicted. Decades later, Armenians could still reach a rabid pitch at the very mention of the episode, spitting out obscenities that time did not soften.

To make matters worse, anachronistic priests and ineffective leadership during its early years also plagued the church. The old-country adage held true in America: "When a group of Armenians gathers and the conversation turns to the . . . priests, practically everyone has a Boccaccio-like episode to tell."[44] Often older, more dogmatic, and less well educated than their congregations, the old-country priests stumbled to meet the demands of the new-world church. Painfully aware of this weakness, the immigrant press warned the community that the church had turned into "a feeble, breathless creature." Once the beacon of the world's first Christian nation, the church now helped ritualize Christimas and Easter for the faithful remnant. The situation led some in the community to conclude that the leaderless church was on the precipice.[45]

In time a combination of factors redeemed the church. Some were tied to the ingrained belief that religious orthodoxy was synonymous with being Armenian; others sprang from the positive effect of America on Armenians' social awareness. For example, in 1906 women were permitted to vote on some issues in parish churches. They used this power to organize auxiliary groups and committees that created practical support for parish activities. Someone, after all, had to cook and bake for those money-making bazaars that welded the community. In addition, as a younger generation of Armenian-Americans came of age, a few became interested in joining the priesthood. With time these young men balanced the effect of the old-country priests by using American know-how to serve their Armenian faith.

Though much fewer, the Protestant Armenians had also founded churches, often in meager circumstances. Unfortunately, the Protestants—mostly because of their affiliation with the American mission—attracted the distrust of the larger community, who felt they stood for eventual assimilation. Their newspaper, *Gotchnag,* advised pre-1915 immigrants to stay in America, sensing the Armenians had no future in the Ottoman Empire.[46] Attending an Evangelical Armenian church tends to confirm these early feelings: the language used is generally English, and the service lacks the ritual power of the Divine Liturgy of the Apostolic church. Yet charges that the evangelicals are somehow less Armenian grossly underestimate the positive reforming effect of this movement on Armenian life the world over.

In appraising the importance of religion in Armenian-American life, one is left with a series of hyphenated images: the Sunday liturgy is usually performed with all the old rituals and language intact, but the incense trails through imposing—and often, sparsely filled—edifices American millions have built; baptisms and Easter services are attended by many whose tie to Armenian culture stretches only to the sign of the Cross, while old women in jersey dresses and recent Armenian immigrants constitute the body of Christ the other fifty weeks of the year; and picnics are held where the chants of the grape blessing by the parish priest vie with the calls of the bingo game yards away—played to make more money for the church. What is undeniable in all this is that no matter how modified, the church is still a major force, not because of its religious sanctions, but as a clearinghouse of activities in the Armenian diaspora.

Yet another communal force in the New World, particularly in the earlier decades, were the various compatriotic groups. Like immigrants from other countries, Armenians identified themselves by the village or region they came from rather than the general national designation. The mountainous geography of the Old Country had emphasized such localized ties. Accordingly, once in America, immigrants were deeply sensitive to the needs of their regions and organized to alleviate financial pressure on the village: "Schools, famine, hospitals, orphanges"[47]—each required and received assistance. Proud of their ability to care for their own, Armenians also helped their needy in America, holding aloof from the help of the non-Armenian. Besides their practical purpose, such groups reknit the social ties of the village. Every few weeks or so, they might meet, collect money for needy survivors in the Middle East, make plans for fund-raising with summer picnics or a winter *hantes* (indoor picnic). Yet others worked for the sustenance of the Armenian

SSR. Imbued with a zest that transformed old pains into service, these often humble organizations channeled a far-reaching compassion. Cutting across local interest, the most powerful philanthropic organization is the Armenian General Benevolent Union (AGBU). Since its founding in 1906, it has undertaken extensive relief projects for the benefit of Armenian refugees in Turkey, Russia, and the Middle East. More recently, it has sponsored projects to help preserve the Armenian heritage in America: day schools, summer camps, relief, counseling and job assistance to newcomers, and cultural activities, especially in dance and literature.

Newspapers were yet another way of centering the immigrant community. From the very beginnings of settlement, Armenians had access to information about their affairs and the surrounding culture through Armenian-language newspapers (often bulletins and handbills). Even in the Ottoman Empire, their literacy and interest in communicating national and international news had allowed them to be much better informed than the Turks. In America, free from censorship and harassment, Armenians were even more at liberty to broadcast their views, educate immigrants who did not speak English, and reinforce old biases through articles on social and religious issues. In addition, they kept the Armenians connected to their literature. Typically, the writing lacked humor and sensationalism.[48] The first papers were private labors of love. Because editors relied on students and poor factory workers for financial support, many early publications did not last more than a few months or years. Others fared better because of political advocates eager to spread their gospels. Here one found all the exaggeration and knife-edged satire the Armenian was capable of directing against his political foes.[49]

Although some were often too poor to subscribe to a private issue of a paper, they read them thin whenever they had the chance, especially in the coffeehouses where men congregated to drink coffee and play backgammon.[50] The titles of these publications were fiery and lyrical, as illustrated in the earliest revolutionary bulletins: *Gaidsag* (lightning), *Shant* (thunderbolt), *Harvads* (blow), and *Loosnag* (little moon). Among others, one could also read *Gotchnag* (church bell), the implacably unbiased organ of the Armenian Protestants, which first appeared in 1901, and *Louyce* (light), concerned with educating the immigrant on "science, philosophy, education, health, as well as on modern ways of doing things: preparing the soil, preparing seeds, preserving eggs, and the like."[51] As decades passed, English-language newspapers filled less urgent community issues, keeping the second and third generations informed about the intricacies of Armenian weddings and picnics, and more recently, crises related to events in Soviet Armenia and congressional resolutions related to the genocide.

One English-language journal of special interest is *Armenia,* a monthly first published in 1903 under the sponsorship of the Reformed Hunchagians. Its purpose was "to offer English-speaking peoples a full and rounded view of Armenians, to provide a taste of Armenian history, literature, culture, art, and architecture, instead of the usual recitals of massacres and persecution."[52] And this it did. The pages of *Armenia* were filled with a hodgepodge of articles, ranging from an appreciation of Armenian embroidery, to clippings about Turkish iniquities, to translations of Raffi's novel, *Jelaleddin.* Here Armenian scholars and political figures interested in the Armenian question could also present their findings. Because of its educational slant, the journal became an impassioned forum where Armenians, Americans, and knowledgeable Europeans exchanged information and opinion. Its honorary editorial borad was as distinguished as the journal, including Julia Ward Howe, Charlotte Perkins Gilman, William Lloyd Garrison, and Edwin Mead. Though internal disputes interrupted its publications for a few years, it informed Americans about Armenia until the 1920s.

More currently, another noteworthy journal is *Ararat,* a publication of the AGBU devoted to cultural and literary topics. It is the only place where one can find a body of Armenian-American literature regularly published. Poetry, fiction, dramas, and reviews, along with articles about artists, writers, and general cultural history, make this a valuable resource, both for the Armenian community and those interested in American ethnic experience.

FREE TIME

> Saturday was the one night I had free. There was a German fellow—a Nazi—who lived at Mrs. Daly's boardinghouse with me. We were about the same age and usually we'd spend Saturday night passing time together. He'd share the cakes his mother sent him from Hamburg, and I'd take him to an Armenian restaurant in Chicago. The first time I ordered *khemah* [raw lamb kneaded with cracked wheat], he didn't want to eat it—but after he tasted it, it became our standard Saturday night supper—just like in the Old Country.[53]

Besides the Armenian restaurant, a standard meeting place for Armenian men, particularly the unmarried or those without wives in America, was the Armenian coffeehouse. Untidy, unsanitary, the food less than palatable, these national institutions, combining the features of a lyceum, entertainment center, and boxing ring, offered a place where immigrant men drank heavy Turkish coffee, played pinochle and *tavloo* (backgammon), argued, backslapped, and swapped stories and information about the Old Country and recent arrivals.[54] Though they were often raided for gambling, the companionship and relaxation they provided warranted their existence. Except for gaming, major crimes were almost unknown among the immigrants.[55]

Coffee formed the basis for a cherished leisure ritual. This was not the bland and watered-down American version but *gaiffa,* a thick, bittersweet brew served in tiny porcelain cups. Although it can be offered any time, coffee is especially welcome in the afternoon—after a Saturday spent cleaning and then bathing away fatigue, after a nap, toward the end of a visit with friends. The preparations and service can be as stylized as the Japanese tea ceremony. The coffee is ground by hand in a brass grinder, brought to a boil with sugar and water in a small brass pot (*jezzveh*), and the foam (the more the better) if skillfully poured rises to the top, a tiny island of volatility. The coffee is slowly and thoughtfully sipped; perhaps one token cigarette is taken or a sweet such as *lokhoom* or *rojig*. However presented, the aroma of coffee has permeated many Armenian households, as this passage from "Dreamers" by A. I Bezzerides suggests:

> Gradually I noticed a strange odor in the room, not the choking smell of tobacco nor of anything nameable, but simply an odor of the old country. Such an odor my Grand Aunt had brought with her when she had come from Turkey. . . . Anna came and Hajji said "Gaiffa," and she shuffled away to return soon with two tiny cups of coffee not much larger than thimbles. The odor of the thick, black Turkish coffee dispelled the other odor.[56]

The ritual ends with the cups "turned over in order to tell their fortunes. A moment upside down and the cups were righted again, inspected, exchanged and carefully inspected once more."[57] The more creative the fortune-teller, the better, for the grounds form miniature Rorschachs and the fortune-teller's aim is to free the dreams of the listener.

Another event that brought the community together was the Armenian picnic. Here not only unattached men but every member of the group could find a social outlet. At first these picnics were sponsored by the immigrant political parties as informal opportunities to air ideology. To this day, some of the picnics in the larger Armenian centers are given under these anachronistic auspices. As time went on, the church, fraternal organizations, and benevolent unions also found in the picnic an easy way to raise money and promote fellowship. But as the decades have passed, the raucous spirit of the old-time picnic has faded. Picnics, of course, symbolized more than communal ties, as portrayed in Sonia Shiragian's "A Visit to Armenia." After a childhood in which her father and his compatriots fill the little girl's mind with visions of a lost paradise they will someday reclaim, the child manages to break the spell these men "had cast to ward off assimilation" when she demands to be taken to this homeland. The Armenia her dumbfounded father conjures up is the only one accessible by car, and in the middle of a rented grove in America he points out: "Aha—kezee Haiastan" ("There you have it—Armenia!"). The girl finds the scene of clannish intimacy among large, laden tables exhilarating:

> [M]en and women were reaching out and taking what they wanted and, with familiar gestures, offering each other samples. The sounds of the Armenian language mingled with the reedy, clanging, titillating sounds of music and the smell of meat being turned over a fire and the whirl of movement and the rhythmic clapping of hands.[58]

The indoor equivalent of the picnic was the *hantes*. Held in the evening or on Sundays, the *hantes* was "a get-together with speeches, recitations, plays, folk dances and food."[59] Here, too, a common motive was money making for immigrant organizations. So pervasive was the profit motive that many wryly concluded that everything was for fund-raising.[60] The speeches at the *hantes,* as at the picnic, were models of long-windedness. Frequently, after 1915, tears would punctuate the comments, followed by complaints from the audience to cut it short. Other beloved pastimes included recitations and plays. These dramatic exercises, accompanied by the usual Armenian hubbub, resulted in scenes where the dispersed Armenian could once more deify the past before a crowded theater:

> "The Garden of Eden, according to tradition, was situated in Armenia. . . . There have been contemporary empires of the Per-

> sian, Babylonian, Grecian, and Roman, but today there is not one to represent them, while the Armenians have a living history. While the nations of Europe were yet barbarians . . . the Armenian empire was a civilized and law-abiding government."[61]

The play itself might be pure wish fulfillment: Kurdish tribesmen abducting beautiful Armenian maidens with the Armenians annihilating the enemy in return. But the audiences gobbled up the fantasy; as William Saroyan recorded in one of his short stories: "What language! What energy! What wisdom! What magnificent roaring!"[62]

Occasionally, groups of Armenians would also form clubs. Two in Reedley, California, are representative. Here a dozen Armenian couples came together in 1921 and decided to mark their self-appointed elevation in the community by meeting once a week. The women gathered under the auspices of the Leisure Club; the men came together as the Midnight Club, discussing books, history, and politics until 12:00 P.M. Through the late 1950s, when they stopped, the meetings remained formal and elegant, as if to strike some distinction against the rural norm.

Music, the most evocative spur to memory, accompanied all forms of recreation, whether through folk songs sung at picnics, the lone clarinetist at the boardinghouse, or the stringed beauty of the oud. Often music erupted into exuberant dance, where the cocky display of the solo male was in strong contrast to the languid line dances of young women. In other areas, though some early immigrants scorned the adolescent play of the Americans, many Armenians enthusiastically participated in American sports. Athletic urges became even more insistent as the second generation entered school, and football, basketball, and baseball regulated the seasons.

Aside from social gatherings and the usual forms of recreation, Armenian immigrants could use free time in yet another way: night school. Long won over to the advantages of literacy, many of them appreciated that to prosper in the United States, skills were essential:

> When I came to America I first worked washing cars at night. Then I got a job at Donian's ice cream factory. And finally I became an inspector at the Western Union company. Going to night school helped me get ahead quicker. I took two subjects: English and algebra.[63]

Besides book learning, night school could offer a valuable social education:

> After beginning night school, I noticed my hair was starting to thin; nothing I tried made it stop. I was embarrassed to show my ugly head, so I stayed away from school. One day I got a note from Mr. Spitler, the algebra teacher, asking me about my absence. Well, I figured if he was interested enough to ask, I should be interested enough to show up. So I returned wearing a hat—I had shaved off my hair to make it grow again. When I explained the hat, he got serious and said, "Perfectly all right, perfectly all right." Then he smiled, "Don't you see my own head? I don't wear a hat to cover up my baldness!" Well, I still felt funny, so I sat down with my hat on. Finally when the class began to fill up, one of the girls walked by and knocked it off—"What's this?" And that was that.[64]

In general, Armenians took advantage of every educational opportunity they could. As early as 1921, they had proportionally the most students enrolled in colleges of any immigrant group.[65] Most of them worked their way through. Industrious and serious, they earned the respect of teachers and fellow students. At first, language difficulties and the weak pull of a sporadically developed Turkish-Armenian intellectual tradition drew many to the sciences. It is not surprising, therefore, that the first generation produced few English-language writers of note. Yet this zest for education led to astonishing social mobility; for example, oral history interviews with Armenian survivors of the 1915 massacres reveal "that their most common occupations were in unskilled or semi-skilled labor, but that their children were largely in medicine, engineering, or teaching. This upward mobility accelerated further in the third generation."[66] Statistics such as these suggest how much drive had been repressed in the Ottoman Empire and demonstrate the speed with which Armenians used new educational opportunities.

THE FAMILY

We were orphaned so young. All we could do was think about our mothers. We looked everywhere for them. Later when we had children of our own, it was is if all that longing was poured into them. We craved their well-being more than life.[67]

> A family belongs together—why do you go off and live so far away? We don't know what you're doing away from us all alone.[68]

The immigrant family was a womb where time and again children had to tear themselves loose. In capturing the accompanying ambivalence, Armenian-American writing taps into universal themes; as one writer asks, "How is it possible for us to be other than ambivalent about our ethnicity? For a writer, at any rate, can there be a more ideal condition? Is it not, after all, the *human* condition?"[69] Even the writers who have only recreated the stereotypes of the Armenian family have sensed that the deepest issues of cultural identity often wear an intimate, family garb.

Like other ethnic groups, Armenians carried notions about courtship, marriage, and child rearing to America, ideas ingrained in their attitude toward the family as a survival unit that insured economic well-being and physical safety. Unable to organize themselves on a large scale, the Armenians had developed skills of passive accommodation to protect family members. Richard La Piere in "The Armenian Colony in Fresno County, California" describes the severe constraints that weighed on the Armenian family in the Ottoman Empire. The core value was a loyalty and cooperation that bound the family into a tight network capable of great productivity, as well as "guile, trickery, and deceit that were the chief weapons against hostile Kurds, Moslems, and the supporting sanctions of the government." During those times when massacres swept the countryside, trust was not freely given; even friends and neighbors might turn treacherous under threat of persecution. In such a situation, "filial loyalty" based on "identity of objectives, sympathy, [and] respect" became essential: "Since friction within the family will lessen loyalty to the group, the Armenians have made distinct provision for adjusting family organization to various situations within the group, always with the aim of promoting those desired qualities, loyalty, and respect."[70]

The pressure the family unit had to bear in the Old Country would prefigure conflicts it would face in the United States. In the Old World, the father had control over family concerns; because he oversaw communal interests, family members bestowed him with respect and "explicit obedience." Primary "interest in the group rather than self" molded the individual's every perception and decision; this priority also provided a rationale for many suppressive customs. For example, a strong patriarchal bias and the need for streamlined decision making discouraged female input, especially the inexperienced opinions of young daughters-in-law, who were reared to remain in the background and speak to their elders through an intermediary. Any threat to family integrity was guarded against, and the father ideally merited respect for his administrative skill and generosity. Divorce was practically nonexistent; because marriages did not primarily spring from love but social appropriateness, their continuation did not depend on wavering emotions. Although similar customs and prohibitions inform other cultures, the reasons for their hold are different. For the Armenians, after centuries of social insecurity and torment, the family had become a small fortress.

As with any institution where power is held by a central authority, though, Armenian fatherhood could get out of hand and trap the family in contradictory feelings. The hysterical humor of Raffi Arzoomanian's allusive play, *The Moths,* underscores the autocratic grip of a wealthy Armenian father, Alexandre Zanickyan, on his family and friends in America. Though "ethnic realism is prohibited" in the opening stage directions, fantastic and macabre scenes allegorically depict the ethnic father as the ego stretched to its limits; bound by hopeless confusion, characters take part in "a Mardi Gras for the deranged, the ridiculed, the disowned."[71]

Drawn to his deathbed, children and friends circle Alex like moths, magnetized by a will that projects omnipotence and omniscience. Repelled, insulted, diminished, they still find in him the source of meaning. Though Alex taunts them with advice to "discover themselves," to "recognize" themselves, apart from their relation to him, there is no discovery. Further caricaturing the Armenian father, Alex fears his family will be "doomed" without him and die in "separate gutters, in separate cubicles, of separate diseases" (181). He is so strongly identified with his family that he threatens to supervise their mass death. But behind his truculence is a frightening vulnerability; like Mephistopheles, with whom he compares himself (144), he is caught by the contradictions of his role and his disbelief in his sovereignty. The truth about Alex's character surfaces through hallucinations that erupt from his inner void; denied primary nurturing, he resembles nothing so much as the fornicating elephant of his waking nightmare. Amid this network of emotional dependency and carnage, the fact of his own father's massacre in the Old Country is a gratuitous detail. The play ends without a release: Alex can neither delay his own death nor kill off his dependents;

and as his family and friends enter into a mad dance with his corpse, the blackout is immediate.

Reinforcing the prerogatives of the old-world family, the authority of the village was also absolute. Families had often been interrelated, and geographical isolation, dialect variation, and inadequate transportation reinforced a close communal identity. In this macrocosm of the family, neighborliness was characteristic, and individual families felt few inhibitions interfering in the affairs of other clans.

Marriage was the central rite of passage, an obligation to the community as well as to the family. Thus as the first Armenian immigrants arrived in America, they tuned in to far-off expectations. Most who came between 1899 and 1915 were male, and of these most were unmarried. Because bachelorhood was deemed unnatural and because the immigrants also feared "absorption and extinction" in America, young men were urged to marry. The problem was finding enough Armenian women to meet the demand. Sometimes the arrangements were plainly outrageous, as contemporary newspaper accounts indicate: "One immigrant with two daughters was accused of bartering them to prospective bridegrooms for $200. Another . . . sold his fourteen-year-old daughter to a forty-year-old suitor for $100."[72]

Usually a couple was brought together through a matchmaker, often a woman. The girls, for the most part young, sometimes had no choice in the matter, finding themselves wed to the "ignorant, old or unlearned." Men who had no luck in America or who preferred more pristine versions of Armenian womanhood could find wives in the Old Country, "either by traveling to Constantinople, writing letters, or exchanging photographs."[73] After 1915 they could search the countries of the diaspora for suitable mates: Syria, Lebanon, France. The lure of an American-Armenian with a secure job and means was strong; for refugee parents from death caravans, these assets outweighed compatibility, age, education. Because Armenian girls had been raised to serve and obey, they usually submitted to parental wishes.

Some Armenian-American writers have been sensitive to the cruelty of such arrangements. "Crossroads in Wasteland," a short story by H. H. Kelikian, describes a fairly typical situation: an older Armenian in America requesting a young girl "from the orphanage in Aleppo or Istanbul under the pretext of salvaging the remnants of their vanishing race." This was after the fallout of 1915, and because the orphanages were soon to close, the girls had no choice except to marry.[74] As we soon discover, the photograph the young woman has of her fiancé is old—like him. The only advantage of such a marriage is that she "will be a rich young widow someday," for as the story unfolds, we find that Baron Hagop, like many Armenian men, had contracted venereal disease in his younger days in the United States. The syphilis has not only put his libido "to sleep" but ends up depriving Anna of children. To complete the unrelieved melodrama of her life, Anna later turns into a religious fanatic and, "uptight" to the end, is killed by two holdup thugs for refusing to give them a safe combination. One of her admirers puts the blame on the "goody-goody heads" of the orphanage, who have taught their charges to repress their instincts. He then asks: "Wouldn't she have been better off if after the First World War the authorities had left her in the ***haremlik*** (Turkish harem) where she might have spawned a brood of children who couldn't help but be beautiful if they inherited a fraction of her beauty?"[75] Although the only alternative offered Anna is the ironic chance to breed more children, such tragedies rose out of a more complex situation than depicted here, a long tradition of female compliance that the orphanages merely embellished. It is a theme that has yet to receive sustained attention in Armenian-American literature.

In the early decades of settlement, if the fortunes of young married women were limited, the plight of the unmarried woman was even worse. As Mardikian writes, "In the eyes of the Armenian people a man can be thirty or even forty and still be marriageable. But a girl who reaches the age of twenty-two or twenty-three and still remains single is in real danger of being a *dunmena* [left-at-home] for the rest of her life."[76] "Home in Exile," by Hapet Kharibian, is a compassionate depiction of the circumscribed life of an Armenian spinster told through the perspective of her American-born nephew. Already thirty when she arrived here with her extended family, she remains "a child-woman among the adults themselves half-lost, outcasts and wanderers," reliving through family picnics "the times past in their own fields and vineyards." Unlike young mothers who adapt by meeting their children's needs, in Auntie "something had shattered . . . during those years of flight and survival. She had not healed properly."[77] Bereft of her mother and the sole caretaker of her father, ignorant of English and any adult sophistication, Auntie is a shadowy Armenian grotesque. Sometimes she bolts out of the apartment into the streets:

> Once the young man had seen her walking down Atlantic Avenue toward City Hospital, her apron flapping, clumping along in shoes which she insisted on getting a size too large because of the heavy woolen stockings she wore; a small, dumpy figure,

> almost a waif in her large, homemade sweater, looking straight ahead, not seeing, and with a half-smile of contentment on her soft, pliable features. (7)

Other times, emotional claustrophobia forces her to break through the rigid obedience that binds her to her family; as her nephew notes: "Isn't there one in every family? Isn't there one who does the slave work? Some do it quietly and become shadows. Some shout and fight back; and, because they fight, take substance and take on character. When she shouted and shook her fist, she was keeping herself from going insane(7). For the most part, however, she spends her time simply, too simply; her only errands take her to a corner store where she buys beans for Armenian *fasoolia* and endless cans of Ajax cleanser, her sole tie with modern American housekeeping. The bulk of her life is spent looking out of a window—on a neighborhood long abandoned by other Armenians—absently picking her nose.

Ironically, the incident that sets her stunted life into sharp relief is connected to the humiliation of her old father. Unable to undo the drawstring to his pants, the old man relieves himself in his underwear. His grandson, trying to cut the knot, cuts his aunt's hand too, releasing decades of suppressed hostility. Yet even here, innocence and helplessness trap her rage, and she becomes yet another emblem of Armenian history. Her nephew's parting glance shows her

> peeping through the curtains with her half-frowning, half-weeping face gazing at him and at a world she scarcely understood. He stopped the car and waved cheerily at her until the pain left her face and she wore, once more, the half-smile which she had worn when he had first come in. Then he continued on his way with that peculiar anguish which he alone bore.(8)

The plight of the aging spinster vied with the frustration of the marriageable daugther. One difficult issue for such women was finding second-generation Armenian men of compatible age. Because traditionally the male was older than the bride by about eight years, the only suitable grooms were immigrants. A few young women refused to compromise their preferences and took up with non-Armenians; others, by marrying immigrants, delayed final assimilation.[78]

Sons of early immigrants who upheld inherited notions of male authority and family unity sought out other Armenian girls. Even though some were aware of the damaging controls that had been placed on these young women, they prized traits that would insure an unruffled marriage. Though the girls were not trained in American social rituals and had minimal contacts with males outside the family, Armenian males often preferred their provinciality to the less inhibited style of non-Armenians. This attitude is aptly expressed in a young Armenian's classic testimony from the 1930s:

> An Armenian girl will stick with you longer and put up with more than an American girl. The Armenian girls have been brought up to believe that the man is the boss of the household and that marriage is a sacred thing not to be revoked, and, for better or worse, a woman must stick with her husband. And stick they do. Likewise from their earliest years they are taught cooking, sewing, and all the other essentials which one would like to have in a wife and which one so seldom finds in one now. They are taught the value, indeed the virtue, of economy and will save with a man. Economy is something which is apparently looked down upon in this country, especially among the more illiterate class of people.[79]

From such comments and actual observation of Armenian marriages in the United States, one concludes that these "unspoiled and sensible" wives were instrumental in promoting the economic and emotional stability of their husbands—even if it cost them their own. They helped save the pennies that bought land, and cooked the stews and pilafs that kept the church solvent and vital. And if they questioned cultural sanctions that reined them in, they did so privately and discreetly.

Intermarriage, an issue alive throughout the diaspora, did jar complacency, though. For example, Shahan Shanour, the French-Armenian author of *Retreat without Song,* described the prevailing ambivalence in his depiction of young Armenian exiles of the 1920s. These men speak of Armenian girls left abandoned far away, seeing them as "essential for our blood, despite their ugliness, their dry pride and tendency to become mothers immediately and grow old."[80] Yet falling in love with a succession of French, German, Italian, Greek, and Russian women, they close the door behind themselves, leaving the Armenian girl "a memory with two fat legs and a slight moustache"(88). A similar ambivalence would capture many Armenian men in America. For the most part, in the early decades of settlement, the community discouraged it; although immigrant spokesmen acknowledged that professional men could marry non-Armenians happily, common workmen had not lived here long enough to "discriminate between good and bad American girls."[81] Mardikian tells a humorous anecdote about his own experience with an American fiancée and the reasons why he broke off the engagement: "I had to admit that if I said 'Eof!' [a common Armenian interjection] to Betty when she wasn't feeling well, I wouldn't stand much of a chance of getting attention. She would expect me to hug her, and tell her how sorry I was, and cook the dinner."[82]

But if the imperatives were clear for the immigrant, offspring had to pioneer new forms of relationships between the sexes. For the parents, direct contacts between boys and girls had been unthinkable. However, the custom of allowing boys greater freedom than girls was undermined the moment children entered American schools, where the restrictions placed on "free-and-easy" contact between the sexes lifted, leaving them "different, shy, and abnormally interested in each other":

> "It is amusing," says a teacher who has taught in a school having many Armenian pupils, "to watch the Armenian boys and girls get acquainted. At first they seem like complete strangers to each other, though often I know that they live in the same neighborhood, and the antics which they go through in getting acquainted are most ridiculous.[83]

Though education provided a legitimate excuse to leave their parents' supervision, the latter usually scrutinized their daughters' activities and often felt no compunction forbidding them to go away to school. Denied free association with Armenian girls, young men turned elsewhere. As one young Armenian relates in La Piere's study:

> It is absolutely out of the question for me to go to an Armenian girl's home and expect to go out with her. In the same way, I can't take a girl home alone after one of our Armenian or school social activities. Such a liberty would be intolerable to her folks. The only possible and proper way for me to get acquainted, in their estimation, is to take my folks along with me for a visit at her home. Even then it is impossible for me to be alone for a moment with the girl. We must be under the constant vigilance of her parents.[84]

Such standards made secrecy inevitable. If deceit came to light, it hurt and confused the parents. But the burden it placed on the children was even heavier, a load of guilt, suppressed anger, and bewilderment seldom resolved. More often, those caught were young women torn between parental autocracy and the lure of American freedom. As this contemporary Armenian woman recalls her adolescence, her mother's deference to her father's authority made even the most innocent outing "a big deal": "I must have been in college. I would sometimes go out without asking them. I came home one night from a date. [My father] hadn't slept well. He asked me, '*Oor manatzer?*' I translate it, where did you get left? I didn't go and get left anyplace."[85]

"The Silk Tie" by Edward O. Dorian is one of the few stories by an Armenian-American that addresses this issue, although the root of the tension is not named or explored. Like the Auntie of "Home in Exile," Nhartouhi (Nata) feels a suffocation that periodically pushes her out of the house, beyond her grandmother's "protection." As a child she has been nurtured on an ingrained paranoia that does not allow children out of sight: " '[Y]ou're good, Nhartoui. Grandma loves to have you swim close so she can see you. How beautiful you swim. But stay close—within sight. . . . Nhartoui! You won't go out far, Dear. Hear?' "[86] The girl's response is normal. She doesn't want to hurt her grandmother, but she does want to move beyond the boundaries laid out for her as an Armenian girl, to enjoy the casual and "brazen" sensuality of the barbershop she likes to pass by: "She envied and found exciting that foreign, adult atmosphere in which a man could indulge in a personal (indeed to her, intimate!) ritual—vainly, visibly, and relaxed"(21). Hoping to emulate them, she takes to walking out to the wharf—not dressed like Auntie in an oversize sweater that signals her otherness, but in nylons and high heels, once symbols of liberated American womanhood. Yet even in these clothes, she does not know what she is fleeing. So confusing is the "not knowing" that once, thinking she has swum beyond her grandmother's range and then told she has not, she realizes she needs to destroy the old woman as she lives inside her own psyche. But as this passage suggests, she does not know how: "She turned—deliberately, slowly—and, numb, submerged herself deep into the water, bound, now knowing, not feeling, in anguish" (24).

The double bind tightens when Nata leaves her grandmother; unable to rein herself in any longer, she does not find a viable identity in the American mainstream. Kneeling beside a pool in a luxurious Los Angeles apartment, she tries to convince herself she belongs: "Like the plants, I'm smooth. Like the rocks I'm firm. Like the tiles, I glisten. But within her a growing, nauseous pit of fear echoed back: Like the plants, you're grotesque; like the rocks, you're brittle; like the tiles, you're counterfeit"(18). Only after a one-night stand with a man who touches the grief can she find brief release in tears. Despite its sketchiness, this story depicts some of the pain of a young woman trying to find herself independent of the immigrant household or the American mainstream, forced into false poses through her lack of role models. Nata's story is emblematic of all second-generation daughters who risked family censure by dating, by eloping, by swimming beyond parental bounds and finding a life outside Armenian culture.

The psychological challenges faced by Armenian women in America deserve a full-length study. But here, at least, it should be noted that as the decades have passed, the old expectations of Armenian wives and daughters have not entirely disappeared from some segments of the community. Depending on when their families immigrated, where they live, their political affiliation within the community, and the attitudes of their parents toward education and marriage, Armenian-American women now voice a wide spectrum of beliefs and responses to their sexual conditioning. This spectrum not only reflects the diversifying effect of the dispersion and American culture on the roles and behaviors of Armenian women, but the continuing hold of an ethos that values individual tenacity—in both males and females—as much as it values the loyalty of individuals to the family.

For the Armenian-American child, entry into American culture presented yet another set of challenges. It was a journey no one had taken before him, with no rites of passage to ease the transition—except for those he fashioned himself. Many, like the child addressed in this passage from Helene Pilibosian's "With the Bait of Bread," were cast into a sea swollen with ancestral desires:

> Child, you were and
> you learned to be.
> For a while, Armenian was
> a wish you could not fathom.
> It is still a sea
> and we fish in it for food
> with the bait of forgotten bread.[87]

For the child born to Armenian immigrants, "the bait of forgotten bread" was dense with expectations. The following statement in La Piere's study describes how one young man of an earlier generation perceived his home life as distinct from the non-Armenian home:

> To the Armenian the home is sacred, the children are the center and the very purpose of home life. . . . This intense interest is

> carried even to the point of parents selecting the wives and husbands of their children. . . . [I]n varying degrees, no Armenian child can escape the influence of the Armenian family. . . . The Armenian home develops finer values, higher ethical codes, and stronger moral qualities, than can the typical American home for it is a stronger influence in the life of the people. Yet it has its detrimental qualities considering the accepted standards of American society. The life of the Armenian youth is stunted. He does not have the contacts and experience which would give him full social development for the life outside the home which he will have to live.[88]

This high-minded sense of morality and respect for family life, added to the pull of the American milieu outside, could trigger severe confusion and guilt in the child. Haunted by the memories and traditions of his elders—a past he often did not understand—and their Armenian-colored vision of American culture, the child might create a world of his own. This world was neither Armenian nor American, somewhere between actuality and illusion, a landscape alive with half-seen mythic figures and ghosts rising from the Armenian psyche, a realm barbed with grown-up mores and prejudices that edged his growth.

"Juno in the Pine Ring" by Karl J. Kalfaian is a sensitive depiction of an Armenian child's journey to wholeness. It movingly explores that prerational and fluid consciousness where our first heroes hold imaginative reign, where unedited experiences are woven into a pristine worldview, where language—still a toy—expresses the child's distinctive heritage and molds his perceptions. The first paragraph of the story symbolically locates the child of Armenian immigrants before he left the security of old-world values:

> It was a black wool day for Juno in the ring of the woods he had fashioned for himself out of a row of trees growing as a border between the sacramental land of his parents' legislation and the lawlessness of the American boys prowling with their fearful blue eyes and pink faces inhabited by the also demon spirits of his mother's fears, his mother who saw peril in all the hard cruel world of boys and men, the world of American impieties.[89]

Only here, in this charmed borderland between two worlds can Juno be himself. In the magical circle of the pines, he is free to shape and make sense of his world, a sanctuary with himself as high priest, investing each object with religious meaning. His catalog of prized possessions not only shows a young boy's fascination with junk, but also stands for the many strands of reality he tries to unite ritually: "Magic white stones, a rusted jack knife, marbles, iron nails, bits of mirror, the skull of a dead cat, a shoe horn, and an old *raki* bottle, along with a Mah Jong set—the strangest and most prized." Unobserved, he acts out Armenian history as he has internalized it and applies his child wisdom to contemporary American conflicts; he debates whether to reenact the battle of Vartan against the Persians, St. Gregory against the heathen gods of Armenia, or perhaps to envision how Lord Jesus might send "angel armies to defeat the wicked Japanese and Germans" (4).

As the story unfolds, the interrelated tensions that govern this child's life emerge. On "black wool" days, while his extended family enters the womb of *their* youth, where they talk of "ancient atrocity and never seen cities," the "blood of martyrs" and "strange wars fought," Juno is tormented "in his own youth that preferred no longer to hear of grandparents murdered, of uncles mutilated and of a horrible world of terror that nevertheless was better than this America he really did not know"(3). This then is his first predicament: sensing the contradiction in his family's attitude toward America and not yet having the resources to resolve it.

Using his pet dog and cat—Skippy and Pinky—as colleagues in elaborate play that mingles Platonic dialogue, Christian mysticism, and mumbo jumbo, Juno berates the pets for behaving "like all the bad Americans at school." These children have beaten Juno because he did not share their idolatry of the New York Yankees; most damning, he has shouted back: " 'Papa thinks you Americans are stupid people for wasting time on ball games when you should be studying or working' "(3). Papa, after all, is omniscient Armenian manhood; not wanting to lose face as a coward, Juno protects his parents from his shame and suffers persecution for attitudes not his own. To further maintain his equilibrium, the child playacts his elders, projecting his own protests onto his pets. He refuses to translate his speech into English for them, accusing them of aping the aliens and enjoying the "curious stories" the teachers read at school. But when the dog dares "to remind him that Mrs. Martin had told Juno he was a son of the American Fathers too, by adoption, Juno thrust him out of the pine ring" (4).

Into this ghost-ridden childhood, American society finally intrudes in the form of two "Amerikatsi" soldiers who help Skippy out of a dogfight. Having survived this brush with pollution in the "Valley of the Yellow-Haired People," Juno addresses his ever obliging pets in the cadences of sacred Armenian lingo: "Now my lord Fido and my lady Anahit, let us rejoice in heart for we have seen the places of terror and have overcome this world of evil by our living faith, to the overthrow of all heathen imaginings"(7). Armed with the ancient faith of his people, he even accepts a ride home with the soldiers—noting their dark hair and eyes; though wary of his fall into the "sink of filial depravity," he thus begins to build a bridge of trust and an identity that spans Armenian and American. As his first step, expressing his exhilaration in the jeep ride, he offers the most powerful of his possessions, his name: " 'I am named Karl at school.' (He felt it advisable to use his alien name in this company)." The typical American GI response follows: " 'Hey, you can talk! I am named Joe at camp' "(7). Having at last found American role models who reflect the "virile vigor" valued in his heritage, Juno may now enter normality.

Called to war, his two friends leave him with a St. Christopher medal, which becomes his most precious possession, "the most solemn sign of deep affection." For the first time, as he listens to the old ones replay the tape of their distrust, Juno becomes conscious of how divided his loyalty actually is; that night, he falls into the unifying space of dream clutching the amulet in one hand and a piece of holy bread—an Armenian charm—in the other. But when Juno awakens and finds the alien object gone, he realizes that he must now tell the truth no matter what. In a providential response, the family matriarch Mairig devises the new formula, the necessary accommodation, that will keep the clan intact, yet allow Juno his self-respect. Speaking on behalf of the child, she states that the family has been divinely led to this juncture. As aliens in this land, it is they who must recognize the Protestant and Roman faiths; though they have distorted the "true Gospel," their God is still Christian: "They are not Muslims like the Turks. Therefore, in this land let us recognize the Catholic and Protestant sacred things. My child, keep the amulet of your warriors and never forsake the love God has given you for them. Pray for them. Honor their holy amulet. Friendship is more noble than blood"(10–11). The old woman thus deftly resolves the dilemma: by the time the Armenians left or were forced to leave their homeland in the early part of the century, the essence of their ethnic identity was symbolized by their adherence to Christianity in the face of annihilation by Moslem Turks; presumably, as long as Juno did not convert to Islam and kept loyal to Christianity, his Armenianness would stay intact.

Because the more difficult issue—his unbroken tie to his Armenian Christian heritage—is put to rest, Juno's discovery of a peer, a little boy worthy of Mairig's ideal of friendship, is only a matter of time; Jimmie—a yellow-haired devil who upsets Juno's isolated school lunch one day—becomes the final link to an integrated childhood as Armenian-American. Taking him home, Juno watches Mairig feed him yogurt (a symbolic act of integration if there is one) and then draws him into the pine ring, enacting one final ritual that uses the Armenian liturgy to forge a common American identity:

> "Behold, ye spirits, this *Amerikatsi* and I, son of Armenia, are now brothers of one blood and spirit. The enmity is broken and we are one." With that last phrase the ancient ceremony of the holy kiss in his church came to Juno's mind, and imitating the ritual of the Armenian church, Juno gave Jimmie the salute of the peace called *voyhchuyn*.(11)

With the instinct of one who has imbibed the essence of his ethnicity, Juno in a moment of inspiration here reverses Mairig's accommodation: though the old woman helped move Juno out of his heritage to embrace the new, Juno's holy kiss initiates the new friend back into this tradition. Either way, the margins of the Armenian and the American traditions are broadened, allowing new life to take root. The story ends with American friendship cemented "over shovels and clams in the muck of the low tide mud banks of Shark River" and it lasts "long after Juno had forever become Karl and forgotten his pine ring." This forgetting of the pine ring is entirely appropriate, for like any other magical space, it disappears once it has worked its alchemy.

I have explicated this story at such length because it is one of the clearest illustrations of what Jack Danielian defines as ethnic awareness: "Ethnic awareness really means ethnic self-awareness, that is to say, in the case of Armenians, not only *what* the youngster knows about Armenians but *how he feels* about his own Armenian identity, especially in the context of an overwhelmingly non-Armenian country"[90]. Quite rightly, both Danielian and Kalfaian see in childhood the period where the personality absorbs the most decisive aspects of culture, a conditioning that may not be easily identifiable as the years pass, but is nevertheless pervasive. As Michael M. J. Fischer states in "Ethnicity and the Post-Modern Arts of Memory," as "a deeply rooted emotional component of identity, [ethnicity] is often transmitted less through cognitive language or learning . . . than through processes analogous to the dreaming and transference of psychoanalytic encounters."[91] For a child of Armenian immigrants, one major perception would have been that of belonging to a small minority in an alien world. In Juno, Kalfaian has not only created a character who is a typical child and an Armenian, but given us a unique human being whose language, behavior, and dreamlike exploration of ethnicity are distinctive. He is therefore an apt vehicle for presenting the existential concerns each Armenian must confront alone. Yet, because the author shapes elements of Armenian history and culture into myth as this child absorbs and lives it, we also trace the uniquely evolving profile of these people as a whole—aliens in an alien land no doubt, but also the recognizable progeny of David and Vartan, Anahid and Gregory. As Danielian continues, this investigation of "the inner coherence of culture," whether through art or other disciplines, can be undertaken only by those "attuned to Armenian sentiments and who have an inner-life grasp of the significance of Armenian traditions and the Armenian life-style" (192). Obviously, the corollary to his observation is equally valid: only a reader with a strong sense of the inner coherence of any cultural ethos will be able to distinguish between surface treatment and genuine art.

REMEMBRANCE

> Sometimes [the old people] sat for long periods, without sound or movement, virtually a setting of statues. It was as though some irretrievably lost memories, having torn themselves free of their cages, were communing with each other confidentially, in the mute tongue of spirits, and they were sitting there quietly, intently trying to make out their intimate exchanges.[92]

As this passage from "The Cup of Bitterness," a short story by Antranig Antreassian, shows, when the old cannot speak, silence itself fulfills the longing for intimacy. The notion that stories and works of art heal us by helping us take control of our memories is as old as wisdom. The Isha Upanishad enjoins, "O mind, remember Brahman. O mind, remember thy past deeds."[93] Similarly, Scheherezade cures her king with a thousand and one tales, each helping reweave the unraveled strands of his psyche. The themes of exile, remembrance, and chronicling are thus woven together in Armenian-American experience and literature. Wherever memory has been suppressed or split off, the psyche has been damaged. "Unmaking It in America," a biographical sketch of his father by Leo Hamalian, presents the silent pain suffered by a man wounded through exile. "Forced to flourish or wither" in this land, he has left no track on the "hard soil" of this country:

> It is as though a silent camera had been trained on his life; and when, as I do more often now, I let my mind drift back to my youthful relationship to him, I remember him as a ghost who gestures, paces, talks, but makes no sound, not even the sound of mourning, nor the smallest murmur of that grief which I now realize he had held within himself like a stone for twenty-five years.[94]

Watching the progressive Americanization of his children, he becomes more adamant: the family speaks Armenian, eats Armenian food, sees Armenian friends. The father feels that keeping his children "Armenian" will regain him his past: "He would triumph in this way over the Turk, who had sought to destroy Armenian identity."[95] The guilt of survival freezes life into patterns that only drive the trauma deeper.

For Armenian immigrants who were survivors of the massacres and deportations, two million corpses were the backdrop to all memory. The Isha Upanishad teaches that healing is a function of "re-membering" the past against the universal backdrop. In this realm stories work their magic by welding the parts to the whole; and as the Armenian folk heroes knew so well, the by-product of shared stories is sanity itself. The Armenians who had grown up listening to stories, unconsciously absorbing their wisdom and memorizing them for the sake of *their* children, already knew the power of the medium. As Walter Benjamin describes their effect in "The Storyteller," the cadences of the stories penetrated deep because they had been intertwined with the rhythms of daily weaving and spinning. Rooted in work, they helped integrate the collective psyche. Even—or perhaps especially—the most humble stories, conjured as a minor anecdote was framed in a time and place, were radioactive nodes, capable of releasing energy indefinitely.[96] Magically, the "self-forgetful" listening sparked the "gift of retelling" in the next generation; magically, the young learned which stories to choose for any occasion, and how to arrange them to restore harmony to the listener's heart.

As time passed and fewer contemporaries remained to re-create the Old Country and share the nightmare of the dispersion, story telling became even more vital for immigrants. But the opportunities dwindled. Who would listen? Who had the time in a hustling America to indulge in time-consuming side trips, whimsy, verbal embroidery? Children trained to value information shunned oral history and lost their childhood delight in repetition: "I've heard that story a hundred times before! Can't you talk about something else?" They had little energy left after carving out their identities, scant patience with stories unrelated to their predicaments. By ignoring these accounts, children deprived themselves of a link to their destiny. Meanwhile the old, stranded in the past, became captive to the mesmerizing, paralyzing pull of the formulaic. This interdependency between the generations is articulated in the crisp observations of James Baloian's "Destiny":

There is only so much one can say
for the rooms of telephones and
lights that bleach the skin white
There is only so much one can say
for the holymen disappearing
To repeat yourself is not history

What is the use of ancients
in a modern world
but to be disciples
And what are disciples
but the fruits of execution

The roots of man are the paradise
and with establishing the sanctity
of paradise
Comes the courage and the strength
of the man

The trees drop fruit
seeds thrown to the wind
To the water where soaking
in the light of the sun

Destiny is born[97]

As our century keeps insisting, "there is only so much one can say" about the self-replicating rites of fragmentation: "To repeat yourself is not history." The only way out of this dead end, to sire a fruitful future, is to reactivate our belief in a paradise that roots up from deep down.

Some of the most eloquent evangelists of this paradise will always be story "seeds thrown to the wind," freely dropping their burden as they bind old and new.

Like the ultimate compression of the story, names also affected healthy transplantation. Bestowed at birth, our names frame our lives, yet one more symbol of Baloian's "destiny." For immigrants and their offspring, names carried a special charge from the beginning of their lives in this country: "When I arrived in this country, my cousin wrote me a letter: he told me to remember I came from a proud family and that I should never do anything in this country to dishonor our name. Whenever I was having a hard time here, I remembered that letter."[98]

Strange as many of these names sounded to the Americans, they were one of the immigrants' few secure links with the past. Yet for this very reason, two opposing attitudes toward names recur in Armenian-American life. Most cherished the long, unusual names that ended in *ian* or *yan* (literally, "of"). They bridled at ignorant suggestions—whether made by inspectors at Ellis Island or schoolteachers inland—to abandon these beloved possessions, as this anecdote cited by Mirak demonstrates:

> Baghdasar Baghdigian walked up to the registration desk of a Kansas City night school and struggled through an application. The teacher glanced at the Armenian name and snapped: "Oh, give that up and change your name to Smith, Jones or a name like that and become Americanized. Give up everything you brought with you from the Old Country. You did not bring anything worthwhile anyway." Baghdigian froze into group consciousness. "The Turkish sword," he told himself, "did not succeed in making me a Turk, and now this hare-brained woman is trying to make an American out of me. I defy her to do it." After that, Baghdigian recalled later, "I was more of an Armenian patriot than I had ever thought of being."[99]

Sometimes, however, the sneers and smirks, the mutilations these names suffered on American tongues, drove the young especially into repudiating their birthright. "The Reunion," a short story by Laura Kalpakian, shows how central a name is to preserving and developing a secure identity. Ridiculed at school for her imposing name (Pahkrahdoui Harkoosanian), the little girl demands a change. Her schoolteacher supports her, even asking her parents not to speak Armenian at home anymore. Acquiescing, the parents go so far as to change their names to Harry and Martha Harker. Made powerless by this change, they are forced to watch their daughter don and cast off a string of American names through the years—Sally, Mary, Mabel, Enid—until she discovers herself as Ginger. By the end of the story, Ginger Harker has become yet another grotesque, behaving as Pahkrahdoui Harkoosanian would never have dared. As the athletic and "violent energy" of the girl confronts them, the adults are mesmerized: "Her short skirt draped just below her knees; she wore silk stockings and high heeled shoes in the American way. . . . Ginger's mouth was unnaturally red and full, her hair was bobbed and lay around her face in shingles. She had Harry's nose."[100] Her appearance—"neither fish nor fowl"—hides the void within under a disdainful facade. As she leaves on a date, the wail of the car horn only distances her family further from the urban maw or "whatever else it was that Ginger Harker went to find."

In a much more complex short story, the themes of remembrance and name, the genocide and its spasmodic grip on Armenian destiny are skillfully explored. Michael Krekorian's "Avedis" is a fine work that deals with these issues through a clean, purposefully dispassionate prose. Avoiding a conventional linear narrative, the story is a series of related fragments. Krekorian has pulled apart the chronology of Armenian history since 1915 and carefully reassembled the pieces to communicate what a more traditional form might not. The Avedis of the title is a survivor of the massacres, haunted by memories that do not fade. As an old man, he returns to Marseilles from the United States, and surrounded by a cacophany of radical and socialist student protests, he takes out a tattered book from a chest he has been carrying. There under a statue of the positivist Auguste Comte, patron saint of sense perceptions as the definitive way to truth, Avedis begins to read an alphabetical catalog of last names—the names of Armenians slaughtered in the genocide. Though nothing in the story suggests that Avedis's name is emblematic, it is ironically fitting whether intended or not, for the name literally means "herald" or "one who tells of glad tidings."

Interspersed with Avedis's roll call of names-as-memories are nonchronological reports of Armenian assassinations of Turkish diplomats; these alternate with regular denials by the Turkish government that the genocide ever happened. Three months after the then twenty-four-year-old myth is again "erased" from world memory, "Hitler orders the mass extermination of the Polish people with these words: 'Who remembers today the extermination of the Armenians.' "[101] The clinical, noneditorialized presentation of facts sets the events in high relief. Yet the cyclically repeated psychic patterns contrast with the objective, yet poetic refrain that appears twice: "Genocide victims fade from the memory like the details in an overexposed photograph. Survivors scatter across the globe like the smear of constellations across a winter sky"(57). As the story demonstrates, the more victims fade from the world's memory and the survivors form a scattered nation-constellation, the more the collective memory of the Armenians is fortified, especially in the minds of those who, like Avedis, have not changed their Armenian names when entering the country.

But because "Avedis" focuses on the collapse of psychic time and the tiresome round of retribution that goes nowhere, it also effectively portrays the poignant split between Avedis and his son George. George has moved to Santa Barbara as a young man, leaving his father in Providence, Rhode Island, in his grocery store, surrounded by bags of gold buried in all the directions of the world, "just in case." Yet just as the Turkish nation cannot avoid the repercussions that fell their diplomats, George too becomes part of a worldwide net of memory. Seemingly isolated in his "glassed-in living room," looking out at fruit trees "dying from a rare disease of the soil" and then the "still ocean far below," George Der Zakarian is nevertheless a target of history trying to catch up with itself. Receiving a letter that Gourgen Yanikian (an aged Armenian assassin) has sent to the Armenian commuinity in Santa Barbara, George feels his hands shake in identification: he remembers that at age thirteen he locked his shop teacher in the basement over the weekend for joking about "starving Armenians." He tried to explain to his father why; he did not confess in school. Now Yanikian, the alter ego of all Armenians who have wanted to bare the lie, is condemned to life imprisonment in a country whose government and legal system collude with the perpetrators. George, in a futile attempt to preserve the specifics behind these eruptions from the past, tries "to recall every word Avedis ever uttered" about the homeland and the death marches; he "wishes he had written it all down." But his father's cane rocker "rests empty" in the corner of the living room, an image of a void that can no longer be filled. This remarkable story, in which the whole is much greater than the sum of its fragments, ends with Avedis nearing the end of his catalog in France, a country where the Armenian genocide and its avenging angels are treated with a much fuller measure of justice than in the United States. The national sympathy, however, does not ultimately soften the tragedy of an old man wakened by wolves' cries: alone, he "learns how the wolves establish territories, raise families, always travel in groups" (69). As Avedis stalls on the last of the names, "Zakarian Zakarian Zakarian," the story ends with a final, allusive image: "The wolves wander the high plains and mountains of his homeland." Without our having to be told, we know that it is a homeland now nearly devoid of its former inhabitants, and that the wandering wolves speak for possibilities denied the Armenians.

Food also serves memory in a positive way through the rituals of daily life. In America, most people's first and sometimes only awareness of ethnic groups stems from the cuisines sampled in restaurants, school bazaars, cooking classes, and the aromas of parts of the city. Understanding a people's food customs—the diet, the means of preparation, the rituals associated with them—can unlock a cultural history. The very idea of a cuisine as a well-balanced diet is an apt metaphor of culture itself.

Like other immigrants, the Armenians did not quickly abandon their food preferences in America. Immigrants opened up Armenian food specialty stores or restaurants to satisfy old-world appetites. In many ways, their food reflected their character. In the Old Country, daily fare had been simple: lots of bread, pilafs made of cracked wheat or lentils, yogurt, fruits and vegetables—food that is easy to digest, filling, and conducive to long life. In the village, food and work had been inseparable; farmers ate four or five meals a day to fuel bodies laboring over the earth and celebrated harvests with feasts of bread and wine.

This tie between work and that most satisfying hunger, appetite born of hard physical labor, loosened as immigrants left an agrarian life-style. What took its place was the belief that food transmits history, an unspoken awareness that kept Armenian housewives hunting for grape leaves in the middle of the industrial Northeast and motivated George Mardikian's journey to San Lazzaro, where he unearthed archaic Armenian recipes. Always, food set free more stories, whether of David of Sassoun stealing buttered porridge from huge cauldrons steaming in the village square, or pagan kings celebrating victory with special soups, or the Sunday fast broken over the stewed head of the lamb. Yet even immigrant parents shaking their heads as children gobbled up the hybrid pizzas, tacos, and chop sueys that formed *their* birthright could remember their first taste of America, a promise of serendipities to come: "The first thing I ate in this country was a vanilla ice cream cone I had at Ellis Island. It was the most delicious thing I'd ever tasted."[102]

ENCOUNTERING AMERICA: IMAGES AND STEREOTYPES

A major chore in understanding any ethnic group and its literature is identifying a few of the types and stereotypes that define the group in the larger culture. If stories and their adjuncts aid remembrance, stereotypes get in the way: they limit, distort, and oversimplify. Usually, ethnic stereotypes are based on aspects of group behavior or attitudes perceived as representative by another culture. For the Armenians, there is a modest body of literature written by non-Armenians where recognizable stereotypes recur. Leo Hamalian in "The Armenian in Fiction" explores these categories, noting the metaphorical use of each:

> For male characters, these are: the Armenian as a tradesman or commercial figure; second, as a citizen of the world; third, as a warrior; fourth, as a guru or spiritual leader or pretender; and finally as Dionysius or physically-magnetic earth-figure. Among the women, the Armenian is portrayed as the sex goddess or the earth-mother; as the loose woman brought low by circumstance; as the virginal and innocent maiden; and finally as the strong, powerful earth-mother or "mairig."[103]

As Hamalian notes, the predictability of these images suggests how little the Armenians were known by most of the world until the dispersion. Tied to a small pocket of rugged land in the Caucasus, their main contact with foreigners came from invading armies advancing east and west. Nevertheless, their skill as middlemen and merchants during and after the Crusades, their military gifts, and ability to adapt within other cultures has occasionally caught the notice of writers searching for convenient ways to express independence, peasant grit, or charged eroticism.[104]

Armenians have identified with self-generated images, extracted from three thousand years of history. Occasionally a work in Armenian-American literature will stereotype some of these images to set ethnic experience in comic relief. For example, Marjorie Housepian's engaging novel, *A Houseful of Love* (1954), introduces us to standard frustrations and stock characters from immigrant Armenian life: scholars hankering to show off their abstruse knowledge of Armenian history, young immigrants hoping to make a fortune selling yogurt, feeble survivors in their nineties who knit all day, archbishops of the church plagued by the chronic indigestion of their calling, proverbs about the wily Nasredine Hoja, which act like "Confucius says" asides, and arguments about Armenian politics.

The familiar issue this work addresses emerges in a debate over Easter lunch: "What our enemies failed to do in fifteen hundred years our friends succeed in doing in one generation."[105] Once more, these immigrants fear the "cultural extermination" of life in America. But after the financial rise of the crafty kinsman Levon Dai and his courtship of an *odar* (non-Armenian) bride, one feels that the deeper roots of frustration in these people's lives have been veiled, only hinted at in the matter-of-fact comments of the narrator, a young Armenian girl. Miraculously, Levon Dai's American in-laws take to all that is Armenian—language, history, food—winning over the clannish Armenians with such energy that one of them drops his former resistance to intermarriage: "I ask them, 'what do you want to do? Keep eternally inbreeding? Wrap your culture up in a ball like an egg and sit on it? who cares, Effendi? Look beyond your horizons.' "[106] And what is the reason for this reversal? The happy discovery that the Adams are not Americans at all, but part German, part Welsh—that is, they too are ethnic!

By contrast, some Armenian-American writers have pitted their Armenian characters against American types to explore the stereotypes we cast on ourselves and others. In James P. Terzian's "The Return of Johnny Calendar," the Armenian protagonist exemplifies the marginal [man] of history, soulmate to "the beatnik and hipster."[107] But the main character has merely taken refuge in the role of "crazy Armenian," earning his living as a café poet in the East Village, spinning wild apocalyptic poems that tout his alienation from his ethnic group. His mask not only limits him creatively, but reflects the self-complacency of the beatniks who come to hear "the truth" about life. Though the dilemma remains unresolved, the story points out a central problem in ethnic experience: having developed a facade as a self-protective measure, Johnny Calendar sees the mask taken seriously by the larger culture when he no longer needs it. Out of its insecurities, the surrounding culture can even *insist* that the mask stay put, plunging him into a huge predicament: whether to go along or to expend the enormous energy self-definition demands.

Unlike Terzian, who explores an Armenian's lack of sustaining identity as a "crazy" poet, Harry Barba's "The Armenian Cowboy" goes in a different direction entirely. This short story, an excerpt from the novel *For the Grape Season* (1960), follows the adventures of Bachelor Bedros, who has come to Wyoming determined to act out an escapade interrupted in the Old Country. As this wonderfully improbable story weaves in and out of Bedros's mind, America emerges afresh, a land that thrives "on men who would not give up, even when their days of glory were behind them."[108] Longing to relive his battles against the Kurds, Bedros has come to help a posse chasing three troublemakers. Plunked into a farcical domesticity in the American wilderness, Bedros remembers childhood adventures dripping with slaughter and devises the ploy by which the outlaws are caught, the same ruse he has remembered with nostalgia and regret for decades. Though it works and satisfies a lifelong fantasy, Bachelor Bedros is left stranded in the middle of reality when he then notices his drooping moustache reflected in a window: "Looking close, Bachelor Bedros saw it was mostly grey. Suddenly he knew—This was what had to happen when a man attempted more than what a man could hope to recapture."[109] Oddly, his response reminds one of Nathaniel Hawthorne's as he searched this country for the shadows of romance and psychological nuance, and found only sun-drenched nature. But what pulls us to this story is not only a caricatured America, but the profile of the aging Armenian etched against the Western landscape. Without adequate challenges, Bedros, the reincarnation of the Armenian "man on horseback," quick-witted in guerilla warfare, only draws laughter and pity.

Other works highlight the social vulnerability of Armenian immigrants and their offspring, and the innate sense of superiority that surfaces in contact with the non-Armenian. The following passage from Shiragian's essay describes how the mask of formality could be assumed at any moment, protecting the "peculiar Armenian self" from defilement. Surprised out of their natural gaiety by meeting a non-Armenian on their walk, the father and daughter fall into the stilted ways of the "foreigner," adopting a formal mask to soften the intrusion. Later in the courtyard of their apartment, they pause politely to hear "doleful depression tales":

> My parents were friendly to everyone in the building, and responded to the usual neighborhood requests with a pleased fuss, as if a minor celebrity were asking for a cup of sugar. (Invariably, they forced two on the borrower.) But they were convinced of their moral superiority—their Armenianness: their ability to work hard, make sacrifices, and survive.[110]

Sometimes the injustices of this society would catch the immigrant off guard, shaking cherished values and idealistic views of America. In

"The Sombrero," a rich autobiographical short story by Leon Surmelian, a young man comes to terms with several interrelated issues: his relationship to the land, its creed, and the treatment of ethnic minorities in the American Midwest. Proud of his "cowboy gait" and his overalls (his "American uniform"), the young man strolls into a small-town Nebraska store and buys a sombrero to protect his head as he works on a university experimental farm. Immediately afterward, he notices a sight common to many parts of the country: Mexicans laboring in 100°+ temperatures, doing the work no one else wants to do. Close to their place of labor he sees a sign at a hamburger stand: For Whites Only. We Do Not Cater to Mexicans. His response typifies the liberal outsider: "I shook my head and walked away, thinking I'd rather have equality before this hamburger stand than equality before the law."[111]

But the story takes on more pointed meaning when a barber denies the young man a haircut, identifying him as Mexican because of the sombrero. "Betrayed by his own class," the young man recoils from the man's white-coated harshness: "You heard me, get out. This shop's only for whites." His response is immediate:

> I wanted to shout at him, "Don't you talk to me like that! I am *not* Mexican." I stood glaring at him which a Mexican wasn't likely to do. But again, I could not say a word. I did not want to tell him—and these other men—my nationality. I did not want this barber to touch me. . . . I could have killed [him]. But I realized I could *never strike an American.* It would be like striking at America, slapping Uncle Sam in the face, smashing a dream, a vision, I knew I would never give up.(32)

His divided loyalty is significant: he is torn between protectiveness toward his own nationality (never named in the story, but implied through "glaring" responses) and his love of American ideals. It is a tension basic to a multiethnic society, and its resolutions are as distinct as the persons caught by the predicament. In "The Sombrero," the young man returns to the solace of the Nebraska landscape and heals the inner split through poetry, which both frees him and makes him feel more American; as he faces the core issue of his wholeness, he muses on the split between his poet nature, comfortable with the emotions, and his American self, which is trying to be "all utilitarian logic and iron will": "Emotions were messy affairs, explosions of irrational dark forces within us, sheer anarchy, but the point was that the heart took over when I wrote a poem, and try as I would I could not abolish my heart"(33).

Again, this passage shows reticence; it seems to identify the inner split as a conflict between reason and emotion. But in the context of the story, the real split is between the forces of integration and the need to identify with an exclusive label; the belief that a Mexican cannot be an American with full rights; that an Armenian should not wear a sombrero; that a farmer is cut off from the balm of poetry. Such splits—imposed or self-created—force the choices that cut us off from our sources, casting long shadows that turn the rejected parts of our lives "anarchic" and outward. The labels or roles that do "win out" suffer through the choice. Here, the young man welds the dichotomies he feels by mystically identifying the Nebraska earth with the land of his birth as he watches a thunderstorm: "I had the sensation of being in the boundless aboriginal forests of America and at the same time—that was the wonderful thing about this summer shower—in the woods of my childhood"(33). This natural baptism ("If there are moments that destroy a world, there are also moments that remake it") may not lead to resolution for every member of an ethnic group, but it does symbolize the task each faces: translating the Old World into the New by tapping into universal energies that serve life in the present.

Armenian American

LITERATURE

INTRODUCTION

The Revolt from the Past in American Culture and the Armenian/American Writer

As the young poet of "The Sombrero" learns, only the universal—expressed for him through art—can heal the split between the ideal and the actual. For the Armenians, the massive dispersions of recent history have tested their cultural and artistic inventiveness; here too their ancient megaliths speak of the cleansing made possible as the waters of affirmative group traditions soothe a stony grief.

For a model of the nurturing role of communal traditions in North America, we need not look beyond the American Indian, whose ceremonies expressed a sophisticated psychology. As described in Robert Beverley's *The History and Present State of Virginia* (1705), stones and water were divine hieroglyphics in the Indian's cosmology; by worshiping these "Pyramidical Stones, and Pillars," he contacted the sacred source of their "permanency and immutability." Similarly, they also offered "Sacrifice to Running Streams, which by the perpetuity of their Motion, typifie the Eternity of God."[1]

The United States, whose social streams have swelled with a perpetual tide of immigrants, has both evaded and typified this notion of the eternal as only a young, multiethnic society could. Here, where the meanings of our origins so quickly fade, old-world traditions and identities were steamed and shoveled out as American destiny manifested.

The welding of democratic ideals, which theoretically raise the individual to heights of self-determination, to the fast pace of a technologically precocious economy has created possibilities for social development unknown before. The full realization of these possibilities, however, has been shaped in many ways by the complex social interactions and loyalties of an ethnically diversified population. Placing Armenian-American literature in context thus requires a brief look at one of the major themes in American literature from the eighteenth, nineteenth, and twentieth centuries, as well as an overview of the tensions within American ethnic writing at large and an assessment of the degree to which Armenian-American writers have been shaped by the literary traditions of the Old World.

In some of the more important works of mainstream American literature, the rise and fall of our dominant ethnic group stems from the devaluation of inherited traditions and the ambivalent relation to the land and its native population. Successive confrontations between the radically self-reliant white man and the New World begin with the arrival of the Puritans. William Bradford, one of the leaders of the Separatist migration to New England in 1620 and later governor of Plymouth Colony, gives a firsthand account of the Puritans' hardships in his narrative "Of Plymouth Plantation." During the "sharp and violent" winters, the untamed land came to symbolize worldly vanity, and its desolation forced men's eyes upward, shielding them from their inner demons: "What could they see but a hideous and desolate wilderness, full of wild beasts and wild men—and what multitudes there might be of them they knew not . . . which way soever they turned their eyes (save upward to the heavens) they could have little solace or content in respect of any outward objects."[2]

The Puritans established a society in this "desolate" environment with a spirit of self-reliance, an attitude that informs Solomon Stoddard's "Concerning Ancestors." Stoddard insists that each generation must reexamine the "practices of [the] fathers," rejecting any that bar the "reformation" of society: "we have no sufficient reason to take practices upon trust from them. Let them have as high a character as belongs to them, yet we may not look upon their principles as oracles."[3] Yet as Michael Novak in *The Rise of the Unmeltable Ethnics* argues, what came to be our dominant ethnic group was not only guided by a spirit of communal cohesion, but "a tradition of subjection." Combining the prerogatives of the church, the commonwealth, and the school, the seventeenth-century Puritan family instilled stern principles of government into its members. In time this "severe internalization of order" would manifest as a "suspicion of looser ethnic groups" and give "historical depth to our perception of the symbolic meaning of 'law and order.' "[4] Though this respect for order ensured the survival of the Plymouth colonists and Puritan self-reliance helped spur the settlement of America, the rigid fear of the "other" that Novak cites would cost everyone who came in contact with it.

By the middle of the nineteenth century, Henry David Thoreau's life and writings—imbued with an even more radical self-reliance—warned the reader of these costs and urged him to look beyond the secular arms of law and order for social stability. Following the Indians' lead, Thoreau found in the interplay of stones and water a spiritual injunction: "Time is but the stream I go a-fishing in. I drink at it; but while I drink I see the sandy bottom and detect how shallow it is. Its thin current slides away, but eternity remains. I would drink deeper; fish in the sky, whose bottom is pebbly with stars."[5] Finding the "emblem of all progress" in the Concord and Merrimack rivers, Thoreau looked to the American Indian as a guide for how Americans might eventually inhabit this land. Significantly, he admired the Indian's "aloofness" from civilization, the wary self-sufficiency that allowed unbroken "intercourse with native gods," and "the steady illumination" of a spiritual genius that contrasted with the "dazzling but ineffectual and short-lived blaze" of modern man.[6]

Thoreau's delight in the twilit spaces of the forest where the Indian "recognized" his gods was not shared by all. His fellow townsman, Nathaniel Hawthorne, would express lifelong ambivalence toward the American wilderness. He bemoaned America's lack of ancient, evocative ruins and found himself drawn to the shadows of the American forest, where the imagination—like the heroine of his *Scarlet Letter,* Hester Prynne—could shake its tresses free. Nevertheless, true to his Puritan heritage, Hawthorne shied away from the Indian, who guarded this shadowy sanctuary.[7]

The darkest side of the American character emerges in Herman Melville's work, particularly in *Moby Dick,* where he drove the American brand of order to its fatal end. In Ahab we find a distinctive type: the white man isolated from his past, defying and subjugating the countryside, secularizing the mysteries of nature. Though Melville's "bulky" allegory cannot be reduced to any one reading, the following observations are pertinent to this study. Ahab's American ship *Pequod* (named after one of the first Indian tribes to inhabit New England) is manned by diverse national types, who enact their democratic ideal—their "conceit of attainable felicity"[8]—as they "squeeze hands all around," extracting the life sperm from the whale of national abundance. But both ship and crew are hindered from fully expressing their democratic impulses. Under the absolute control of Ahab—his one leg symbolizing his isolation, his facial scar signaling his bifurcated vision—the ship of state runs into disaster. The more Ahab tries to impose his notion of law and order on a cosmos whose authority defies scrutiny, the more constricted his path becomes.

Self-exiled from his past and the lifeline of tradition—shown by his alienation from family, crew, and natural forces—Ahab curses "all things that cast man's eyes aloft to that heaven, whose live vividness but scorches him" (634). Nothing could be further from Thoreau's nonchalant communion with the starry streams of time than Ahab's outright rejection of the sun. Without a past, he has no story except "madness maddened" (226) and no compass except his blind will. Like Satan, the brightest star in heaven before he mistook the reflection of God's light for his own—leading one-third of the heavenly host into hell—Ahab repudiates his own soul. And throughout the chase for the elusive whale, we are aware of a persistent irony: just as the American wilderness remained aloof and unfathomable to the uninitiated white man—even as he was plundering its riches—even so, Moby Dick "does not seek" Ahab (716). In retrospect, we know that Melville's brooding epic was prophetic. Groaning for the "Time, Strength, Cash, and Patience" (196) to complete his story, he experienced America as the coffin of the white man's will to power. But though he, like others, detected the horror behind the American show of "confidence" and realized that Ishmael's only hope of salvation lay in embracing the coffin of the Indian Queequeg, his warnings were unheeded by the culture at large.

In between Melville's response to romantic optimism and the eruption of modernism, naturalistic writers depicted the individual even further alienated from the natural order and group loyalties. Stretched thin by nineteenth-century American expansionism to the West and superficial notions of Darwinism, the optimistic veneer of democracy cracked. Heir to the ideal of the isolated white man battling an unfriendly wilderness, the naturalistic "hero" came from nowhere and had nowhere to go; symbolically lacking a father, he never learned the words or rituals that ease us into communion with alien forces. Thus, Frank Norris's McTeague, as blundering a protagonist as we will find, pulls teeth in the farthest reaches of the West, San Francisco, his occupation mirroring his inarticulate and brutish personality. Like Ahab, whose ship becomes a hearse on the oceanic desert, McTeague dies in the "chaotic desolation" of Death Valley, handcuffed to the corpse of a man he has killed for gold, which in turn symbolizes the only gratification left naturalist man—the material and sensual.[9]

The Revolt from the Past

Untethered individualism leads to nihilism: by the time modernism overtook our consciousness, American history had already illustrated this axiom. As "new time" assaulted the communal sanctions of the Western world and the transforming charm of the old myths vanished like dew under a microscope, many mourned their passing. The inversion of the natural order is lyrically evoked in Walter Benjamin's "The Storyteller" when he recalls a time when the stones of the earth and the planets of the sky were in communion with humanity, unlike the present when the heavens and the earth have "grown indifferent to the fates of the sons of men and no voice speaks to them from anywhere, let alone does their bidding."[10] Driven underground by the secular triumvirate of Darwin, Marx, and Freud, "the vanquished powers" of nature were, in the words of W. H. Auden, "glad / To be invisible and free: without remorse / Struck down the sons who strayed into their course, / And ravished the daughters, and drove the fathers mad."[11] Even when writers such as T. S. Eliot returned to myth and upheld traditions that led to psychospiritual wholeness, their views were often marred by the old mistrust of the "other," as hinted at in this oft-quoted passage from "Tradition and the Individual Talent"; Eliot pronounces the historical sense essential for artistic maturation:

> [T]he historical sense compels a man to write not merely with his own generation in his bones, but with a feeling that the whole of the literature of Europe from Homer and within it the whole of the literature of his own country has a simultaneous existence and composes a simultaneous order. The historical sense, which is a sense of the timeless and of the temporal together, is what makes a writer traditional. And it is at the same time what makes a writer most acutely conscious of his place in time, of his contemporaneity.[12]

In the context of this study, what makes this passage noteworthy is Eliot's seeming indifference to traditions excluded from "the literature of Europe from Homer" on. Without pause, he bars writers who do not enter American culture through the Homeric gateway from adding to the "order" of our national literature, leaving many unsure of their "place in time" and of their "contemporaneity" with their countrymen.

In summarizing the general condition of the American hero, Daniel Hoffman examines the implications set up by this pattern of isolationism within American literature. Plagued with the aftereffects of a radical individualism that has kept him a child, waylaid in the wilderness, unwilling to contract the "sacred marriage" and return to responsible social action, the American hero eludes the time-tested condition for psychological maturity, what Hoffman terms "a full commitment to fixed values" once derived from sacred sanctions; he also forfeits the redemption derived from service to these values. As Hoffman comments, "Before the submission to this immutable pattern . . . the child-spirit can envisage any or all fulfillments of the potentialities of its psychic energies. In the American folk hero the transformations are metamorphoses without being rebirths."[13] By losing sight of the values that sprang from the sacred, we have lost our way in a wilderness of our own making—and, as we keep discovering, recovering our cultural and spiritual sources is not as easy as preparing instant oatmeal or tearing out a subdivision. Unwilling to refine our "psychic energies" through discipline to values filtered through history, fearing the emasculation and idolatry of traditions that lead to personal integration and transcendence, Americans dissipate youth, energy, and commitment to action in what Hoffman sees as "linear motion through as many conditions of 'reality' as possible."

Our collective ambivalence toward the past peaks in the atomic fallout of much postwar literature. In "The White Negro," an essay on the beatnik and the hipster, Norman Mailer isolates "the psychopathic element of Hip which has almost no interest in viewing human nature, or better, in judging human nature from . . . standards inherited from the past."[14] Precisely this isolation from the past makes Hip behavior psychopathic. Mailer continues:

> The only Hip morality (but of course it is an ever-present morality) is to do what one feels whenever and wherever it is possible, and—this is how the war of the Hip and the Square begins—to be engaged in one primal battle: to open the limits of the possible for oneself, for oneself alone, because that is one's need. Yet in widening the arena of the possible, one widens it reciprocally for others as well, so that the nihilistic fulfillment of each man's desire contains its antithesis of human cooperation.[15]

As Mailer is aware, his "Hip morality" is indeed "ever-present" in our culture, and he is kin to a long line of American writers who have rebelled against the "encrustations" of history. Narrowly defining history as an agent of victimization, Mailer opens his ideal of human cooperation to the psychotic logic of its opposite: do what you feel like before it gets done to you.

The extremism of Mailer's position is balanced by the moderating ethos of writers such as Gary Snyder. Reminiscent of the transcendentalism of Thoreau, Snyder's poetry renews his contract with the earth and points Americans away from "nihilistic fulfillment" toward discipline and cooperation. In the following poem, he returns to the archetypal play of water and rocks, joyously invoking their creative interplay:

O waters
wash us, me,
under the wrinkled granite
straight-up slab,

and sitting by camp in the pine shade
Nanao sleeping,
mountains humming and crumbling
snowfields melting
soil
building on tiny ledges
for wild onions and the flowers
Blue
Pelemonium

great
earth
sangha[16]

The waters that loosen and irrigate the hardened earth rush through this poem, whose form and content are as spare and nurturing as a slab of "wrinkled granite." Line by line, life takes over the rock—the ultimate emblem of our planet—and leads us into the beautitude of the "great earth sangha," the brotherhood of being. Finally, a new chapter in the story of the universal sangha is signaled when Snyder transforms Ahab's nemeses into living microcosms of Mother Earth:

The whales turn and glisten
plunge and
Sound and rise again
Flowing like breathing planets
In the sparkling whorls
Of living light.[17]

Against the lonely and violent journey of the radically self-reliant white man stand other works that shift our prespective. For while the Ahabs and McTeagues were confronting their personal limits in the wilderness, and while the Eliots and Pounds were trying to escape theirs by expatriating, millions of immigrants from diverse nations were cultivating the abandoned wasteland with myths and rituals from another world. The staggering fact is that from 1820 to 1971, forty-five million people poured into the United States from the Old World. It was a vision that thrilled Walt Whitman, who remains one of our greatest seers; Whitman looked beyond the inevitable social tensions this influx would aggravate and recognized its role in creating a democratic "physiology," a "Form complete" worthy of our highest Muse. "Without check with original energy," his "barbaric yawp" voiced all that the expansive American Self might become, secure in the belief that his country had received "the best of time and space, and was never measured and never [would] be measured."[18]

Although the effect of immigration and ethnicity on American life and literature has become the focus of much scholarship in the 1970s and 1980s, the subject remains massive and intriguing. Scholars who have written on American ethnic experience in general present differing views on the durability and even desirability of ethnicity in American culture. For example, Gordon D. Morgan in *America without Ethnicity* (1981) argues that "America is not a good place for cultural pluralism and ethnicity to flourish. It defeats all efforts of individuals or groups to remain separate."[19] Arthur Mann in *The One and the Many* (1979) studies the exploitation of ethnicity by parties, groups, and individuals, suggesting that without community traditions, shared stories and aspirations to fertilize its diversifying tendency, ethnic ties lead to social devisiveness and embitterment.[20] Thomas Sowell in *Ethnic America* (1981) examines the sociology of nine prominent American ethnic groups, concluding that "cultures are not 'superior' or 'inferior.' They are better or worse adapted to a particular set of circumstances."[21] Only when we place an ethnic group in the context of these circumstances can we begin to understand the interplay between the culture of origin and that of America.

At a more subjective level, literature enables us to enter the internal awareness of an ethnic group. The work of collecting, sifting through, evaluating, and making ethnic writing available to a larger audience will occupy scholars and critics for decades to come, offering many the opportunity to engage in original research. As this body of multicultural writing permeates our awareness, it will in Wayne Miller's words, force us to "deal with cultural consciousness and the ways in which literature becomes an element in the creation of that consciousness."[22] Hence, the very persistence and vitality of American ethnic writing refutes Gordon's claim that "cultural pluralism seems to have very little future in America in the long run."[23] The thematic thrust of some of the more distinguished American literature that deals with ethnicity—whether it is Toni Morrison's *Song of Solomon,* Leslie Marmon Silko's *Ceremony,* Maxine Hong Kingston's *The Woman Warrior,* or Philip Roth's "Eli the Fanatic," to name a few selections out of hundreds—focuses on just this consciousness: what does it mean to live out an ethnic identity in America? The responses, as varied as the individuals within any ethnic group, are as striking as the recurring question.

Several recent studies of American ethnic writing highlight some of the paradoxes ethnic writers work within and argue for the revitalizing effect of ethnicity on American culture. Marcus Klein in *Foreigners* (1981) sums up the contributions of "marginal" writers of the thirties, particularly white ethnic and black writers such as Mike Gold, James T. Farrell, and Richard Wright, with this statement: "The underlying truth of America itself was its cultural dissolution, from which circumstance there followed necessity, in literature, for acts of artifice."[24] Writers born into immigrant families—and some not—mined their origins in the "masses," as members of the "proletariat," to attain literary legitimacy. Finding modernist ideology irrelevant to the daily struggles of the working classes, such writers turned to "the lower depths" and its habitats, such as the ghetto, for inspiration. Klein argues that the cultural pot that holds us all has always bubbled over; because of the dominant sense of "marginality," our writers have rejected or created "the cultural fact of America," but they have never "merely accepted [it] because in an abruptly urbanized, industrialized, radicalized, and ghettoized society, there has been no American culture available for mere acceptance."[25]

Werner Sollors in *Beyond Ethnicity* (1986) reiterates that the theme of the outsider is a dominant American cultural trait.[26] But in the most fruitful part of his discussion, he challenges the validity of the separation Klein sees between modernism and ethnic culture in America. Sollors clarifies the relationship by aptly stating, "We quite instinctively tend to equate America with modernity and ethnicity with tradition, without much regard for the astounding evidence which contradicts that assumption."[27] He then cites Ulf Hannerz, who states the experiential fact: " 'The desire to maintain ethnic boundaries may be a source of cultural vitality in a multiethnic society.' "[28] The work of Armenian-American writers and artists illustrates how modernity and ethnicity fuse in new forms of "cultural vitality."

Finally, Michael M. J. Fischer in "Ethnicity and the Post-Modern Arts of Memory" goes even further by describing how ethnicity itself is reinvented or reinterpreted in the works of American ethnic writers such as Maxine Hong Kingston and Michael J. Arlen. I cite the major points of his discussion because each bears directly on my treatment of Armenian-American literature and the perspective I return to throughout. First, Fischer writes that as a deeply rooted emotional component of identity, ethnicity is primarily transmitted "through processes analogous to the dreaming and transference of psychoanalytic encounters."[29] This point suggests how limited some disciplines such as sociology have been in identifying the psychological nuances of ethnic experience and rightly argues for the symbolic, creative resources that ethnicity offers an individual.

Second, Fischer makes a much needed distinction between ethnicity as an inherited label and as a created identity: "to be Chinese American [or any variant of ethnicity] is not the same thing as being Chinese in America. In this sense there is no role model for becoming Chinese-American."[30] Once this distinction is made, we can view the struggles of writers and individuals such as Juno in his Pine Ring to discover their American ethnicity as essential to their devising a personal mythology. This distinction helps clarify the predicaments of most of the characters in the coming sections, binding such diverse characters as Paul Aroian, Lexy, and Michael J. Arlen into a fraternity of the imagination.

Third, Fischer asserts that "the search or struggle for a sense of ethnic identity is a (re-)invention and discovery of a vision, both ethical and future-oriented. Though the search for coherence is grounded in a connection to the past, the meaning abstracted from that past, an important criterion of coherence, is an ethic workable for the future."[31] This point too is important in assessing the actual concerns of many ethnic artists, and particularly Armenian-American writers and artists such as Peter Najarian, Peter Balakian, and Arshile Gorky, who seek to complete an aesthetic and ethical arc that begins in the Old World and curves over into the New. It may well be that this ability to forge affirmative visions *related to,* but *not determined by,* the past is the most subversive contribution ethnic writers can make to American culture.

As with other American ethnic groups, a body of literature by Armenians formed in stages, first emerging with the arrival of earlier immigrants in the late nineteenth and early twentieth centuries. Among immigrant groups of this period, the Armenians were exceptional in one important way: ninety percent of them were literate.[32] This engagement with the written word brought the outspoken immigrant press an eager audience. These newspapers also published some of the first Armenian literature written in America, with poetry and fiction describing the challenges of American life and nostalgia toward the Old Country a staple. However, in the larger context of the worldwide dispersion of Armenians, much of the literature written by Armenians in the years after World War I would fail to purge the traumas of the recent past. Though the Armenians had managed to support a far-reaching, active press in the Ottoman Empire, and gifted poets and short-story writers had depicted the Armenian character with depth, the massacres and deportations absorbed many writers into a dream world, away from the betrayal of history. In the words of Vahé Oshagan:

> Now there was the added sense of being rejected by the hostile world and haunted by the macabre dimensions of the tragedy which defied reason and language. The inability of self-expression had the effect of imprisoning the Armenians more and more in their pain, the obsessive mood of dereliction. . . . For the traumatized, penniless survivors, young and old, the world had shrunk to the dimensions of their forlorn existences.[33]

In America, this "disarray" would first work itself out through literature written in Armenian. Immigrant writers such as Vahé Haig would achieve recognition not only in the Armenian communities of the United States, but in the Middle East and Soviet Armenia. Their contributions were enhanced as others wrote in English of themes related to the Old Country, dispersion, and life in America. Writers such as Emmanuel Varandyan and William Saroyan published their first work in the 1930s, and it is from this period that I draw my earliest sources. For many, two of the most compelling reasons for self-expression lay in related issues: first, the need to express at least part of the wounding Armenians had sustained early in the century and second, to relate this task to their transitional position in this country. As described by Harry Keyishian in a discussion of the Armenian-American novelist, Richard Hagopian, this transitional position is laden with responsibility:

> Only from the troubled second [generation] does the pressure of conflicting loyalties force a unique statement of what it is like to be between worlds, with an understanding of and sympathy for

> each, and the frustrations of being caught in a crossfire of conflicting and sometimes contradictory demands. The experience can confuse and embitter, or it can sharpen sensitivity and expand the consciousness of the person who always observes his society through cultural bi-focals, who can bring to bear on his experiences an understanding impossible to those whose awareness comes from only one source.[34]

Although Sollors rightly questions the extent to which we can understand ethnic experience in terms of the generations, some of the most compelling Armenian-American literature (as well as American ethnic writing in general) is written by the children of immigrants; for whether they like it or not, the second generation fills the paradoxical role of cutting edge and buffer, pioneer and middleman. Torn by the frictions between Armenian and American sensibilities, some of them join the childhood persona of William Saroyan in defying the nativist furnace with a taunting otherness: "we're here, too, now, and if you can't stand the only way we can be Americans, too, we'll go right on being Armenians";[35] others, like the poet Harold Bond, enter the dark spaces between two worlds and make it "brilliant with the welder's spark."[36] No matter where they end up, each is directed by a vision only "cultural bi-focals" can give.

Forced to either make sense of a three thousand-year-old Armenian past in the land of their birth or disperse the accumulated power of their names, the writers examined in the following pages bear a historical sense that T. S. Eliot himself might have envied. Skeptical of a redemption that lies outside history, they are in active and personal relationship to it, responsive to both the Armenian and the American. Though this dual outlook often locates these writers at the social and psychological margins where they wander like the persona of Peter Balakian's "Oriental Rug" through "a century mapped by nations wandering," or places them like the Aram Tomasian of Peter Najarian's *Voyages* before mirrors that symbolize their double-consciousness,[37] they do not inhabit what Christopher Lasch describes as "the barren world of the borderline," where faith in language is devalued and the main tenet of belief is the illusory nature of the world.[38] Like other American ethnic writers, they are preoccupied with the more profound issue of psychological integration, a task whose success requires more than a change of clothes, a well-groomed manner, and dexterity in standard English. In their journeys toward wholeness they tend—like Juno in the pine ring—to discover affirmative emblems of change and continuity that help us decode the interplay of two cultures.

One obstacle preventing a careful appraisal of Armenian-American experience is the assumption that any piece written by an author with an Armenian surname focusing on a conventional range of Armenian-American subject matter automatically ranks it. Much more needs to happen, as these writers demonstrate. There are many fine American writers of Armenian heritage whose work I do not discuss in this next section; pieces by many are used to illustrate themes in Armenian-American life in the previous section. In choosing to concentrate on the work of the following writers, I have been led by concerns central to this study. As a group, they not only raise issues critical to understanding Armenian-American life, but show in varying ways the creative potential of a hybrid identity; not until the perspectives presented here are recognized as central is it possible to critically evaluate Armenian-American literature in general. Individually, each writes significantly about the more complex *psychological* facets of Armenian or Armenian-American experience in a substantial body of work or important single work; each one writes not only of what Michael Fischer calls the "search for [a] coherence grounded in the past," but tries to discover the meaning of that past in the attempt to find "an ethic workable for the future." The latter ambition makes this writing of pivotal importance to a wide audience, no matter what its ethnic background, for by reading these works, we are challenged to engage in a corresponding seach for our own moorings.

In the case of Emmanuel Varandyan, a keen psychological probing into the ethos of an Armenian village in Persia at the turn of the century focuses our attention on "the cultural DNA" that programs group mores; written over a half century ago, *The Well of Ararat* still challenges sentimental notions about life in the Old Country. In the work of Peter Sourian, depth of characterization and insight into the conflicting motivations that pull the psyche rephrases the question of what ethnicity is after all—weapon, prop, veil, nuisance, medium of communication? Peter Najarian's poetic fiction charts the inner journey by which the individual integrates conflicting facets of identity, ethnic and otherwise, into a visionary whole. Michael J. Arlen's autobiographical accounts also trace a journey, this time to the cultural roots of identity. Richard Hagopian's fiction offers a tender, bittersweet look at Armenian immigrants caught and liberated by their dreams. His writing reiterates a thesis central to this study, that sympathetic communication between the immigrant generation and their children is the mainstay of cultural vitality. William Saroyan's prolific work spans all these topics, but in the chapter I devote to his writing, I examine some of the undergrowth tangling his Armenian-American self.

Each of the poets whom I discuss develops an important theme in ethnic writing in general. Diana Der Hovanessian's evocative poems convince as no other argument could that the Armenian language remains a living vehicle of history; David Kherdian's sketches of immigrant figures and poems that describe the generational transition from the Old Country to the New speak with clarity of the healing passage of time and of loyalties many will identify with; Harold Bond's poetry explores the mystery of creation and the relationship of art to an ethnic past; and Peter Balakian's work translates history into the images of daily life, masterfully weaving a tragic awareness of the Armenian past into poems located in America. As a coda to this last section, I discuss the life and work of the Armenian-American artist, Arshile Gorky. Gorky's abstract expressionism refutes views of modern art in which the artist creates independently of the past, and his life illustrates the special difficulties and opportunities of the immigrant artist (as opposed to those of the second and third generations). Throughout, his work argues that an intimate knowledge of the artistic and cultural traditions of one's native land enables one to meet the present and envision the future with creative authority.

For the most part, this literature is not a direct outgrowth of the mainstream of Armenian literature. For two millennia, the epic and poetic resources of Armenian literature channeled through troubadors and bards, contemplatives and revolutionaries, have fed the Armenian imagination and shaped a durable, unmistakable self-image. Nevertheless, the writers discussed here are not easily placed in the line of Mesrob, Nareg, Sayat Nova, Raffi, Varoujan, Baronian, or the bards who celebrated *David of Sassoun*. Their relationship to Armenian literature is one of spirit, of ancestral sympathies, burdens, responsibilities; like other writers of the Armenian diaspora and of Soviet Armenia, these writers register the pain of exile and alienation as they weave images of yearning and loss, celebration and futuristic vision into their writing. But for the most part, Armenian-American writers are not dominantly schooled in traditional Armenian literature, no matter how great their admiration and feelings of kinship toward that literature; non-Armenian literary influences echo through their work with much more effect than the Armenian. What I find so striking about this literature as a whole is its *American*-ness: its rhythms, idioms, preoccupations, the very *context* of the writing locate it in an American literary landscape. These traits are made more striking only as the reader listens to an Armenian voice trying to make sense of transplantation. As we hear in the stylized originality of Saroyan's best prose, the medium is still the message: often translating Armenian idioms word for word into English without missing a beat, Saroyan harnesses the creative power of the in-betweener in search of a language.

Through their crossroads identity in America, these writers add to our understanding of the Armenian diaspora. Despite the disorienting effect and speed of American life, this country thrives, in Arshile Gorky's words, on "the clash of new and opposing ideas." Thus some of the more interesting questions about contemporary Armenian identity have arisen in this country. By responding to these and in portraying one ethnic group re-collecting and re-forging its stories, this literature helps us do the same. Though much psychological territory stays unexplored,[39] even in what has been addressed, the ethnic dimension sheds light on related issues such as sexuality and the relationship between the generations. Sometimes, ethnicity is shown to unite people only through an outworn, fear-ridden past; at other times, it is a bridge crossed on the way toward realizing the more universal identity of the "sangha"; in its most potent form, it leads to the deepest stratum of the psyche, where empowering myths and dreams filter an age-old light and language resumes its original role, to create and heal.

As a final note, I must reemphasize that in tagging these writers "Armenian-American," I do not mean to mine their work for some uniform essence, for no one image encompasses the diversity of modern Armenian experience. Though there will be many echoes as these works speak to each other, their cumulative power lies elsewhere, in the sustained challenge they offer to one another and the reader to look beyond the obvious and clichéd for more truthful "measurements" of Armenian-American identity. As Snyder's poem and the progress of Armenian history show, it takes a long time for the waters of creation to loosen and soak through a past dense with cultural imperatives. With a subject as involving as ethnicity, the writing can skim the surface with the stereotypical and melodramatic. Sifting through to the authentic—no matter what the genre, the style, or the voice—tests assumptions; more often than not, what we thought was "Armenian" turns out to have been the movies.

EMMANUEL VARANDYAN Culture as Entrapment

Nineteen thirty-eight. As the United States harvested grapes of wrath and depression, the nation's ruddy optimism darkened. For many, home had become a wasteland, breeding hunger, unemployment, and Dust Bowl desolation. Literature responded by sidestepping the abstract and venting the reformer's zeal. The Armenians entered the thirties with vigor, settling into the rhythms of a hyphenated life. Though many were losing farms to foreclosure in the San Joaquin and others put in grueling hours in the factories of the East, they were weathering the temporary collapse of the capitalist dynamo by finding time to collect money for the young Armenian homeland, continuing fearsome political squabbles, picnicking on Sundays.

Toward the end of this disillusioned decade a novel appeared that looked backward, winning critical attention by its unusual detachment from breadlines and alphabet-soup government agencies.[1] But in retrospect, one questions the nature of this detachment: in its way, this novel was as severe a sociological critique of the Old World as the *The Grapes of Wrath* had been of America. As a work of fiction, *The Well of Ararat* stands apart in Armenian-American literature, a tightly layered melodrama that captures the sobering patterns of life in a Persian-Armenian village. It portrays a way of life so meticulously ruled by ritual and custom that individuals are betrayed by its impersonal demands.

Varandyan's background suited him for the treatment of what he has called the "anthropological" material of this first novel. Born in 1904 in Urumia, Iran, he immigrated to the United States in 1926. Right before *The Well of Ararat* was published, he worked as a researcher in Turkish and Persian manuscripts at the Clemens Library. Later he was a distinguished teacher of English and Middle Eastern culture at Ohio State University, and has served in advisory capacities for offices of cultural information and Armenian studies organizations. In addition, he is an accomplished linguist in eight Near Eastern and European languages.

The wealth of this personal and intellectual understanding is woven into the *The Well of Ararat*. Here, Varandyan depicts the patterns of rural Armenian life in Persia at the turn of the century. Though the merchant class of the Armenian colony had achieved distinction and power through centuries of entreprenurial service to the Persian shahs, the rural Armenians were trapped by a conservatism that tied them to the narrow sanctions of the church and the family, and expressed itself through a superficial idealism and lyricism. In the novel, we see these mores in action as a village prepares for an Armenian wedding, the rite that epitomizes the unity of life. By filtering the details of the preparation through the eyes and emotions of a young man entering puberty, Varandyan shows the psychological effect of these customs on one of the most basic human drives, sexuality. Through its sustained irony and its faithful account of peasant mores, the story not only tests the value of rigid cultural traditions, but is a notable contrast to the undistinguished and sentimental literature that was being produced by Armenians in Persia at this time.[2]

In keeping with its themes, the prose is as colorful and densely textured as a Persian carpet, by turns heated with the passions of the central characters, imbued with the stately rhythms of a bridal procession, laden with metaphors that suggest the pagan past and the earthier idioms of the Armenian language. Even the structure reflects the symmetry of an oriental carpet with the shorter first and third parts framing the central section, which forms the wedding description. It is against this backdrop of ritual that Varandyan sets in motion his intense story of a love quadrangle with the bride at its heart.

The story is told by Sassoon, a fiery and sensitive boy entering puberty. Its basic plot as outlined in the introduction to the book is timeless:

> Sassoon's Uncle Ardavaz returns from Russia and becomes betrothed to Marina, a beautiful girl for whom Sassoon has con-

> ceived a deep, adolescent passion. To him, wrapped in the romantic idealism of youth, she symbolizes all the beauty, the sorrow and mystery of life itself. Ardavaz, chagrined by Marina's reluctance to marry him misunderstands Sassoon's adoration, and punishes him brutally. Then he discovers the true reason for Marina's diffidence—she is in love with Aris, Ardavaz' friend, who was . . . best man at the gay peasant wedding. Ardavaz challenges Aris to a duel with whips.

During the brutal encounter between the two men, Marina poisons herself and dies.

Driven by emerging sexual drives, Sassoon is hardly a detached observer. Bothered by goings-on he does not understand, he surrenders himself to the instinctual urge to "find out." His endless fascination with everything concerning the bride, his impatience to mature, and his uncanny ability to disconcert his elders demonstrate the power and intuitive guile of the id. Because his more direct ploys knock against the stern reticence of his family, Sassoon becomes a resourceful—and sometimes reckless—voyeur. He peeps through cracks in walls and doorways, steals away whenever he catches a hint of intrigue or an irregularity in the daily routine, shamelessly manipulates the affections of his family to uncover more clues. All the while his behavior suggests that the burden of sexuality not fully recognized and expressed is one of the most complex of mysteries.

A similar lack of self-control inflames other characters as well, erupting into scenes of great ambivalence and irony. Sassoon's relationship with the two men who love Marina is slowly colored by his jealousy. From the beginning of his uncle's return, the forwardness of the boy grates against Ardavaz's military formality and veneer of self-discipline. This alienation only deepens as he sees the boy encroaching closer and closer to the bride. Yet Ardavaz's wrath merely reflects the anger of his thwarted passion, used to the less rigid mores of Russia. Thus each time Sassoon openly admires the bride, Ardavaz's hostility kindles.

For all his eagerness to know, however, Sassoon's first contact with the "mystery" is traumatic. Like many children encountering the carnality of sex, he is repulsed as he steals a look at his uncle kissing Marina for the first time. The following passage indicates his mixed emotions:

> I . . . saw Uncle kissing Marina over and over again. She seemed to be in the arms of a baboon. Every time he kissed her, he gave her, according to custom, first a piece of gold then a piece of

> silver. She tossed the money away and ran back into the main room, crying. . . . The guests ate the melons and laughed. I couldn't eat; I couldn't laugh; and I couldn't look straight into Uncle Ardavaz' face. He seemed to me to be dipped in slime.[3]

But despite his antipathy toward his uncle's "modern" and aggressive sexuality, Sassoon also identifies with him. From childhood, Ardavaz has been a role model, the intrepid explorer of foreign lands who has now come back to assume the ultimate hero's role as bridegroom. Sassoon's ambivalence, one of the major sources of tension in the book, finally tips in the uncle's favor when he overhears Marina and Aris declare their continuing love. His response leaves him as fierce as his uncle: "she belonged to somebody else, not to Uncle either. For the first time in my life I realized what love meant. But there was nothing that I could do" (304).

More of what one critic calls "the sophisticated ambiguity"[4] of the novel emerges as the characters become enmeshed in the many armed ritual of the wedding; depending on their role in the drama, their passions intensify or die when controlled and directed through elaborate communal customs. Thus, Ardavaz's rising lust during the forty days of ceremony contrasts against Marina's limp acquiescence. Her response—emblematic of her upbringing as a model Armenian daughter, adept at sublimating desire to parental pressure—indirectly causes her death, which discredits Maxwell Geismar's assertion that the romance follows a "typically American pattern."[5] As an icon in the sacred feast, the bride is a mystery to be known. But as a human being, her preferences are ignored by parents eager to marry her off. The structure of the book reinforces this irony: long pages show the life cycle stimulated through ritual, with each part of the ceremony laden with mystical nuance. Yet the bride's overt reluctance taints the life force with a sense of obligation gone wrong, and the "Second Gate of life," which the Islamic Mullah describes as "the brightest landmark in the lives" of the Oriental peoples (6), leads right through the Third Gate of death.

The sacrificial role of the bride is supported by the social setting of the wedding: rural Armenian life circumscribed by poverty and the threat of violence from Moslem foes. This threat helps explain the marriage arrangements. In a story told only after the wedding journey has begun with precautions to insure the bride's safety, we learn that the girl is being married relatively young—at the age of sixteen—to protect her and her family. Recently, while she attacked a snake in her father's garden, the Tartar Son of Bey has tried to steal her into his harem.

Though she manages to escape, he vows "to finish off" her parents and abduct her. This detail brings a centuries-old pattern to the foreground and reminds us that for the Armenian, the family was first of all a fortress. Romantic love was usually an unaffordable luxury; constancy, trust, and courage were valued more than personal preferences. But the choice of Ardavaz over Aris has less to do with safety than finances: Aris, though suitable in other ways, comes from a poor family.

Besides lifting the fear of abduction, the wedding adds grace to lives coarsened by deprivation and separation. Like Sassoon's father, many of the men labor as seasonal workers and traders, *garibs,* who migrate to the steppes and oil fields of Russia and return home with the snow, "their bags filled with gaudy gifts and their earnings sewed up in their belts" (9). A view of life governed by basic needs permeates the wedding sequence in particular where food and jubilation mingle: "the eternal Time was obliterated and the ever-present Universe was nonexistent (187). These people's joy in eating increases only because it is done en masse. Each of them lives in an extended family where the concerns of each member are shared with every other. Matters of honor especially are of group interest. Thus when Sassoon finds out Marina's secret, he warns her: "If they catch you . . . don't you remember what they did to Nazo's daughter? I saw the red splotch on the snow" (312). If the sanctions of the family should fail, those of the village provide a strong back-up. This line of authority explains what appear to a modern sensibility unnatural intrusions on privacy, such as the custom of the Seveners inspecting the marriage bed after the first week of cohabitation. As reported by a young woman witnessing Marina's and Aris's emergence:

> Suddenly the door opened and the bride and the bridegroom amid cheers and applause walked down the steps. The Seveners and Grandma then walked into the room; and while we were waiting anxiously, as throughout this whole week, they came back soon, happy, laughing, and declared that everything was all right. (291)

Scenes such as this transform the book into a sustained exposition of the old-world ethic—especially the Persian-Armenian variant—in which the individual's place in the universe can never be self-determined but must harmonize with the needs of the whole. As one of the wedding guests puts it: "Our marriages, our births, and our deaths have been common joys and common sorrows" (208).

At this point, Balakian's comment about this novel's "extraordinary detachment" from the rest of the world comes to mind. Indirect hints that form ironic counterpoints to what would shortly befall the Armenians elsewhere, in the Ottoman Empire, suggest that Varandyan was well aware of the sociohistorical context of his tale. For one thing, Sassoon notes that this story occurs some years before the Great War, the conflict that would overturn his family's way of life. Second, he makes repeated references to the social and psychological effect of the communal feasts: "It had taken people centuries . . . to learn the art of living; no place was there such a felicitous blending of natural beauty, simplicity and ecstatic abandon" (22). This passage is doubly significant as an indirect commentary on the Armenians' ability to survive: constant turmoil helped them develop the art of total presence to the joys of the moment. Despite their modesty and indirection, these people are not repressed or crippled by an inability to express their emotions. Sassoon's accounts of some telling digs at modern Western ideas of progress underscore this point. For example, he hears his great uncle tell Marina's father that regularity and method are the watchwords of the twentieth century. To this the father replies:

> A machine in their pockets is their most regular companion. A machine on the walls tells them what time they should begin to eat, and what time end. They sleep by machines; they work with machines; travel by machines; write with machines; talk by machines over long distances; dance like machines, so many steps, no more or less; travel by machines on the ground, above the ground, and under the ground; climb up high buildings by machines—I wager they are machines themselves. I don't care for that kind of stuff. I like to forget time. When I am drinking my bowl of wine, I like to be drinking wine, nothing else. (44)

Nevertheless, though the absence of isolation, anxiety, and nihilistic self-absorption—disorders tied to the exclusive identification with a particular time and place—offer an implicit criticism of modern life, this peasant's attempt to annihilate time comes as much from the dangers of the moment as an attitude of transcendence.

The well where the village youths congregate to review prospective brides symbolizes this nontemporal realm at its most idealized. As in the works of nineteenth-century Armenian poets such as Medzarentz, the village spring draws a twilit hope: "hallowed with tradition and revered as a holy source of life," the spring draws girls and brides who dress up and show off their bodies as their carry the earthen jugs filled with water (27). Here, the same water that cooks the food, cleans the family on Saturday, and brings together the village youth also serves as an effective cosmetic: "They were wont to wash and massage themselves with cold water, before going to the spring, until their bodies became ruddy and vibrant, and when the winter air played on their cheeks and calves, they flushed with pink-and-white vigor" (27).

Another custom that unites the community is story telling. Amid the wedding festivities, two troubadours vie for the honor of regaling the bride and groom. The winner's legend will christen their journey into the garden of life. But though Ashig Jivany tells a spellbinding narrative, the story does not release the listeners from entrapment. A careful reading of the tale unveils striking parallels to the main action. Both are set into motion by Moslem holy men and interlaced with journeys—caravans and migrations, bridal processions and exiles—reflecting the waywardness of life. In the troubadour's tale, the characters are pushed far from their course by an indifferent fate. And when they do try to outsmart destiny, the attempt backfires, as in the main story. This view of destiny—in Armenian called *jagadakir* (literally "that which is written on one's forehead")—as a stern given reflects a typical Oriental attitude. Like the *karma* of Hinduism, destiny cannot be avoided, only accepted, worked out, and sometimes transcended. Exhibiting an Oriental love of the ideal—in which virtue can be found in the most evil characters—the tale also teaches undying faith, even at the cost of life. Similarly Marina, later discovered in her love for Aris, shouts at Sassoon: "I shall love him even in my grave. There! Go, go, go to the housetops, go to the church tower and cry out to the whole village, to the whole world" (313–14).

In both stories, the most important communication is indirect. In the wedding story, poetry sung to the accompaniment of the stringed *taar* even bends the will of natural forces and reveals the true identity of the lover. Later, when the truth of Aris's and Marina's love is about to rend the family, the stage for the confrontation between the men is set through an extended sharing of song. This entertainment culminates when Shakira, Sassoon's aunt, accompanies Ardavaz in a song that foreshadows tragedy: "Oh, mountains! lofty mountains, bury me in your everlasting bosom, the day has ended, perchance I may find rest in the eternal dream of your breast!" (326). Through indirection, music and story telling allow the listener to find a personal message in the hearing, a message that speaks to the intuition. As a result, the bride and groom find their conflicting desires reinforced as they listen. But at no time do they share their doubts. To a modern sensibility raised on "openness," such reticence seems pointless. Yet both the main story and the wedding tale emphasize the axiomatic importance of knowing when to keep quiet. As we learn, though, it is a rule that can backfire.

Finally, cushioning one's attachment to life or death, both stories portray life as a dream, a view basic to the cosmologies of the Orient. As in a fairy tale, identities shift according to roles: wandering merchants become troubadours and maidens turn into mysterious brides. But none of it is forever, not even this way of life that has evolved through millennia. As the Mullah tells Sassoon at the beginning of the story: "We are only children enticed by butterflies. But it's delightful to chase them" (3). Here we find the final irony. For though the peasants have tried to recreate the experience of the Eternal amid their hard lives, the abrupt end of the marriage suggests their limited power. Who, after all, is guiding the journey? Sassoon's sense of helplessness after discovering Marina's secret illustrates that even the greatest passion must yield to fate: "These thoughts and questions oppressed me like nightmares; I felt, with pangs, over and over again, that they were beyond my solution. . . . I was helpless; so was Uncle, so was Marina, so was Aris" (309). Somewhat like naturalistic characters caught between the urgency of their needs and the unsympathetic sanctions of the community, these poeple burst with desire. Once released, their passions must, like a magician's charm, take their full, disruptive course through a world trembling between hard dualities.

Although contemporary reviews of *The Wall of Ararat* were generally favorable, they did not do justice to its strengths. The headings for reviews in two major publications ignored the actual ethnic focus of the book: the *New York Times* review by Alfred Kazin is entitled "A Tale of Persia" and Courtlandt Canby's in *The Saturday Review* reads "Persian Wedding." Kazin's treatment in the *Times,* while praising the stylistic strengths of the novel and the village cameos it presents, fails to capture its complex depiction of peasant *Armenian* mores. Although he compliments the peasants for their "poetry of association, the gift of binding everything together so naturally that what is true seems whole,"[6] by neglecting to identify these peasants as Armenian he brings no insight into the cultural sanctions that precipitate the ending tragedy. Canby comes closer to the mark when he writes: "There is something in the book that raises it above a mere *genre* scene, and that is the quietly insistent emphasis on the modern innovations which were filtering into this and other villages from Russia in the days just before the war."[7]

Despite the merits of this novel, Varandyan has published only one other, *The Moon Sails* (1971). Balakian notes that this story of war at sea, based on personal experience, "is almost Conradian in its ambition, but as fiction it fails to rise to the metaphoric level it suggests."[8] But elsewhere in his work we do find the same psychological depth, irony, and lyricism that distinguish *The Well of Ararat,* particularly in the short story "Ahsaddhur: The Gift of God." Here too, the story is recounted by a young boy on the trail of a secret—this time death—and the action centers on a Persian-Armenian village, where harsh mores help destroy an innocent life.

As in *The Well of Ararat,* the peasants of this story find relief from "the tyranny of Shahs, Sultans, and Czars" through song and festival. In the middle of one such celebration, a pageant commemorating the life of a revered poet, we meet the central characters: Baron Torose, a sadistic schoolmaster consumed by the love of order, as symbolized by the clock; and Ara Balian, a young boy who has just lost his brother because of the schoolmaster's uncontrolled sense of discipline. Baron Tórose is an engrossing portrait of evil, coalescing the shadows of the peasant ethos. His desire for perfection defeats his students: he paces the length of the classroom ("some said this was his way of keeping warm,"[9]); takes delight in speedy mathematical gymnastics; "lifts his index of release" only after the bell rings twice; maneuvers the class like "a master chess-player." Significantly, he comes from Tiflis and has been educated in Moscow: a lover like Ardavaz of depersonalized rituals.

Ironically, Ara's brother and sister arrive late to school one morning because the family cannot afford a clock. Like Sassoon's father, Ara's father works in the Russian coal fields. The penalty for tardiness is exile into the snow, from which the young boy eventually develops a fever and dies. Ara's subconscious response is to merge time and Death in the figure of the satanic schoolmaster: "I passionately hated Death" (8). This response reminds the reader of analogous references in *The Well,* especially the passage about machines. But though the peasants of the earlier story obliterate time restrictions through their rituals, in this narrative the children are at the mercy of the teacher's obsession with time. Parents deliver up their children, instructing the teacher: " 'Here, Master, I have brought this child to you—make a man out of him. *Misse kezi, voscorn indzi.*' This meant you can dicipline him anyway you wish; use the rod, his flesh can take it; but please don't break his bones: the trained frame and brain must be left for his father and mother" (15). Trying to make men of these children—able to fight off the tyranny of shahs, sultans, and czars—the social structure sacrifices them to brutal pedagogues. The scene in which the children are ordered into the snowy field poignantly foreshadows deportations to come elsewhere:

> They walked across the veranda to the courtyard, which was as smooth as a clean carpet of fleece. Arpia held Ahsso's hand, like a young mother anxious for the life of her baby. She was nine or ten and Ahsso seven. . . . For a few seconds they lingered at the edge of the veranda, where the snow had not made any inroads. They recoiled from entering the field of snow. They looked back in a wistful manner. Baron Torose was watching them through the center window. He raised his index finger and ordered them to proceed. They stepped into the snow, first timidly, shrinkingly, pawing the flakes with their toes, then listlessly, as though it were a matter of fate, not choice. (13)

To complete the irony, religious values bow to superstition. Because the family cannot afford a doctor from the city, Gulo-bajy, the priest's wife, is called to examine the little boy. But the same intuitive antipathy between Sassoon and Ardavaz flares up between the village crone and Ara. Her rough treatment and clumsy folk methods of lancing the fever sore prove fatal, echoing the sinister movements of Baron Torose: "Gulo-bajy stuck her right index finger into his mouth, and with a sudden jerk pressed the swelling on the right side of his throat" (19). As in the novel, ambivalence also surrounds the authority of religious ceremonies. Though the church doctrine teaches salvation through faith, Baron Torose's manifesto overrules faith with satanic "knowledge": "To challenge God is to know God. . . . One who dares to taste of the fruits of knowledge has the key to the mystery of God's paradoxes" (9). Thus, the greatest paradox by the end of this story is that an innocent child—the "gift of God"—whose voice Baron Torose especially loved is the victim of his desire for an abstract perfection.

As depicted in these two works, Varandyan's Armenians—whether it be the lustful Ardavaz, the evil aesthete Baron Torose, or the passionate adolescents Sassoon and Ara—are not bucolic peasants. Against the strict codes of a village society where the penalties for trespass are ruthless, their emotions pulse through the unguarded cracks with destructive force. Despite his acute awareness of the limitations inherent in this worldview, though, Varandyan is equally skeptical about more modern alternatives. Symbolized by the clock and the machine, these impersonal agents merely enforce new forms of regulation. Throughout, as the innocent suffer, their life force weakening "like the tick of a broken watch" (343), we sense the utter fragility of what is most beautiful and promising before such subjection. For Varandyan, the past is thus not an object of naive longing, nor a golden age when problems were simple. Instead, it holds up a warning mirror to any era or culture that violates the most sacred of laws: whenever and however we try to regiment the human heart, the dawn brings death.

PETER SOURIAN The Trap of Multiplicity

If Emmanuel Varandyan presents culture as a carefully wired maze of right and wrong, Peter Sourian explores the imprisoning patterns of contemporary life. The more his characters fumble to escape the past and the pressure of their ethnicity, the more they fall victim to it. Yet a grasp of how history might serve dislocated lives remains elusive. Here the themes that have become the special props of modern Western life—spiritual isolation, uncertainty about place and role, attachment to the moment—take on a unique pathos in the lives of immigrants and their children. By focusing on what Nona Balakian calls "the psychological strains and defenses that an ethnic background aggravates,"[1] Sourian shows how ethnics afloat in the mainstream, even when superficially assimilated, intensify the insecurities of the culture at large.

For Sourian, these issues become more urgent with successive works, as seen by comparing his first novel, *Miri* (1957), with his third, *The Gate* (1965). In both, characters are sabotaged by family and ethnic dynamics. In *Miri,* published when Sourian was twenty-three, the same story is told three times from different points of view: by Miri, a young Greek war refugee; by Josh, a gentle guilt-ridden WASP smitten with her; and by Lexy, her American-born cousin and roommate to Josh. Each telling reveals the limiting effects of background on perception.

Though Lexy's highly defined Greek heritage challenges him to chart new patterns of behavior with immigrant parents, it will also sustain him as he accepts his male Greek prerogatives. His security contrasts with the stereotypical guilt and competitiveness of his roommate, Josh. Josh, the blond and blue-eyed son of duty-bound WASPs, proves that sampling other ethnic traditions highlights the best and worst in one's own: he envies his Greek friend's casual ability to concentrate and relax with all the flexibility of Varandyan's peasants, his ability to tell stories, the exotic food, the young women with their strange accents, the sense of belonging. About Lexy, he tells his friends, " 'Yes, his father's some big shipowner,' . . . as if some of the wealth and security had rubbed off on me."[2] In his parents' house he admits to himself: "I had no home, not even a self that I could clutch to Josh, and say, This is me, the way Lexy seemed to cry it whenever he was awake, the way he seemed to dream it and know it, under the blanket on his filthy mattress" (105).

By contrast, although Lexy's Greek background sharpens his insight into the surrounding culture ("It's funny the way people are always skirting around their pleasures, isn't it, paying out good currency and coming out with nothing") (117), we see his sexist father paying next to nothing to give momentary pleasure to the typically harassed immigrant women in his family. Faced with the inconsistencies of his father's life and the wartime sufferings of his cousin Miri, Lexy's central challenge is "in this day and age, how can I, me, become a man?" (206). Unable to repeat the past, yet discontent with a culture that undermines his Greek manhood, Lexy struggles toward complete intimacy with another.

This desire helps explain his instinctive attraction to his Greek cousin; as he wonders at this pull, we find the split characteristic of many children of immigrants. On the one hand, his wish that his children be "all Greek" voices an intuition that here, at least, is a way to have a "self"; on the other hand, he vaguely feels that in a country where we do not have to marry within our native group, such an attraction is oddly incestuous: "I used to think, if I get married I'll have to marry a Greek girl, because otherwise my children won't be all Greek. For my children not to be all Greek seemed a terrible thing, I don't know why." But as he grows older and begins to feel attracted to girls, he finds all the Greek girls he has met "unattractive": "The idea of sleeping with one of them seemed unimaginable, just plain impossible. I don't know why" (185). Even more than the ending resolution, where Lexy enters manhood by confronting his father, this issue so lightly touched on here gives the novel a special interest. For in a land where so many "flavors" of sexuality are available, the second-generation will always feel the responsibility of "hybridizing" or maintaining the blood line. How children work through this question, the cutting edge of assimilation, remains a charged issue in American ethnic experience in general.

Commenting on Sourian's work in general, Balakian observes: "It is not too often today that one encounters a writer who can so skillfully convey the multiple impulses and subtle influences that shape feeling and attitude."[3] We find this attention to "multiple impulses" in *Miri,* where Lexy falls asleep at the end weighing possibilities: "She is not like these Modern Youth, I thought, in the phrase of my father, and then thought, I don't even know about that. She is pure . . . and then thought, I don't know, maybe she isn't" (219). Similarly fragmented sensibilities swing back and forth through *The Gate,* Sourian's longer and more complex novel about Armenian immigrants unable to adjust to exile in America.

The action takes place in New York City. Throughout, much is going on: flashbacks to the Hamidean massacres of 1894–95 and the events leading up to 1915, vignettes of immigrant experience in the 1920s, many scenes in which we meet a spectrum of Armenian and American urban types. Ostensibly, the story is told by Paul Stepanyan, the son of an immigrant architect, Sarkis Stepanyan. Describing his writing intentions, Paul hopes to "concoct something" out of his family's "immigrant past," to create out of this raw material "a remarkable alchemy . . . and pour out a molten fool's gold of narrative."[4] A major question facing the reader is whether the narrative ever achieves this "remarkable alchemy," the synthesis needed to make sense of the diverse episodes and layers of report. For not only is the story laced with newspaper and documentary accounts, letters and journals, anecdotes and flashbacks, conversation and interior monologue, but the narrative voice keeps shifting, from first to third person, from an objective view of a given character to a minute transcript of his mind and senses at play. Through form and content, the novel thus reflects Paul's view of truth: "The truth seemed like a large fish which never existed whole, except as an imaginary ideal form, splintered into living minnows, darting every which way, to be caught one by one—only a few of them—until sunset, supper, sleep" (233). Unable to see the fish whole, the characters also dart every which way, failing to integrate the warring stimuli that liven consciousness. And because they are not able to achieve inner consistency, communication is distorted by ambivalent and half-hearted signals.

Insecure and outraged, the Armenian characters show how the great events of history—that objective foundation that we cling to for guidance, caution, and inspiration—spring from split motives, which are in turn manipulated by fanatics bent on violent ends. As a study of such fanaticism and human inconsistency, the novel forces us to reexamine the treacheries of the Armenian past. The two characters who play out the central melodrama are Boghos Boghosian, a would-be Armenian intellectual of the most humorless type, and Sarkis Stepanyan, Paul's father. We follow the relationship of these immigrants from its beginnings in Constantinople to its tragic end in America, decades later.

On the surface, the men are opposites in almost every way. Boghosian is an old-country "intellectual" of fatiguing seriousness who thinks cracked wheat vulgar and who will "not spare one drop of his own or anyone else's blood for the nation" (313). Like narrow chauvinists before him, Boghosian spends years writing yet another history of Armenia "for the people," embarrassing for its dullness; as Paul remarks, his only memorable trait is "his ineptness with the language" (153). Though the sight of a man touching a woman is enough to make him turn away and he seems devoid of passion and spontaneity, he tries to breathe life into long-lost heroes and values. As in the hands of all true believers, his mythical heroes—"David of Sassun, Tigranes the Great, the mountaineers of Zeitun"—prop a psychotic desire for vengeance.

Personified by Boghosian, fanatic excess becomes the touchstone of recent Armenian history as we piece together interspersed accounts of Kurdish marauders, Turkish massacres, the assassination of Talaat Bey by an Armenian revolutionary, infighting among Armenian factions, and the murder of Archbishop Tourian. Yet watching the seductive play of dice in a backgammon game between the Armenian nationalist, Hagopian, and a partner who is beating him, we see the idea of Armenia reduced to a mechanical reflex of the conscience, whipping the forgetful flesh. As he fights conflicting instincts, Hagopian fumes about the game while an inner voice insists: "*Forget Armenia.*" While his eyes follow his partner's lucky dice, that voice asks: "How can Hagopian forget Armenia? What else is there? *This?* Am I an animal, a cold, tiny lizard-brain?" (202). Coming to the end of the game, Hagopian puts into words the dilemma these Armenian immigrants face as daily needs fog over their dreams. Failing to grasp the "large fish" of an ideal fragmented by time and genocide, Hagopian succumbs to the cheaper thrills of the moment:

> Armenia, what was Armenia? How could one grasp it? It was everything, yet it was not in the air, not in a room, like a chair or a table. But with this—with this gambling, awaiting the outcome of the dice your chest tightened as if in the grip of passion;

> blood throbbed through your heart, and a resolution always followed, a sterile event. (204)

Boghosian has none of Hagopian's frankness, clutching an outdated notion of Armenia, which in time becomes a weapon, a foil for psychosis. A true literalist, he has accepted without reservation a simplistic code; admitting the complexity of the world, he nevertheless insists, " 'But . . . some things are black and white' " (194). After Paul informs him that his history is not publishable, Boghosian asks why Paul does not write about his people; it is a question he already knows the answer to: "It was because I was definitely, fatally evil. I would triumph, as true Armenians never triumphed" (194).

Ironically, Paul's father, Sarkis, who has repudiated as much of his heritage as possible, is like Boghosian an absolutist. He does not want his prejudiced view of Armenians contradicted and scorns the common and embarrassing aspects of his Armenian past. In a revealing passage, he compliments the Nordic calm of the Swedes and the English, and then complains about the obsessive treatment of the genocide in Armenian newspapers. The contradictions in his feelings emerge when he admits that he "can't help" hating the Turks himself:

> But those Armenians are *so proud* of what they went through. Why can't they be proud of themselves today? I'll tell you why. Because they haven't done anything for themselves as individual people. They suffered and so they think it's up to the world to live for them. So they've suffered. It was horrible. It was. So what? (214)

Like Boghosian, Sarkis stereotypes the attitudes of an entire group. But though the pathetic "Old World codger" clutches the past, Sarkis tries to bury what he has not faced. Thus, at one point, when Paul asks Sarkis to translate from his own father's journals, the unresolved pain briefly surfaces as he reads the first line—"*With God's help I will come back along this road again*"—and then freezes. Trying to take up the text again, in a trembling and "chastened" voice, he reads his own name twice, closes the books, starts to weep, and adds an unneeded coda: " 'I can't any more' " (131).

Because so much remains unclarified through actual confrontation, Sarkis's ambivalence intensifies. Much as he makes fun—like Boghosian—of the "peasant cracked wheat stuff" that feeds the Armenian-American heritage, he also admits that despite the "stupidity" of being

Armenian, " 'I'm crazy enough to be more Armenian than any one of them' " (249). Similarly, though he refuses to teach his children Armenian (" 'You can ruin your children, leave them with a broken English and a broken heart' " (121), he uses Armenian all the time. And railing against the insularity of the Armenian church and wishing to erect a "human Christ" instead of "an Armenian Christ," he nevertheless wants this Christ to reflect "His suffering" rather than "His glory" (210). As to his motives for even bothering with a project that involves his ethnic group, he again admits he "can't help it": "I don't know why the Armenians should have a cathedral, but I have to do this" (218).

The image that most fully captures Sarkis's ongoing tie to his culture appears when Paul opens the family refrigerator and discovers it bare "except for the large bowl of yoghurt my mother made every week for Father, always covered with the same old plate, and a half-empty bottle of prune juice and a cut lemon, all for Father's breakfasts. Same as always" (107). This prosaic image of change and continuity—an American refrigerator containing something so typically Armenian—suggests how deeply embedded old habits can be. If the breakfasts are the "same as always," what about all the other relics of ethnicity rooted in the psyche, beyond the reach of reason or hostility, holding firm against erosion? As Balakian comments, though Sarkis "wants to free himself of an oppressive past," he defies "assimilation into a society emotionally antithetical to him" (57).

Over the years, Sarkis's inconsistency aggravates Boghosian's frustration as he rationalizes that "no appropriate outlet" remains for personal and political grievance. Although Sarkis is the son of the Armenian patriot who sends him to America, Boghosian sees his life as an unbroken affront to himself and to Armenia. But this hatred is aggravated by his unacknowledged resemblance to the architect; plagued by his shadow, Boghosian twists so much that he can stalk and kill Sarkis with the same Velo-Dog pistol that Sarkis's mother gave him in 1915 in Armenia. As an ironic side note, April 24, 1915— Sarkis's eleventh birthday—sparks the senseless chain of events that leads to his own equally pointless murder.

In retrospect, the killing—the ultimate perversion of a stagnant, sentimental chauvinism—helps us place other, earlier scenes in context, as when Sarkis imagines a conversation between his mother-in-law and Greta Garbo, skewering the faddish tastes that unite people in the name of a quaint ethnicity. Sarkis muses that the old woman and the screen star would hit it off perfectly, spending their time talking about body ailments and health tonics: "and he could hardly imagine Greta Garbo's excitement when she learned that Mrs. Dorian had been cooking cracked wheat all her life" (277–78). At the other extreme, Boghosian's bogus love of abstractions, his use of "Armenia" to shield his own weakness, is mirrored by Paul's girlfriend, who invokes "the abstract mass of suffering humanity" to enlarge and protect herself. Bloated at either extreme by the "ill-digested panaceas of our time," the spirit seldom rests in moments of bravery. For the most part, even a phone call from his father triggers Paul's ambivalence, making him wonder if he feels "annoyed or friendly." Thus, divided in will, unable to remain loyal to absolutes, people fall into annihilating contradictions.

This realization sheds final light on an odd turn of phrase Paul uses earlier in the book and helps us see his entire account, at one level, as a symbolic reenactment of Armenian history—history not as ideals embodied through recorded events, but as a chronicle of individual irrationalities that erupt into collective tragedy. Trying to assure Sarkis that he is hard at work writing, Paul admits: "He did not believe me; but, during those years, *until I wrote out my massacre,* I assured him at rhythmically timed questionings that it was indeed true; so he believed me" (86; emphasis mine). This cryptic passage simultaneously collects and disperses the strands that make up the novel. Throughout, truth and individual purpose are "massacred" by the fluctuations of the mind, and many leads are left unintegrated, so that we sense a comment or gesture is significant without understanding why. Though this confusion may reflect the perpetual limbo in which the mind works, it also leaves the reader with a vague dissatisfaction—what *did* that reference to real estate mean? Why *does* Paul ask his brother-in-law about his father's death? Though we can concoct an answer out of the random clues and half-developed patterns of the whole, we are never sure the solution fits. In denying the reader a tidy certainty, Sourian joins other avant-garde writers of this century. Succinctly described by Christopher Lasch, these writers insist "that art—like life itself—is a fiction: the arbitrary imposition of meaning on experiences otherwise meaningless. Modern writers have reversed Ibsen's formula: the reality they wish to re-create in their works is that of illusion."[5] But such reversals are risky because they frustrate a basic human urge: to make sense out of the multiplicity. As the novel ends, the gate into meaning stays locked, stripping the massacres themselves of significance: we are stranded with a group of highly evocative portraits.

PETER NAJARIAN Voyaging Back to America

Describing his first novel, *Voyages,* Peter Najarian has referred to it as a "young man's book," which it is. As such, it has aroused acute responses among the Armenians who have read it. Some, like the middle-aged Armenian woman I once met at a Sunday picnic, deflated my enthusiasm for the work with, "That book! So much filthy language! I don't find anything in it." At the other extreme, Mark Malkasian finds in this novel and in the author a hero fit for other young Armenian men. I cite the beginning paragraphs of his extended critique of what he calls the Armenian-Americans' confusion between art and public relations:

> All Armenian heroes are outcasts and failures. That has been our destiny in this world.
>
> My most recent hero is Peter Najarian: genius, rebel, madman, failure.
>
> He understands the Armenians. He understands them too well, and in 1971 his terrible knowledge gushed forth into a book (*Voyages*). It is a work of love, but Najarian speaks with the voice of a lover enraged, with anger, hatred, and honesty that stings the eyes. Most of his books are now safely packed away in an AGBU warehouse. Najarian never received an answer to his wail of agony. I imagine that whatever burned in his belly thir-

> teen years ago has eaten away his insides by this time and has left little more than a brittle shell.[1]

The "belly-burning" frustration of this reviewer also torments the hero of *Voyages*. There is just enough truth to what Malkasian says to make the reader reconsider his statements one more time; take, for example, his first line: "All Armenian heroes are outcasts and failures. That has been our destiny in this world." In one sense most heroes are rebels. But the "Armenian" dynamic here has to do with a self-image reinforced by much postmassacre literature. Describing the dominant mood of these writings as defeat, Vahé Oshagan notes that they focus on "the pathetic lives of misfits who try to justify their failure by referring to the Genocide which, like some fatality, casts its long shadow in their souls and on their lives."[2] Although it is true that the genocide has cast a far-reaching shadow through the generations, it is not necessarily the shadow of "fatality." The subjective nature of this darkness is what the protagonist of *Voyages* will have to explore.

Peter Najarian was born in 1940 in New Jersey; he attended Rutgers University before "getting kicked out in my sophomore year." He has lived in Greenwich Village and London, and received a Creative Writing Fellowship from Stanford in 1967. He now lives in Berkeley, California. Najarian is a fine visual artist as well as a writer, giving the Armenian figure a sensitivity that brings it uniquely to light. Besides *Voyages,* he has published a volume of sketches about children of immigrants, *Wash Me On Home, Mama* (1978), and *Daughters of Memory* (1986). Neither madman nor failure, he is a deeply reflective writer, capable of seeing beyond the polarities that tear history apart.

Like other protagonists in this literature, the hero of *Voyages* finds himself stranded at the crossroads where American and Armenian history meet. Heir to a labyrinthine history, Aram Tomasian traces the futile descent of the generations from the Armenian Plateau, "where once Urartu girls opened their legs to Armens."[3] After Medes, Greeks, Mongols, and Arabs take turns ravishing the race, its struggles come to a whimpering end in America, its shame beheld in "a bald sterile creature masturbating in the mirror" (39). If the young narrator of *The Well of Ararat* is stifled by the constraints of a rigid old-world ethos, the narrator of *Voyages* is confused by the mismatches and frayed edges of the democratic ideal. More an extended prose poem than a novel, *Voyages* shows a young Armenian-American unknotting a past that overlays his identity. Images and refrains that invoke the myth of the New World as depicted by our major writers and the lyrical exploration of America's debilitating effect on the immigrant family rephrase the critical tension each American must face: the distance between the ideal raised as the Statue of Liberty and "the Old Bitch gone in the teeth" (76) she seems to have become.

Plundered of her elasticity, America is old before her time, her complexion flushed with a neon overlay; her landscape supports "banks that look like churches and churches that look like banks" (16–17); her cities look "innocent from a distance" (22), but after three hundred years as foster home to the nations, "the New World .[is] stone, the green mildewed, the marrowbone sucked dry" (46). Though some of her finest writers boast of the perpetual sunrise that graces the country, "there is more to day than dawn," and in time the hope turns false: none can achieve full human potential in this land of dwindling alternatives as "we live and think within horizons and there's no room left, no way out" (74).

This image of America forms a counterpoint to Aram's feelings about his family. The desolation, the betrayal, the human waste he experiences as the history of his people is reflected in America, "the last nation, the dump of refugees, dreg of all that blood" (49). As he chronicles the sorrows of each family member and various Armenian acquaintances, we watch America becoming increasingly tainted. He laments, "It was once my country, a child's country. And then? From Queequeg and Daniel Boone I became no one, an amanuensis for an immigrant" (31). But it is the necessary fall from grace, from a carefree association with the national myth to a painful confrontation with our private histories to bridge the gap between the one and the many, the real and the ideal. Thus, Aram takes Whitman to heart: "And so, *starting across the river from where I was born, well-begotten, and raised by a perfect mother, I did strike up for a New World*" (11). By the end of the book what seems an ironic statement of intent turns into literal truth.

As in other works by Armenian-American writers, the uneasy bonds between an immigrant father and his son aggravate and symbolize a more general confusion or dissatisfaction. Here, Aram tries to rest his father's ghost, "the broken voice" of a man victimized in two worlds—the Old World whose flat tiled roofs formed a secure playground until he had to flee the Turkish army, and the New World, which systematically unmans him: shaving his head at Ellis Island, forcing him to abandon his artistic talent to find work, finally crippling him with a stroke that leaves him a vegetable during the last years of his life. As Aram perceives it, Petrus Tomasian's tragedy crystallizes Armenia's final catastrophe. In passages such as the following, the full extent of the damage is hinted at as Petrus muses on an ancient birthright ripped by massacre and left to drift by an indifferent America:

> Pieces of himself floating in the wind, the drawings he left behind, fumes of garlic and tobacco, oud and zither waves, the purl of charcoal in the breeze: honey in the sand with the childhood he left behind and the golden chattel of his mother's kitchen, hieroglyphic brass, and all the talismans, occult buttons and teeth, buried with the garbage: somewhere between the River Kura and the Caspian Sea, Ecbatana and the Cilician Taurus.
>
> "What do you say, Petrus?"
>
> *You look like a Jew—I don't fuck Jews.* (48–49)

Like the narrator of Leon Surmelian's "The Sombrero," to the extent that he is not one of America's chosen—white Anglo-Saxon Protestant—Petrus's legacy to his son is that of an outcast, wandering through a spiritual wasteland, reenacting the genocide.

His mother's story further complicates Aram's dilemma. Like other young women who survived the massacres, she has been raised in an orphanage and is eventually brought over to marry a man she has never seen before, Petrus's nephew. Once married, though, she does not fall into the expected pattern, sacrificing her needs to a false sense of duty. Listening to another woman survivor "embroidering" an oud solo, she admits the emptiness of her situation: "I had not learned how to be happy: where was *kef* for the orphan without a home, that dumb donkey who never learned how to love her husband because he was forced upon her?" (62).

Fiercely honest, she breaks one of the strictest Armenian taboos: she leaves her husband, divorces him, and with her first son, Yero, sets up a home alone in the middle of an alien country. Only after she grows strong in herself does she marry the man she really loves. Though Melina is in many ways a typical Armenian mother (symbolically, sending food in bottles and plastic bags with her son wherever he goes), she has not acted conventionally. Momentarily giving us a glimpse into the double bind many Armenian women have found themselves in, Melina aligns herself with her son's sense of isolation when she confesses: "I was different. . . . Why do you think I don't tremble like other mothers when their sons go out with Italian or Irish girls? Petrus remembered his father's house and it meant everything to him, but what did it mean to me, *Armenian,* except that it made me an orphan?" (58). Interpreting his parents' ethnicity as impotence, defeat, the inability to fit in, Aram is caught in a double bind of his own, uncomfortable as either Armenian or American. His search for a positive model is further thwarted when he considers his half brother, Yero, who is a walking contradiction, who uses American gadgets and speaks inane—and loaded—"profundities like *Let the dead bury the dead*." At the other extreme has has married Armenian and sends his children to Armenian school. More American and more Armenian than Aram, he still carries the sadness of two unreconciled traditions; as Aram asks: "what is the grief that hides between your temples, my brother, my half-brother, O my dispossessed brother?" (88).

Like his stepfather, Yero is unmanned by the rotting American Dream; his creative, "wish-fulfilled" visions of "Indians and settlers, wigwams and cabins, Eskimos and igloos" (107) happy in their diversified coexistence are leveled by the relentless agent of democracy, the public school. But though his house outwardly renounces "the sinuous design of his father's people: all the lines . . . bent straight and hard" (101), he still displays the brown photographs of his ancestors in the recreation room and like his mother, hangs onto the communal shell of family gatherings, kissing "formally on the cheek" when they say "so-long until the next weekend." But as Aram notes, the family unit is "like a paralytic with a blood clot in his brain," and the ritual only delays the day when Yero too will "see his children move not twenty but many miles away" (117).

Viewing his family's compromises only heightens Aram's frustration. He is by turns unwilling to judge ("Let the dead bury—as he said—the dead" (108), yet compelled to do so; disdainful of the choices his brother has made for himself and his children, yet unable to offer alternatives. He finally leaves America for England, driven by the "monster" of his fears—the fear of becoming crippled, of his differentness, of his hopelessness, haunted as the child of two displaced Armenians by a question that has no objective answer: "Do we justify? Do we justify the burping, farting, snorting Turk, full of orgy: the fat Gestapo, the ecstatic bombadier?" (51). He leaves America, having developed poses, masks, and ruses that both hide and reflect his destitution. He dresses like his hero, Cockroach Oskan, an Armenian-American hobo whose home is everywhere and nowhere, carrying stale bread in his pocket for breakfast; he steals to "keep honest"; lopes down the street "like a camel" and stares into the mirror of his collective past, trying to locate the sourcs of his unease in general resemblances to his people:

> But when he looked close and hard and silent and tried to hold on to an image of the past, to some link with an ancestor, to keep

> balance with himself and the past, the nose slowly wavered, swelled into a tumor hiding itself beneath its own growth and the eyes saw not themselves but the vapid gaze of no one in particular, a vague vestigial face. (39)

In England—free, he thinks, of America, parents, and the old self—Aram's masks are forced off one by one. An affair with a woman who refuses to relieve his self-created torment with an Answer leaves him with new questions about whom to blame for his troubles: his country, himself, his mother?—"Of course my mother but that was too deep to understand" (132). His girlfriend Anita herself goes to America, explores his country and visits his family, jarring him with a fresh set of perceptions: "Dear Aram, she wrote in swift smooth letters, it's really amazing how alike you and your brother are. . . . Your mother is a darling. . . . I saw her with all the pleasures I had once ignored, watermelon and corn, a warm rain in Central Park, sunset on the waterfront; she was sending them back to me" (142).

Fed and released by these new images of his home, his true self surfaces one evening as he looks once more into the mirror. Quickly going through his "repertoire of masks," flexing his facial muscles into caricatures of "the awesome Turk, the poor hobo, the tired old man," he finally lets them relax, allowing the transparency of the mirror to reflect his abundance: "It was a gentle face, good, innocent, sad but beautiful and suddenly all the love I ever wanted from Anita, from anyone, came out of me for myself" (145). By the end of the novel, though he still fears the monster, steady light is beginning to enter. He sees that "all parts of the world were related" and that "the stars were always the same" (148); he rekindles faith in the dawn ("It seemed wrong somehow that Hemingway killed himself at dawn") (149); he even wants to go back home. As he reaches the core of the labyrinth that houses the crippling fear and guilt, he vows to "stare in its eyes and squeeze it by the throat and kill it and bury it and carve its picture on my hands, incised deep across the lines of my fortune." Freed of Aram's projections, his father's spirit dispels the final layer of illusion: "My son, he said, I never wanted you to be. Why did you think I did?" (150).

With that final question, this lyrical novel makes us examine the relationship of suffering to being an authentic Armenian. Aram is trapped by a natural but false notion about his Armenian-ness, that to transmit the essence of his heritage he must remanifest the stigmata of group persecution and his parents' pain. But like Ellison's Invisible Man finally hearing the affirmation in his grandfather's voice, the pure acceptance of his own humanity, Aram learns to hear the undertones in his parents' stories. His mother has deliberately taken hold of her happiness, freed herself to dance unashamed; his father has been characterized by his friends as a good, smart, sweet man—not just a paralytic stalking his son's imagination. Neither is *less* Armenian for being a full human being, and vice versa. Similarly, America does not have to be seen as the land of either/or. There are as many ways to inhabit her fruitfully as there are ways to mask ourselves from the responsibility of discovering our individual role. Aram's routine laments—"I felt doomed to be worthless, dull and ugly" (10); "If I were poor, if I were poor enough, then no one, not even a bum could ask me for anything" (22)—mirror adolescent frustration; his mother tells him he needs "something to clean [him] out" (24), again reminding us of the epilogue to *Invisible Man,* where the affirmative trumpet of Louis Armstrong shouts, "Let the Bad Air out." But it is only when Aram—with Anita's nudging—faces his childhood alone, dispassionately, without crippling filters and labels, that he purges the monster and begins to withdraw his shadow from his ethnic group: "the categories I had molded and hardened for so many years began falling apart, mixing together into a thick inchoate puddle of emotions I had to examine all over again" (142).

Once these self-generated stereotypes are shaken and Aram dares to accept the underlying vision of beauty, goodness, and innocence in *himself*—a vision just as much his father's legacy as the senseless suffering—his relationship to America is on the mend as well; for if he can experience the ideal within himself, he will also see it in the world at large. Most important, by refusing to rest in the mechanical role of an amanuensis, parroting a formulaic ethnicity, Aram discovers that the truest "justification" of his identity as an Armenian has been under his Armenian nose all the time, not embedded in any action or belief, but in the unprejudiced acceptance of the past as it culminates in his unadorned self. In this ending *Voyages* goes beyond the stories of defeat that typify so much postmassacre narrative: the misfit fits himself inside his own skin. Significantly, the resolution takes place against the catalyzing American backdrop, suggesting how difficult and how possible it is to find oneself anew in this country.

In *Daughters of Memory,* Najarian takes off on themes first developed in *Voyages*. His third work is an unusual piece, where his drawings enhance the merging of personal and collective history. As in *Voyages,* the narrator is on a quest, this time in search of the eternal feminine. Here, she enfolds all of history with her limitless ability to arouse desire and inspire art. Although the narrator, Zeke, is ostensibly in love with a contemporary woman named Dolores, the most vital feminine force in the story is his mother, a character who appeared in middle age as the Melina of *Voyages*. Now the mother has entered a later period of her life; in prose that captures the beauty and sensuality of aging, Najarian pays homage to a woman increasingly identified with the universal as she enters the last stage of her life: "She's an old woman with a face like Sitting Bull's, her lips disappearing as she takes her teeth out and brushes them with baking soda . . . [her nails] less nail than fungal crust, chtonic and recyclable, her feet like the ground itself, the bunions and calluses like a transition into the world of rocks and trees."[4]

This portrait of a woman who has anchored her son's life with the simplicity and durability of granite is supported by vignettes of old Armenian women of Fresno chewing on gossip as naturally as they suck on pumpkin seeds. Najarian has a sure sense of the rhythms and preoccupations of these women, the way their thoughts are translated from Armenian dialect into American English. The humor and sympathy he brings to these exchanges, interspersed throughout the book, are one of its major strengths; as their miniature dialectics evoke the tragedies of the Armenian past, the mundane betrayals of a transplanted life, and the underlying vitality of their common sense, the old women become an Armenian-American version of a Greek chorus. Their wisdom is no less deep for being homegrown; they have seen it all and time has contracted to a still point from which they see things whole and pure.

As the narrator pursues his vision of wholeness, his travels take him back to the lost country. In *Voyages,* Aram Tomasian fled to England to recover his Armenian and American identities; toward the end of *Daughters of Memory,* Zeke makes his way back to Turkey, once the Armenian homeland. The passages that describe this odyssey relieve any who are numbed to knee-jerk clichés about the filthy Turk and the unerasable hatred of one people toward another. Seventy years after the events of 1915, nature has taken over the historical and political absolutes of the past; the Turkish villages Zeke visits in the back country of Anatolia are spotted with persons who were once Armenian. But now they look, speak, act Turkish; or is it that the Turks now look no different from the Armenians? Both are hospitable and finally harmless: the Armenian Boghos is "less anything than the same creased and stubbled face in the same sienna tan of the same earth he shared with Gambar who was less Moslem than a big smile and brown teeth, both of them holding on to their cows and their wheat in their seasons" (136).

These passages exude a mood of reconciliation, a mood sustained by

Najarian's meditation on the role of art in history. After a catalog of the dead, in which he invokes the spirits of a representative handful of family acquaintances who were either starved, enslaved, raped, or humiliated, Najarian unites the worlds of art and life as surely as he has united the Turk and the Armenian: "the terror of history impossible to draw, all drawing a transformation and every suffering doomed to become art" (140). This conclusion is not so different from the one reached by Arshile Gorky when he turned to the world of abstraction to redeem the pain of exile. But if the focus of Gorky's myth was the Old Country itself, for Najarian it is the ever elusive female who reincarnates as all the women he has ever loved, known, or seen. The drawings, particularly the abundance of nudes, in the volume are thus an appropriate support to the text; stripped of roles and status, these women are laden with the mystery and memories of the author's past and the desire that keeps him drawn and drawing.

As the book ends, the tension between desire and reconciliation is maintained. After watching Zeke make love to a Turkish prostitute, we flash back to Fresno, where the Armenian crones reaffirm the harmony of the life cycle no matter what its pattern:

> What is [your granddaughter] studying?
> Life, she says she's studying life.
> What do you mean she's studying life?
> That's what she told me, she said she was studying life sciences.
> Is there any money in that kind of subject?
> There's money in everything.
> Not in raisins. There's no money in raisins anymore.
> You wait, in a few years there'll be money in raisins again too.
> (157)

Written with a lyricism that places the Armenian past in an affirmative context, *Daughters of Memory* helps the Armenians catch up with themselves and points us toward the love that redeems history. It also brings Armenian-American fiction full circle, moving from the margins of experience to the core.

MICHAEL J. ARLEN   Setting the Fathers Free

Michael J. Arlen is known to most readers as a critic of television, a medium he has written about in several books of essays and as a staff writer for the *New Yorker.* In the introduction to one of these books, *The View from Highway 1,* he writes, "One of the most visible lessons taught by the twentieth century has been the existence, not so much of a number of different realities, but of a number of different lenses with which to see the same reality."[1] One of his gifts as writer is that he so often brings what one commentator calls "a literary" lens to television, using the expressions of one medium to elucidate the other. In a slightly different way, in his two autobiographical works, *Exiles* (1970) and *Passage to Ararat* (1975), Arlen uses the alternating lenses of his family's past and the American past to help him discover the truth of his identity.

Unlike in *Voyages,* it is not the son but the father who wears the mask in these works, smoothing its elegant, urbane contours over a tormented spirit. To retrieve the true image behind the facade, his son journeys to an alien land whose own contours are naked with unfading passion. Together, these two works raise a compendium of questions about ethnic identity, including the relationship between fathers and sons, exiles and their homeland, psychological invisibility and marginality. They poignantly unveil the sorrow that hides behind so much of the Armenian's anger and neurosis. *Exiles* is a series of flashbacks and vignettes about Arlen's parents and his own growing up. After completing this book, Arlen continues to puzzle over his father's past and discovers that he is missing one of the giant pieces of his father's identity—and thereby his own. In *Passage to Ararat* he tries to fill in the huge amount of subjective ethnic content that has been withheld, with the result that the work resembles a journal or notebook of queries and responses much more than a finished report. As a result, Arlen's questions about the Armenian personality and the effects of history on this personality are more provocative than his answers.

The central figure in *Exiles* and the presence that haunts *Passage to Ararat* is Michael Arlen, an Anglo-Armenian novelist whose chief fame rests on a romantic novel that caught the imaginative spirit of the twenties. But though *The Green Hat* "was enormously romantic. And lushly written. And very 'modern,' "[2] the amusing style only drove the author's "nerve and passion" underground. As told by his son, the elder Arlen's story is a classic tale of a "disconnected" psyche, whose surface polish hides a festering irresolution. Only occasionally does the father hint at the cynicism he feels toward his heritage, as in this remark from *The London Life:* "An Armenian in London finds quickly that his nationality is something of a faux-pas" (69). But in the following passage, expansive in its bitterness, he articulates the anguish of a nation betrayed by its will to live:

> Son of an incapable race, born in the musty twilight of an outcast people, inheritor of centuries of ignoble martyrdom and mean escapes, what did I deserve but the anxious and helpless solicitude of the unwanted servant . . . O Armenia, O unlovely courtesan, abasing yourself first before another, why could you not die with dignity, why could you not die with Ninevah, Carthage, Babylon? Then Genghis Khan offered you oblivion. And you got out of that too. Dead, you might perhaps have interested historians of antiquity. . . . You would have made a fairly interesting corpse. But alive, you are a bore to everyone and a burden to your children. The Jews, serving the peoples of the West with their genius, and each other with encouragement, have inherited the earth. You, unable to achieve anything, not even self-harmony, not even unity, not even freedom from jealousy, not even oblivion, have crawled in an orgy of tiresome martyrdom, keening your way at the heels of history, into the

> twentieth century. Poor creature! You didn't want to die—is that it? God gave you life and you cherish your faith in God as you cherished it against Bajazet and Tamerlane. God is a firm believer in the political principles of the twentieth century and the political principles of the twentieth century with [*sic*] you to the devil. . . . The people of the West are no longer able to wring any pleasure from pitying you. They are bored with your Christianity, with your massacre, with your complaints, with your existence. And your children are but litter and rubbish on the face of the earth.[3]

At one level, Arlen is merely stating the obvious. Not only has massacre almost annihilated an entire people but in its fallout inbred group responses have been aggravated: self-pity, hatred, and fanatic factionalism swell the vacuum left by 1915. Even more sobering is Arlen's cold reminder that the world shrugs at the writhings of small, victimized countries unless they are strategically important to "Great Powers." Yet as we saw in *Voyages* and *The Gate,* if the children of this race feel like "litter and rubbish on the face of the earth," it may say less about Armenia than about their own disappointment.

Feeling the same impotence that plagues Aram Tomasian, Arlen tries to efface his Armenian identity, condemning himself and his family to an exile almost as difficult as the one suffered by the survivors of the massacres. The depth of his retreat is suggested by contrast in passages where his son describes the Armenian half of the family—the typical love of gardens, the gregariousness, the business sense, and childlike bonding to family and parents (90–91). Showing their "intense interest" in the lives of their children, the elder Arlen's parents have even sent an Armenian priest to his wedding, fearing he would not be married properly by the Latin church (91).

Arlen senior's adult life is a deliberate denial of this colorful, noisy, often embarrassing background. He and his equally dislocated wife skim the surface of Jazz Age society; send their children to a succession of academies; dress with the meticulous care of the idle or insecure; move through a sunlit youth on the French coast into a later, shadowy life as expatriates. Their son comments on an existence that seems to come out of an F. Scott Figzgerald novel: "the possibilities they . . . were beginning to live with were already then, dimly, unknowingly, beginning to outrun their resources" (25). Though each tries to find a home in the other, both are "deep in exile already by the time they meet" (26). And in the image of the father pacing endlessly in the small room euphemistically called "the library," ending the day reading "in the big green chair in the corner of the room," we find an analogue of the dead end his life has reached.

What the younger Arlen illustrates so movingly in *Exiles* is that there is no escape from the past; one's ethnic origins can complicate life even after the original name has been dropped. Thus Arlen leaves England during the war because his "foreign ancestry" raises questions about his loyalty (37). The double wound—of never completely fitting in because one *cannot* and because one *is not allowed to*—reappears in America, erupting in isolated bursts of anger against the Germans. As the son reviews the past, the father's congenital rage against genocide, as well as his flair for symbolic gesture, emerges when an old friend retells an anecdote: "Do you not remember that time when Goebbels was staying at the Imperial, on the floor below, and stepped onto his balcony, and your father went to the sideboard, mixed a Martini, very exquisitely called down to Goebbels, and poured it on his upturned face?" (130).

What bothers the son is a question central to this study: how can a healthy connection to one's ethnic heritage help one discover a vital place in one's adopted culture? He is wrenched as he repeatedly bumps into the buried potential of his father's life—watching his father trying to be like the "others" and "being in the end so different. Not enhancingly different. Just different. Invisible" (45). The father's ambivalence about his Armenian past unbalances everything else in his life; his desire to be close to his children and not quite knowing how; his deprecation of his professional success; his professed lack of backbone as an Armenian contradicted in action by his wile. The following anecdote illustrates this shrewd business instinct as we learn how Arlen lands his first American job in Hollywood. Responding to Mayer's question about his plans, Arlen replies:

> "I was just talking to Sam Goldwyn . . ." my father began, which was true—he'd met Goldwyn outside in the lobby and Goldwyn had advised him to buy race horses. "How much did he offer you?" Mayer asked quickly. My father thought for a moment. "Not enough," he said. "Would you take fifteen hundred for thirty weeks?" Mayer asked. My father said yes, and went home that afternoon, and called up lots of people to go out to dinner, and told my mother that he was now a screenwriter for M.G.M. (38–39)

But having abandoned his Armenian roots and leaving England for America, the elder Arlen never settles into this country either, and his son intuits the eventual costs to himself of his parents rejecting so much of the adopted culture as they "complain their way through dinner," "sniping and snipping" into what their son feels is "some huge composite American ear, that would surely in turn spew maledictions back at me" (99–100). These observations contrast with the graceful balance achieved by his uncle in Britain:

> And Taki, this marvelous Armenian, not trying to be English or anything as pushy as that. But English all the same, such a fine solid English voice, such fine solid English concerns. He had a reddish face, and a big-hearted laugh, and liked green, and gardens, and vegetables growing in the garden, and small things in the fields outside in the special way that only Englishmen do. Takvor Kouyoumdjian. He was truly a very lovely Englishman. (89)

Takvor Kouyoumdjian (appropriately, Takvor means "king" in Armenian) appears as a brief oasis of stability in the narrative. He displays no quiet angst, no confusion about the labels "Armenian" and "English," no running away from any part of his identity; he stands for a refreshing embrace of the present. The mythology he is connected to is not a system of symbols, but a natural expression of the daily preoccupations of his culture—gardens, vegetables, small things growing in the fields, all that a true Armenian would love as much as a true Englishman. His generosity of spirit can only hearten.

By contrast, the self-exile of Arlen's parents disorients him as well. His experiences of national identity or family solidarity are impoverished: "I realized that there was at least one genuine certifiable 100 percent *English* thing I could do reasonably well, which was to catch a cricket ball" (143). Another time he watches his parents leaving for an elegant evening out and fantasizes: "I watch his hands, the silk, the tiepin. We are in a canoe together. A fishing trip. . . . I feel unbearably happy" (159). But for the most part he feels dislocated and coming to visit his father in Hollywood once, he says of him: "My *father,* I wondered, knowing full well that this man advancing down the platform was inalterably my father. . . . He seemed so small to me, I hadn't realized he was so small, no taller than I was really" (40–41). This realization—that our parentage *is* inalterable and that their histories help shape ours—informs every page of *Exiles,* and leads the son to search out his father's sources.

Passage to Ararat won the National Book Award for contemporary affairs in 1976. Possibly its appeal is based less on its retelling of the Armenian past or its connection to *Exiles* than its dramatic attempt to make sense of the Armenian character and group behavior after the massacres. Early in the narrative, Arlen meets the analogue of the Armenian soul as Ararat. Unlike other childhood legends that diminish with time, he finds this mountain has become "more": it is an impassive god, and for millennia people have created a mythology around it: "Inevitably the Ark! Where else?"[4] It will take a long time to decipher the blank face of this deity that permeates the Armenian soul. In the process, the book shows intellectual observations about the Armenian past yielding to the emotional breakthroughs Arlen must make to align himself with his past.

Through study, Arlen concludes what others have also noted, that though the Armenians have been controlled by other powers for much of their history, they have kept to their own singular path: "They had been hardy mountain people first, perhaps not very cultured or clever—people who grow up in the mountains are rarely cultured or clever—but direct, practical, and physical" (187). With time and conquest splintering their sovereignty over the mountain, Ararat became the visionary ideal that the exiled Armenian revered as a sign of past glory and apocalyptic hope. Like any other group descending into powerlessness, the Armenians eventually became obsessed with the "peaks" of their history, rhythmically intoning lists of hallowed names like a Moslem counting his worry beads. Through the centuries Ararat, by turns firm yet ephemeral, began to reflect the dissociated psyche of Arlen's Armenians.

Plundering the ancient histories, Arlen finds that the bold stream navigated by kings such as Basil II (who blinds fifteen thousand Bulgars before sending them home) once fed a tough-minded self-respect. Responding to his combative instincts, Arlen is drawn to stories of Armenian warriors and soldiers, to accounts of once expressed brutality (77). With the "isolating" experience of Turkish rule, the stream passed underground, the collective psyche retreated, and the Armenians' world shrank to that of the middleman, who traded, interpreted, and made himself "useful" to the Turk. As he brings his research up to date, Arlen pulls away from the handwringing protests of massacre survivors: "Those damned massacres, I thought. That chauvinism, such a chauvinism of misfortune!" (79). But beneath this distaste lies a pressing question: how did the offspring of Tigran become the victims of genocide?

The answer lies in a story of dehumanization at its extreme, and though his conclusions will not satisfy all readers, they serve the more immediate purpose of laying his father's ghost to rest.

As Arlen portrays them, the Turks loom as master provocateurs, playing a subtle and not-so-subtle game of manipulative incitement by which Armenian protests usually lead to "rampage by Turkish mobs" (176). It is the classic case of a bully sneaking up and attacking on the sly, then protesting the victim's cries: there is no evidence, no court of appeal. Usually the oppressor's rage reaches sadistic depths with any suspicion that he is related to his victim, an axiom illustrated in speculations that Abdul Hamid may have been half-Armenian. Like others, Arlen finds that with the implicit approval of the liberal powers, the Turks' authority over the Armenians became absolute. It was thus possible for Talaat Bey, the engineer of the massacres, to indulge a blithe depravity: "We have been reproached . . . for making no distinction between the innocent Armenians and the guilty, but that was utterly impossible, in view of the fact that those who were innocent today might be guilty tomorrow" (234). Though such passges do not probe the Turkish character (for the most part, most massacre accounts do not), they do highlight the cynicism of the Turkish authorities at this time.

Bated in this way, what do a proud and extroverted people do? Arlen concludes that a collective depression settled over the Armenians: "Might not a *people* show signs of listlessness, a glazing of the eyes, a lack of motive, an inability to get out of bed in the morning and look for better work?" (169). Along with this ennervation, he finds feeling itself rechanneled; gazing at the portrait of an Erzerum merchant, he notes the man's resemblance to his own father, the eyes burning in a "frozen face," where the heat has been directed "inward":

> Did he mind it that he could never have a serious place in governing his country, or that his Turkish neighbors sometimes called his son *giaour*—"infidel"? Or did he set his expression, freeze part of himself, his face—all save the eyes, which no man can control—and tap his finger on the coffee cup, and nod, and curl and uncurl his hand inside his well-cut pocket . . . and *manage*? (140–41)

Elsewhere, Arlen notes yet another sign of disorder; the same display of miniature a tourist finds in the museums of Yerevan—where entire stories are carved in the eye of a needle, beneath rough folds of stone—

he sees in Bibles "no larger than a couple of thumbs" (115). Their overworked delicacy reminds him of the tiny carved boxes in an old Armenian man's home in New York: "His whole apartment had a kind of miniature, concentrated, hard-carved look—obsessive and airless, too" (115). This is not the creative gesture of a minor race cultivating the art of miniature, but their nearest approximation of invisibility without self-annihilation.

Reviewing these symptoms, one wonders with Arlen at the fine balance any self-respecting Armenian had to maintain: how could one keep a grip on one's individuality, one's group loyalty, and one's necessary compliance with Turkish oppression without going insane? Thus, Arlen marvels at the toughened daughters of Barav whom he sights in Yerevan: "I had never seen such women: the skin of elephants, the eyes of bears" (79); later he warms to the smiles of old Armenian women, their "nobility, exhausted dignity, and . . . solemn, married charm" (146). That "exhausted dignity," that resignation to a fate one can no longer resist, becomes the more noble pole of other responses whose sum effect is aberration. Arlen connects the uncharacteristic cool control to the more "typical" Armenian excitability as related symptoms, one directed inward, the other outward. He realizes that to have been an Armenian in the Ottoman Empire was to become "something crazy": "Not 'crazy' in the colloquial sense of quirky or charmingly eccentric ('My crazy old man!'), or even of certifiably mad. But crazy: crazed, that deep thing—deep where the deep-sea souls of human beings twist and turn" (142).

So much for conditions leading up to genocide, which Arlen describes as the first triumph of modern communication allied to political violence. As a critic of modern media, Arlen is especially sensitive to the ramifications of this satanic pact, and notes that by controlling the system of "interior" and "exterior" communications, the Turks disconnected the victims from the rest of the world and from one another (244), the final isolation and, on reflection, an ironic analogue to the Armenians' plight psychologically. In the aftermath of genocide, new traumas were generated. Examining these, Arlen cites the same problem met elsewhere in this study, as in Najarian's *Voyages:* how does one emotionally justify surviving, escaping the cemetery of one's homeland and somehow managing to live? Guilt becomes a pivot between remembrance and regeneration, and aggravates an overloaded psyche. As for the shrieking violation—no one outside heard it. Did it even happen? Arlen concludes that such a mass of displaced emotion could only turn into self-hatred:

> One thought of the wailing or hand-wringing quality of so many Armenians—especially the older men, but also the sons—whose physical gestures seemed directed more against themselves than against the alleged object, the Turks. The diatribes against the Turks—tantrums, as it were, carried down now through three generations. Wasn't the surest way of tormenting an angry child as follows: to leave it alone, ignored in its rage? (248)

On the one hand, this hypothesis validates Peter Prescott's assessment of Arlen's television criticism, that he "is able to infer from isolated scraps a thesis of significance."[5] But shaped so completely by models of unhealed wounding (including his father's), Arlen's thesis is also reductive. In many ways his perceptions are accurate—with the wisp of a reminder, sobbing anger still shakes many survivors. Yet this descriptions also drives the thousands of exceptions into even greater invisibility. The wails of those who were forced to watch impotent while wives, parents, and children were brutalized is balanced by the sterner poses of those caught by other dilemmas: those of children orphaned in alien terrain, wives left to carry on alone, old women toughened beyond grief. The image of Aram Tomasian in *Voyages,* who discovers that it is he who pigeonholes his father's legacy and projects it as a crippling monster, warns one against fully accepting Arlen's conclusions: no one set of responses to the massacres speaks for all who went through them, nor does it untangle emotions that can shift with the time of day or the time of life. Such a corrective may undercut theorizing impulses, but it also allows greater justice to those who do not fit the stereotype.

This thesis also ignores another reason for the handwringing. One of the major problems in dealing with contemporary Armenian experience lies in the Armenians' general inability to articulate what the massacres have *meant* to them as a people, not as an event, but as a stepping-stone in the Armenian myth. For if the Armenians were frozen with frustration before the massacres, they were frozen with pain afterward. This account of meaning cannot be given by political history or documentation or even through massacre narratives, of which there are many. What such an unburdening would entail is the kind of story telling that transforms *David of Sassoun* into a high form of group therapy. Tragically, in consigning Meherr to an extended vigil in the Rock of Van, the epic also—symbolically—cuts the Armenians off from a catharsis through the imagination. At the most profound level, only a resumption of the myth by a gifted modern bard can free and heal the collective psyche. The hands are perhaps the most eloquent instruments of physical self-expression, the storyteller's wand. When we wring them compulsively, it is not necessarily from self-hatred; it may be a sign that we cannot put our ideas and feelings into words and must cry with the frustration of not being able to "speak" our sadness, and to relieve our bodies of grief and anger. Thus the retreat of the young into the present everywhere in the diaspora and in Soviet Armenia may not be the purely positive sign Arlen finds it to be. Tired of the war between sympathy and their own inability to alter the past, these "clearheaded, impatient young will begin to set their fathers free" (292). But though the burden of recovery now rests on their instinctive wisdom, it will take a long maturing process to release these instincts in ways that genuinely heal—rather than suppress—the past.

What preoccupies Arlen throughout his research is not only the question of how an entire people might be driven mad, but the personal issue: how am I related to my father? The question tails him to Soviet Armenia, where in an emotional debate about the Turks, his guide accuses Arlen of wanting to tear down his father. Despite Arlen's denial, the guide Sarkis insists: " 'Fatherland, father. It is the same thing. . . . Your father was an Armenian,' he said in a voice that seemed quite hoarse. 'You must respect him' " (136). Before he can be clear about his relationship to his father, Arlen has to be clear about his father's tie to a heritage he rejected. If culture is in part a record and reflection of the vicissitudes weathered by a group of people, we see that even though he distanced himself from them, Michael Arlen the father not only responded to those vicissitudes, but trapped by their primary imprint became one of them. Freeing ourselves from such constraints without losing our bearings requires that we accept them as thresholds of growth. In this process neither Sarkis's deterministic equation—"Fatherland, father. It is the same thing"—nor Arlen's blanket comment that race is "the most basic and unindividual of all characteristics" captures the dynamic connection between the individual and his culture; more like the double helix of DNA, where each strand periodically cross-fertilizes the other, this interplay weaves the inexhaustible patterns of human possibility.

Arlen comes full circle when he suspends critical judgment and, like Aram Tomasian meeting his true face in the mirror, allows the past to flow into the present: "How strange to finally meet one's past: to simply meet it, the way one might finally acknowledge a person who had been in one's company a long while. So, it's you!" (254). Later before the shrine to 1915 martyrs, he releases his father's spirit to the plain dominated by the mountain god and listens to his guide speak of delivering his own father to his rest on the plain of Ararat where "the old man spent the afternoon asleep in the field" (256). Though Arlen does not pursue this image, it becomes a paradigm of integration for all Armenians who wish to land their family ark onto a world ripe for a new creation. The nap leads to that deeper experience of identity, in which the unconscious connects us to our sources. Perhaps only from this level, where we live protected by the unchanging Ararat at the core of the personality, can we contact a self beyond massacre, beyond label.[6] Here, there is hope not only for what Arlen calls the "more modest dreams" of an ordinary life, but a sense of well-being that harmonizes our ethnic self with the other facets of our personality. Such a resolution will not appeal to all, especially to the angry and impatient young eager to repatriate the "homeland." But in the context of Arlen's two works, the only way any of us can end our more basic personal exile is by making that passage to a homeland beyond the shadow of self-denial.

RICHARD HAGOPIAN Unifying the Household

As an Armenian vocation, fatherhood demands virility and administrative skill. As in previous works, where massacre and immigration have tested the traditional sanctions of the Armenian father, Richard Hagopian's three books of fiction—*The Dove Brings Peace* (1944), *Faraway the Spring* (1952), and *Wine for the Living* (1956)—also explore this theme. Here the Armenian incarnates as a little man whose bewildered sense of place and purpose in American life is reflected in his tenuous hold over his family and fortunes. Yet as we read these works, it is hard to say whether depression stems from persecution in the Old Country or the uprooting values of American culture. No matter what their plight, Hagopian's sympathy for his characters remains consistent; the reader senses in the author—who had taught religion and who was for many years before his death a professor of speech at the University of California, Berkeley—a zestful spirit with compassion for the forgotten.

The uncertainty these characters feel about new-world roles emerges in the sad lyricism of the writing. Sparks of beauty in an old peasant song or the birdlike poses of children, the movement of a proud steamer, or the impulse to risk all in a fight for honor—each echoes the desire for transcendence in a world of toil and bitter luck. Hinting at their limited power, Hagopian often shows his Armenians caught in an insanely funny or pathetic dilemma, gambling away a week's salary at backgammon or courting disaster by defending less-than-honest women. Just as the Armenian folk epic *David of Sassoun* mixes humor and pathos that symbolize the rigors of life in the Old Country, in Hagopian's fiction this same tension stands for the uneasy passage into the new.

Although the work that interests me most is *Wine for the Living* because of its fuller treatment of theme, *Faraway the Spring* introduces Hagopian's major concerns. Here, the Armenians have not caught up with the demands of their lives in America, "like lost sheep, hopelessly wandering around, dying penniless."[1] The main character, Setrak Dinjyan, is a "sad Armenian," burdened by a vague defeat caused by "Life." Throughout, life is referred to as a mercurial force, "ready to do things" (52), trapping and "belittling" us. Setrak copes with his constricted existence with a "neat tightness" of bearing, changes shoe-factory jobs often, and feeds his passion for backgammon, where the Armenian ritualizes the zestful play of life.

Setrak has spent much of his adult life evading domestic realities: watching his daughter reminds him of his own narrowed hopes ("Pretty soon she will get out of high school and will go around shoe factories begging for a job as a tag girl. Wonderful girl. Is that a life for her!") (106). His wife, obedient in demeanor, thwarts the last shred of his authority by finding a part-time job washing dishes for the Protestant church socials; her cautious independence highlights the insecurities that keep her husband aloof from a world that does not accept him as he is. The constant sight of a son crippled through his own negligence completes the melodrama of Setrak's life.

In the course of the novel, this little man learns of an opportunity to redeem decades of family sorrow by challenging a Stranger Armenian to a game of *tavloo,* backgammon. It is the one sphere where he is king: "I can spit the dice from my mouth and win. It is the soul, the pure heart!" (82). All the suppressed poetry and masculinity of his meager life are at stake. Thus, when he loses, he severs his one link to dignity and his right to respect as an Armenian father. Not only has he failed to finance his son's medical needs, but in the dejection of losing the game, he steals an Easter hat for his younger daughter, a hat that makes tangible her own yearning for beauty. Yet despite its surface darkness, *Faraway the Spring* is not tragic. Companionship and sensory delights lighten the Armenians' cares. Moments of wry awareness or crazy inspiration (Setrak wanting to order a headstone for the Stranger etched with a tavloo board and dice, 216) suggest this isn't a world of tragedy so much as tragicomedy. The miraculous ending completes this mood: the Stranger, after a mysterious death, bequeaths a large sum of money to Setrak, demonstrating that Life can do many things.

Wine for the Living, a longer, more ambitious novel, is also Hagopian's most interesting work, dotted with episodes that exude a comic sense that again belies surface sadness. The action takes place in Revere, Massachusetts, where Hagopian was born in 1914; it is a city marked by the "fiendish" tourist attractions of the coastal town and the ethnic neighborhoods that give it the "pungency" of an old-world enclave. It is a world where children are cut off from parents who work at low-paying, low-status jobs that require little skill and much physical strength. It is also a world where a moment's chance can destroy the heart's desire with a thrust of death. Nevertheless, the exaggerated proportions of the main characters in the novel—caricatures of Armenian types—tip the balance toward comedy. The main plot centers on another disaffected Armenian father, Ara Aroian, whose emasculation is symbolized by long stretches of leisure spent in his backyard chicken coop. Unlike Setrak Dinjyan, whose rotten luck emphasizes his small stature in an oversize world, Ara's maladies are caused by the intrusion of his brother-in-law, Atanas, into the domestic circle. Even his name, *Atanas,* seems to play with the Armenian for Satan, *Satana.* As the story develops, Atanas's narrow forehead, "round, greasy face," and "wet cat eyes" challenge Ara's ability to unify his household.

To add to his troubles, Ara's wife has become a bitter, peevish semi-invalid, clutching her heart whenever she senses opposition. Her malaise not only stems from unnamed griefs carried from the Old Country but the heartache of losing her first two children to American notions of work and love, a loss aggravated through shrewish intolerance. Years after the tragedies, she still resents her husband:

> John. I saw that strong god of a boy turn into a good-for-nothing, worthless. . . . How many times did I beg him to do something! Break his bones, I would say, but keep him away from that Irish whore. . . . He did not say it is the weakness of our strain. Always, this is a New World, they must be free, they are not like us.[2]

Trapped by this xenophobia, the third and youngest child, Paul, finds himself in the most bewildering position of all, having to juggle—like Juno—parental moods beyond his grasp. To their credit, father and son eventually find their way to each other, overcoming old-country suspicion of American ways. Their reconciliation is enriched by the support of the Italians, who share immigrant status with the Armenians in this Massachusetts community. As elsewhere in Hagopian's work, the Italians share the Armenians' loyalty to the family and their struggles as recent arrivals; they also radiate the lyricism and joy in the moment his Armenians crave.

Burdened by domestic disharmony, Ara Aroian is Hagopian's most endearing character, his bulk a powerful foil to a humility he confesses in the following comment: "There is lots of trouble in the world . . . everyone is unhappy. I do not know the answers. I am not bright" (64). He is the type of man who spends his life getting into "good trouble," which he defines as:

> The kind when you fight the good fight, not to win alone, but where you must take as well as give; where you help the poor by giving them the tips you yourself need; where you take home a drunken stranger only to be berated by his wife as the cause of her man's downfall; where you help a man roof his house on your day off and lose three days of work by falling and spraining your back; when you raise a giant fist and get a black eye and a cut lip defending a Revere Street bum who has drunk too much. Yes, or even when you separate two dogs in a fight, only to have the one who was underneath turn on you and give you a bite in the leg. (11)

The chief task facing such a person is not discerning "good" intentions, but finding a way to use his strength to best advantage, so that he is not left a martyr to his own stupidity. But it takes the first part of the novel for Ara to abandon the symbolic forms of taking control in favor of direct action. Early on, his best friend, the cook, Garo Garabed, informs him that he needs a new hat to cover his "misshapen" Armenian head. He then advises Ara: "You are afraid, that is what is wrong with you. Buy the hat—have no fears. I will help you. Unify your home. Let this be the beginning" (75). Later, responding to the poetic allure of the hat he has just bought, Ara rehearses the speech he will deliver to Paul. Though he never delivers it, the words express the unspoken yearnings of his daily life and the hat—much like the Easter bonnet Setrak Dinjian steals for his daughter—becomes an emblem of self-respect. More than "mere wool and silk," it represents tangible beauty, "the beauty of love, a friendly home, where we are not criticized by those who do not work and who merely find fault." Ara concludes: "It was for the sweat of my brow that its leather band was fashioned and it was for my drab life that this little feather was plucked from some high-flying bird. It is for the pride I take in my humble job as a waiter that it was created" (152–53). However, Ara discovers that no hat can unify a home if the household demons roam free. To prove this point, in one of the most hilarious episodes in the novel, the corrupt Atanas slinks up to the hidden hat and with shoes smeared with cow dung—"ceremoniously, and with great precision" (156)—steps on it. So much for symbolic gestures as a way to domestic peace.

Running as a subtext to the main story is the friendship between Paul and the barber, John Tripo. Like Lucy Aroian, John has a heart condition. But though the Armenian woman turns frustration into bad temper, the Italian tries to realize his dreams by taking voice lessons through correspondence. Inspired by the old man's persistence, Paul showers his thwarted affection on him, only to have his corrupt uncle turn his parents against the friendship by insinuating homosexual charges. Yet, it is indirectly through the barber's death of heart failure that Ara's confusion ends and he is reconciled with his son. One evening after seeing a vision of John, Paul gains insight into his father's drab life; lacking the wealth of the barber's aspirations, Ara's life is rutted in a futile round: Only the dimness of the Grotto and the steady monotony of serving food and drink, the same motions from kitchen to tables and back, which little by little would force the remaining strength out of his father's once strong limbs and back. This and nothing more from sunrise to sunset (269). The son's empathy thaws the father's heart, and he responds in his native tongue in words that express Hagopian's themes: " 'Do not cry,' he said, as he pressed his sobbing son to his chest, 'do not cry. The people of this earth grow used to these things and their pains will lessen one day. The old lose track of time and truth, but in the young must burn some seed for tomorrow' " (269).

Rediscovering himself through his son's compassion, Ara is now free to exorcise his household. After one more symbolic act—a wild self-baptism in the nearby brook from which he arises "like a wet phoenix"—Ara confronts Atanas: "So you have devoured my home, my friends, my boy, the good man, and now it would be me, my own flesh, ha! Here then take it. I give it to you!" (280) After bodily evicting his adversary, Ara resumes his place as an adored Armenian father; Paul's accolade—"Father, you are the strongest in the world" (283)—crowns him as a "tornado of action," a "cleasing wind of undestructive destructiveness."

Equally important, Paul advances on his way to bridging the dichotomies of his life as a second-generation son when he wins a medal for drawing a poster for the Massachusetts Society for the Prevention of Cruelty to Animals. As in "Juno in the Pine Ring," where the St. Christopher medal stands for symbolic entry into a new cultural tradition, here too, a bronze medal welds the Armenian and the American in important ways. Upon presenting the award, the school principal bravely intones: "This is only one victory, one medal, one winner. Life is full of contests, defeats, victories. Strive, strive each and every one of you to win the greatest contest of all—LIFE!" (292). Her exhortation reemphasizes Paul's victory in the first contest of his life, where he excels creatively in a mainstream environment—the school—for the benefit of American society *and* Armenian underdogs! Defending the medal from class bullies also reunites Paul with his best friend, the Italian Mario, from whom he has been estranged. When Paul takes the medal home to show his mother, Mario innocently comments: "My uncle said that the Armenians never helped fight for the Italians, but the Italians fight for them. He said that is why the Armenians are smart and win medals" (300). Though Armenian generals no longer win medals through warfare, their heirs continue the tradition in a transplanted version.

Finally, when Paul shows his mother this prize, the children spot a small deer etched on the bronze—a detail that transports the sick woman to a past before her troubles began: "A little deer. But such a little deer that the eye almost cannot see it. Yes, it is a deer. I know. In my land they lived there by the thousands. Whole families . . ." (303). Her softened tone, the memory of a lost beauty and integrity of life, draws her son closer. Though American ways drove away her older children, here the school prize and her son's sensitivity help heal her. As for Paul, he waits for Ara's homecoming, gripping the token of his achievement, a sign that the family will survive as he continues to bridge the distance between two cultures.

Despite its sentimentality and imperfectly integrated subplots, *Wine for the Living* exudes the warmth and charm of a good homemade wine. In the words of Harry Keyishian, if Hagopian's work does not have "vivacity and relaxed daring, we are recompensed by a steady concern with transmitting truth."[3] In this novel, the major truth transmitted is that impatience alone will not liberate parents from the past; to get the job done, the young must parent their own parents with nonjudgmental sympathy. This is a huge demand given the resistances within Paul's family. Yet in the end, his patient love is the only strategy that frees Ara to act.

The Two Worlds of WILLIAM SAROYAN

> [My] mother's mother Lucy Garoghlanian, said of me before I was much more than fourteen, even, Our Willie is in one place, the world is in another. I knew it, though, before she said it, and I also was entirely willing to believe that this was folly, and even downright stupid and even destructive. All the same, nothing changed. I do indeed mistrust the world, the human race as it puts itself into affairs, all systems, religious, social, economic, and pretty much everything alienated from, or forgetful of, the universe, the solar and time systems, the earth, the unknown, and nature. So what? So let anybody who remembers that I suddenly surprised them by apparently unexpected and unaccountable shutting off of myself from them that I found it altogether necessary to do so. I am working on my own absurdity and vulnerability and fraudulence, I can't work on anybody else's.[1]

This passage from William Saroyan's last autobiography, *Obituaries,* might well serve as an obituary to his life and work. To the end, as he swung between fantasy and reality, Saroyan left a track, an ornately self-justifying trail of clues as to his whereabouts. Many would be charmed by the classic Saroyan poses—the ingenuous rebel, the whimsical seer of the extraordinary in the mundane, the crazy Armenian. Others would feel their brains frying as the lines of undiluted and sometimes unrevised prose rolled on and on, mercilessly avoiding conclusion. His exaggeration, his love of tangents, and his gooey style would make him the butt of many critics' frustrated wit. There are times when Saroyan is flawlessly good, as in the droll short stories of his early years, possibly his best gift to American literature. There are times when his writing is moving through its simplicity—not in the gushy plays and autobiographies that he felt compelled to crank out, but passages secreted here and there, where he settles down to telling the truth about his life. And then there are lots of times when he is plain awful.

Rather than rework old ground and take sides in a critical struggle that pushes and pulls at Saroyan's artistic merit, I would like to focus more directly on matters that contribute to this irresolution in the criticism, the relationship of his Armenian background to other issues that constantly get tangled up in his writing. To begin with, I emphasize that Saroyan could be as rational, clearheaded, and sensitive about Armenia's historical dilemma as anyone else. In "Antranik of Armenia," an essay written in the 1930s, he sums up the betrayals of Armenian hopes by Western powers, the misguided but understandable aims of the revolutionaries, the perpetual ache around the past. Here, as he so often did, he expresses relief that Armenia is freed of the burdens of nationhood, freed of illusory claims to distinction. Reflecting on a visit to Soviet Armenia, he finds Armenia an ideal that transcends limits of space and time:

> [T]he vines were exactly like the vines of California, and the faces of the Armenians of Armenia were exactly like the faces of the Armenians of California. The rivers Arax and Kura moved slowly through the fertile earth of Armenia in the same way that the rivers Kings and San Joaquin moved through the valley of my birthplace. And the sun was warm and kindly, no less than the sun of California.[2]

Yet a careful reading of the works where Saroyan deals with his and his family's ethnicity reveals a confusing complexity of motive that prevents us from taking sentiments such as the above at face value. Though Saroyan writes prolifically about the Armenians, clothing them in nonethnic garb when he moves away from Fresno, he can disguise his "absurdity and vulnerability and fraudulence" with portraits that verge on stereotype. But more often than may be apparent at first, anger and disillusionment—with himself and with the world—stalk his jocularity and determined upbeat mood, peaking at those points where he depicts Armenian fathers and sons subjected to a bullying yet indifferent world.

Saroyan's notions of fatherhood were steeped in the American broth. In *Rock Wagram,* an autobiographical novel published in 1951, he insists: "A man's father is always great. A man's family is always great. How could there be any question about that?"[3] But questions there are. As in *Passage to Ararat,* this attitude indirectly engendered collective trauma when thousands of fathers were murdered, leaving their sons defenseless. Perhaps a similar conflict motivates Saroyan's extensive commentaries on the loss of his father—not in Armenia, but in America; in one of his autobiographies, *Here Comes, There Goes, You Know Who* (1961), he writes of his lifelong preoccupation with death, "most likely because my father died before I was three."[4] This father, only thirty-eight when appendicitis killed him, has left an immigrant's legacy: "He hadn't made it. But as if a special favor to me he had kept a record of it, of the failure, the loss, and the finality" (36). "He'd needed time, and a place. . . . It just wasn't tough enough. . . . There wasn't enough of it."—these personal responses quietly echo collective experience; they remind us of what it means to be a marginal and try to write. For the son, these painstakingly constructed notebooks not only become an emblem of one man's desire to capture an elusive eternity, but of his failure to capture the bittersweet truth of his life. From yet another perspective, in the collective story, the fragments are like colophons from the past, messages from a truncated life that testify to the bitter luck that sweeps the culture bare. Like those persistent medieval monks who hoped someone would retrieve the messages, the father here has recorded—as "a special favor"—"the failure, the loss, the finality." And like other sons in this study, repulsed by the defeated, the crippled, the weeping, Saroyan wishes the writing could have been tougher "for the truth of us."

These notebooks resurface in various forms throughout Saroyan's writings, appearing as the scraps of paper he uses to catch ideas for stories, jottings that reassure him of his grasp of art, power, reality (*Here Comes,* 208). We also find them in a section of *Rock Wagram,* where Rock has a priest decipher an Armenian poem written by his father. Filled with references to Baghesght (Bitlis, the home of the Saroyan clan) and imminent death, the poem is the last Word delivered by Rock's father, who here becomes yet another incarnation of the absolute yet benevolent authority whose hold on the collective memory insured cultural survival. Elaborating on this notion, Rock tells his Jewish director "what Jews and Armenians have in common":

> "We have fathers in common. We're fathers ourselves the minute we're born. We get over being sons quicker than any other people in the world. Our sons do, too. We fix our fathers, and our sons fix us. That's the reason we're intelligent. . . . we're fathers at birth because we want enough of us to be around to receive the accidents." (154)

At one level such comments refocus our attention on those regular bloodlettings in the Ottoman Empire, when if the need arose, a child had to refather—or remother—an entire culture; at a more personal level, they suggest how fully Saroyan had internalized the directives of his role, an image that would strain him emotionally and psychologically.

He would express the poles of this tension in different stages of his career as an overly romanticized depiction of his Armenian family's life in Fresno pulling against a perverse will to see his ethnic group die out. On the surface, the antics and sentiments that entertain Armenians and non-Armenians alike in works such as *My Name Is Aram* are irresistibly charming. In these stories about the Garoghlanian family, Armenian eccentricities are cushioned by the enfolding fruit orchards, the vineyards, the irrigation canals of the San Joaquin Valley. At its pastel best, the Fresno of *My Name Is Aram* is a paradise where guardian angels indulge the fancy: Abbott Darcous of "The Three Young Swimmers" feeds his young visitors canned beans and French bread in the store he runs for "casual Poetry"; the Ojibway Indian of "Locomotive 38" buys a new car just so Aram can go fishing in Mendota. It is a world where human desire can sometimes work wonders, as when Aram chaffeurs the Ojibway Indian all summer "by instinct." Even when outer reality pierces through private mirages of creation or achievement, the stories laud any desire to impose personal notions of beuaty onto the desert of life, as in the famous "The Pomegranate Trees," or to escape mousetrap institutions, as in "The Circus."

Underneath the high spirits of the surface, the pathos of the immigrant experience sometimes breaks through and we get some sense of the hard lives the Armenians and other ethnic groups were living in the Valley. At such moments, ethnic ties not only comfort the lonely, but offer therapy of a high order; thus, in "The Poor and Burning Arab," Uncle Khosrove's silent marathons with a heartbroken refugee are eloquent with sympathy: "They understand one another and don't need to open their mouths. They have nothing to keep back."[5] Well aware that rational speech distorts the true nature of emotional upset, Uncle Khosrove's response to any calamity is embedded in a common Armenian saying: "It is no harm; pay no attention to it." As explained by Aram's mother: "it is simply that he is homesick and such a large man" (13).

In other works, particularly in autobiographies such as *Here Comes, There Goes, You Know Who,* Saroyan paints his family and its customs in even more striking lights and shadows. He describes the ideal supper for a summer night as the typical peasant fare of "cold grapes, flat bread, white cheese, mint, bell peppers, green onions, tomatoes, cucumbers, and cold water" (*Here Comes,* 103). He snuggles into the embrace of the Armenian bed, rhapsodizing about "the order of coverings we slept under: wool from the old country, beaten until light, and sewed into thick blankets" (90). At times he even sketches in the specific behaviors of the immigrant, as when he describes his grandmother giving him a bath, an event that evokes unbridled sentiment:

> Her hardest work was done when she pushed the freshly wet and soapy cloth into my hands and growled, "Get to your privates." She would turn her back a moment, or at any rate look aside, singing anything that was going for her at the time, an angry hymn from the silly Protestants, as she called them, or an Armenian patriotic song, or her own version of *Keep the Home Fires Burning*. . . . "La la la, la la la, now the feet, get them good, you walk a lot." And then a final and total rinse, the old lady saying as she poured the water slowly over the head, "Ohkh." This is not the same as *Ahkh,* which is a lamentation in a dozen different languages. *Ohkh* means, good, *how* good, could anything be better? (121)

The rhythms of her actions, her verbal punctuations, her rough modesty, and the delicious *ohkh* that soothes like a baptismal blessing—all identify her as the immigrant Barav. Inspired by her spunk, her grandson too would become enamored with language, using words to invent and embellish, to pose and to defy. To the end, he would glorify the small, the finite, the particular, and label this love Armenian in slippery, overgeneralizing prose:

> And the Armenian gestures, meaning so much. The slapping of the knee and roaring with laughter. The cursing. The subtle mockery of the world and its big ideas. The word in Armenian, the glance, the gesture, the smile, and through these things the swift rebirth of the race, timeless and again strong, though years have passed, though cities have been destroyed, fathers and brothers and sons killed, places forgotten, dreams violated, living hearts blackened with hate.[6]

The effervescent triumph of such passages does not lift the guilt he can express in the next breath. The family that seemed such a warm focus of nostalgia would not always understand the erratic patterns of the newly dubbed and dissolute artist he became with one swift swing of luck in his twenties. Seeing him come home drunk at daybreak a short while after the publication of his first book, his mother lashes him: "had you been no more than a common laborer at peace with the world, it would have pleased me more than this foolish success and madness" (*Here Comes,* 118). As for the day-to-day realities of a Fresno childhood, like an icy breath they often pierce through the picket fence that guards his idealized childhood. Saroyan grew up at a time when Fresno was reserving its brand of nativist hostility for the Armenians. The gingerbread facades of the city, wealthy from agriculture, were the dream of any young man eager to relive the American dream à la *The Music Man.* But those who inhabited this multiethnic all-American city in the middle of the San Joaquin Valley, especially the Armenians of the early part of the century, were the special targets of a prejudice few ethnic groups have escaped in this country. As documented by Richard La Piere in the 1930s, the following comments by Fresnans were typical, attitudes Saroyan would have been familiar with:

> I have found [the Armenians] ungrateful, deceitful and unreliable without exception.[7] The Armenian witness will tell the truth only if it suits his own needs, he will lie like a trooper if it suits his own interests(339). If you treat them civilly they are ungracious. If you are brutal and rough with them, they respect you. Very few of them ever smile—they have a sour countenance as though every thought was mean, *not sad,* just mean. If their conduct in Turkey is as it is here, no wonder the Turks kill them. Many, many Americans long to run them out of the country(341). They are the only foreigners in Fowler [a farming

> community near Fresno] who think they are just as good as we are. I don't know why they aren't, but we think they aren't.(346)

And an American teacher notes: "Experience in class-room and on the school ground and in public gatherings demonstrates the characteristics named. The children are loud, aggressive, often dispute each other, and demand attention with little ceremony"(343).

So much for "the Armenian gestures, meaning so much." Not all the Fresnans responded negatively, nor were criticisms of the Armenians' pushiness, greed, dishonesty complete fictions. As La Piere notes, the Armenian colony of Fresno had brought a set of behaviors developed over centuries for protection in a hostile environment; they had not made adjustments for the differing ways of the Americans: "Set to resist" persecution, the Armenian was intensely loyal to the family, "tricky . . . in protecting that family; constantly suspicious, questioning always the motives of others, unwilling to accept the obvious since the obvious is but a mask to hide treachery; and ready to abandon all other loyalties . . . in the salvation of the family" (436). Furthermore, La Piere emphasizes that "it was not what the Armenians did that drew antagonism upon them; it was *how they did these things*. They were no more dishonest or aggressive than others but they were tricky, dishonest, and aggressive, in different ways. These ways were those which they had brought with them from Armenia" (447).

Many Armenians were aware of their image in nativist eyes. Responding to Fresno's distaste, Saroyan reserved some of his sharpest—and most self-revealing—criticisms for the public school system of Fresno: "The Armenians were considered inferior, they were pushed around, they were hated, and I was an Armenian. I refused to forget it then, and I refuse to forget it now, but not because being an Armenian had, or has, any particular significance" (*Here Comes,* 139). Nevertheless, "being an Armenian" would remain an issue that he circled around over and over again. Despite his claim that it did not have "any particular significance," he often refers to his challenging and overt identification with a "despised and hated" ethnic group.

As Joe, the protagonist of Saroyan's 1939 play, *The Time of Your Life,* had earlier commented, "It takes a lot of rehearsing for a man to get to be himself."[8] But if one falls into an institution—whether an orphanage or a city school—rehearsals can be thwarted, even forbidden. For Saroyan, the school—along with the Oakland orphanage where he and his siblings stayed for five years while his mother worked as a live-in maid—would serve as his introduction to the "mousetrap world."[9]

Prototypical blocking blocking figures in Saroyan's human comedy thus include some of his teachers at Emerson School in Fresno, humorless and pompous individuals who thwart "swiftness," "casualness," "artlessness," and "innocence." One example of the impudent dialogues Saroyan is fond of re-creating is the immigrant child confronting his WASP teacher in an ethnically diversified classroom. In several ways, the scene is an American classic. It begins by presenting the "running commentary" of a grammar school teacher complaining to her "dark-eyed" ethnic charges about the cultural gaps between herself and them; she wishes they would stop dreaming about Armenia, Syria, Assyria, and that they would stop talking and making fun of her in a strange language. Are they really making fun of her behind her back? The little boy Saroyan responds:

> "No, we just like to talk Armenian once in a while, that's all."
> "But why? This is America, now."
> "The Americans don't like us, so we don't like them."
> "So that's it. Which Americans don't like you?"
> "All of them."
> "Me?"
> "Yes, you."
> "How can you say that? I like or dislike people of all kinds on their own merits."
> "Then, you don't think Armenians have any merits."
> "Some do, and some don't."
> "Sure, but *all* Americans are one hundred percent perfect, aren't they?"
> "You've got to stick together, don't you?"
> "Don't *you? All* of you? Afraid of us? Our loud voices and swift ways? Don't you all stick together, too?"
> "Well, maybe we do, but then, this *is* America, after all."
> "But we're here, too, now, and if you can't stand the only way we can be Americans, too, we'll go right on being Armenians." (*Here Comes,* 68–69)

Like Ardash, "The Armenian Mouse," who is Saroyan's ultimate alter ego, the child here pummels away at snakey authority like a guerilla fighter. Consequences do not matter; what counts is seizing the aesthetic call of the moment. His challenging questions—"Afraid of us? Our loud voices and swift ways?"—come with his ethnic territory, for as Saroyan later boasts, such talk—loud, intense, and self-righteous—is traditional in his family (*Here Comes,* 199). One might add, such talk also aroused a lot of local hostility. Such limber lips pose an extra threat in this instance, for this is more than a dialogue about school behavior, getting at the core of the conflict between the "mainstream" culture (an abstraction like "standard English") and ethnic groups living "in-between." Because language use constitutes the most immediate sign of cultural allegiance, toying with Armenian on school grounds would have been one of the strongest affronts to a system designed to enforce a standard Americanism, pure of ethnic tint and taint.

The background for this childhood melodrama is also significant: a classroom filled with students from different ethnic groups. Though he never developed the interactions between these groups with much depth, Saroyan was always sensitive to the shared concerns of ethnic minorities within "American" society; he saved some of his best digs for the "plain Americans" who cemented the spaces between the Armenians, the Assyrians, the Japanese, the Mexicans, and Native Americans of Fresno. Thus in "Locomotive 38," a story in *My Name Is Aram,* the car salesman sprays Aram with a slick, all-American gratitude: "From now on, son, he said, I want you to regard me as a friend who will give you the shirt off his back. I want to thank you for bringing me this fine Indian gentleman" (178).

Despite the bravado, even for the cocky, the mousetrap gapes. And for the immigrant family, with one leg "still in another world," daily life remained a cat-and-mouse game between the old and the new. The ever shifting dynamics of settlement in America are reflected in a chapter from *Here Comes, There Goes, You Know Who* where Saroyan remembers a cat in the Fresno house falsely encouraging a mouse to escape only to catch it again ("It's an unfair contest of course, but only *after* the mouse has been caught, and a wise mouse doesn't get caught") (125). Retreating from the unadorned truth of their exile in Fresno, Saroyan once more takes cover in the only comfort left, a deliberate imposition of meaning on the emptiness: the people speaking that strange tongue may be gone now and "you could say it was never anything. I don't want to" (126). The narrative goes back and forth, like a Ping-Pong ball, forcing the reader to grope for the meaning of the whole. If the house in Fresno and the life it sheltered "was never anything," how much less substantial are Bitlis and a distant past, especially for a son born in America? On the other hand, "a wise mouse doesn't get caught," either by menacing cats, the limits of time and space—or the tensions of his life.

Yet, depending on the time of *his* life, these tensions were periodically aggravated by personal crises that hurtled Saroyan's trapeze toward complete disillusionment. In the shift, his descriptions of the Armenians became increasingly gloomy, his buoyancy collapsed into self-hatred, and his visions of family life shattered into cynicism and self-parody. These extremes are reflected with especial pain in the three works of the early fifties that fully unleash his anger. Here the sharp edges of a worldview that had been honed on songs relating the Armenians' homelessness, their sad fragmentation after genocide, were wed to the orphan's creed—isolated from communal solace, sinewy and streetwise, marbled with a rigidity that rejects self-pity and forgives slowly.

These three works—a novella entitled *The Assyrian* and two novels, *Rock Wagram* and *The Laughing Matter*—were written in midcareer, as his marriage was falling apart for the second time and the call of mortality becoming louder. With increasing intensity these works suggest that the melancholy that plagues the "dying race"—whether Armenian or otherwise—has seeped into the protagonist's soul, where it can only find a healthy outlet in swift motion—flying, gambling, racing. At rest, the main character finds himself in spiritual limbo, unable to adopt the ethos of his ancestors and equally incapable of creating a viable personal code. Thus in the middle of his writing career Saroyan returned to the theme of his earliest short story, "The Daring Young Man on the Flying Trapeze" (1933), in which the young man's refusal to be saved from starvation by the Salvation Army coupled with his steady motion to the end forms his chief claim to heroism. But though the daring young man was responsible only for his own life, the middle-aged protagonists of the later period face crises of family life, where the models of their ethnic past remind them of their domestic shortcomings. In each successive work, the ethnic group serves a dual purpose, not only mirroring the central character's spiritual uprootedness, but exhorting him to pursue family ideals beyond his grasp.

In *The Assyrian,* the novella that begins the 1950 collection of stories with the same name, Paul Scott reexamines the profiles of his life as he prepares to meet his approaching death. What little we know of his life falls into the typical Saroyan pattern: Scott is a zestful gambler, deriving from the swift throw of the dice a keen sense of personal freedom, the satisfaction of beating the odds against defeat, of riding through inner turmoil on a tide of luck only confident timing and daring can compel. He has come to Lisbon, Portugal, on another gamble, climaxing a lifelong search for an elusive connectedness and transcendence. In following his brief meditation on his past amid the backdrop of this gracious city, where civility soothes his restlessness, the reader finds the key to Scott's character in the constant push against constraint, social and otherwise:

> He had always gone too far, but he had always come back, too. He had always plunged overboard, and then taken a swim, sometimes silently, desperately, knowing that he was struggling for his life, for another chance to find out how far he could go, struggling silently and proudly; sometimes indifferently, scarcely struggling at all, apparently only waiting.[10]

But the cost of compulsively defying boundaries, ricocheting between what is and is not allowed, can be disease. Early in the story, Scott traces the root of his malaise to "bitterness about himself": "He knew he didn't care about anybody else in the world, not even [his daughter] if the truth were told, he cared only about himself, and always had" (18). In both these passages, the repetition of "always" underscores Scott's isolation as a form of now instinctive self-protection.

The anger and shame of Scott's self-recognition will recur in the later works, accompanied by the central character's ambivalent tie to his ethnic heritage, by which the members of a small, dying race urge family bonding. In *The Assyrian,* Paul Scott has responded to his call, having early on sided with "the tired side, the impatient and wise side," hidden in him like a life spring until he reaches puberty. He has even learned the strange language "as if it were a secret shared by only a handful of people miraculously salvaged out of an extinct race" (17–18). He ends his description of adolescent self-discovery with the same paradoxical notion that marks Saroyan's earlier short story, "Seventy Thousand Assyrians": "He began to understand how superior he must be to most other people in that his very race was finished and had no need to clamor for irrelevant rights of any kind" (18). But the skeptical reader can only respond, "What is more relative than the term 'irrelevant'?" For though Scott feels pride at the Assyrians' miraculous escape from extinction, the relief has not lifted him emotionally. Like Theodore Badal, the Assyrian barber of "Seventy Thousand Assyrians," the melancholic Scott confronts himself as essentially alone, asking himself, "How does anybody have a friend?" (21).

Before he leaves Lisbon, Scott dines with a fabulously wealthy Assyrian, an old man of ninety-one.[11] The meeting shows that the spiritual fatigue ascribed to the ethnic group is as much projection as description: one does not have to renounce life with one's people. Thus we find in Curti Urumiya a man vigorous in appetites, as mentally alert as ever, aware that the game of life—like the game of intrigue surrounding his business moves—should at least amuse. Unlike Scott, seeking freedom from his "tiresome" self, the old man radiates well-being, relishing the hours like the delicacies his Greek cook prepares daily. In a similar way, he views his ethnic identity as an aesthetic dimension of his life and rebuts Scott's disavowal of specific national ties ("Being alive is nationality enough for anybody") with vital self-assertion: "the other little bit sometimes, in some cases, seems to make being alive just a little more fun. For instance, I have for many years felt that I have . . . outwitted the foolishness of life, and I must confess it makes me very happy. I mean, I survived, although my race didn't" (56).

Reinforcing this notion of ethnicity as an aesthetic value, the two men's use of Assyrian reminds us of the modern reenactment of an ancient religious rite. The deepest spiritual communion these two wanderers "of the same family" can achieve is to speak their common language. Like priests respectful of ritual time, they reach "a silent agreement that they [will] begin to speak that language without test or preparation, at the proper moment" (50). As they taste the sounds of the old tongue, rescuing each word like a precious relic from the sea of modern European languages around them, we witness the closest analogue to a religious ceremony in this existential space. But because these secret words no longer symbolize ideals applicable in the contemporary world, the language is ultimately reduced to the status of an artifact, briefly uniting connoisseurs like once functional art, without bonding them spiritually.

Significantly, it is not long after this that, feeling death twinges and the old restiveness, Scott ignores a doctor's orders to stay put and boards a plane going east. He carries into death the same willed loneliness that has always urged him "to be done" with the social pretenses, to keep moving: "He'd had it and he was satisfied. 'I never gave a shit for any of it anyway,' he thought. 'There was always a little rhythm anyway, and there still is. I got out here all right, and I'll get on the plane all right, too, the same as the other travelers going east, and I'll get there, too' " (77).

Published a year after *The Assyrian,* in 1951, *Rock Wagram* picks up many of the same concerns as the earlier work, but locates them in a more specific ethnic context. Rock's quick passage into the competitive milieu of Hollywood is most noticeably reflected in his name change from Arak (literally meaning "swift" in Armenian) Vagramian to accommodate his acting career. Despite the steadfast connotations of the new name, the shift in social identity deprives this second-generation Armenian of the old security of Fresno family and friends, and places him in a world where he is cautioned against assuming easy friendships.

In the tradition of the Saroyan picaresque (and American heroes in general), Rock is perpetually on the road, charting the American landscape, seeking contentment in hurtling through "a dream of cities, money, love, danger, oceans, ships, railroads, and highways"(25). But although in the earlier work Paul Scott pursued his independence of family matters, Rock constantly defines himself in the domestic ideal: "A man is a family thing. His meaning is a family meaning" (282). Yet falling into the overriding pattern, when it comes to living up to this ideal, Rock fails. His relationship to his estranged wife is only an intenser version of Scott's marriage; here, the nonethnic spouse is personified as a beautiful, money-hungry, frivolous bitch, who cannot keep faith with her husband's simple code of love and trust.

As if to cushion Rock's marital failure, one of the Armenian women in the novel articulates the immigrant distrust of romantic novelty:

> "To marry a stranger is perhaps an adventure, but the question is, Can the daughter of people who do not understand us be a true wife to one of our sons? Isn't the eye of the stranger's daughter forever out? [a literal rendering of a common Armenian saying about greed]. Is it fitting for one of our sons to marry the daughter of a stranger?" (83)

Nevertheless, we know that Rock's marriage to Ann Ford is not merely abandonment to momentary passion. An offhand observation he makes one day as he recalls the Armenian women of his youth at church picnics indirectly explains why Rock—and perhaps Saroyan—could not have married a nice Armenian girl: "They were like sisters every one of them" (95). As for many ethnics, in-group marriage, though socially prudent, would have smacked of friendly incest. Furthermore, though Rock has a hard time forgiving Ann her frivolities, his mother and grandmother adore her. This detail simultaneously veils the autobiographical truth, that Saroyan's family responded to his young wife with an almost stereotypical xenophobia, and casts Rock's recalcitrance into even sharper relief.[12]

As the novel progresses, we find that Rock's inability to forge a family stems from a deeper stratum of his experience, primarily his uneasy relationship with his now deceased father. This facet of the story returns to the central lack in Saroyan's childhood: a flesh-and-blood father. Rock feels that the Armenian son is a father at birth; fathers are "there" to "receive the accidents," to shield the family from outer chaos. But how can a man become a mature father without earlier security and discipline as a son?

Witnessing the further disintegration of his family with the death of his mother, Rock resolves to "begin again" by trying a reconciliation with his wife. But before doing so, he tries to solve the mystery of his father's legacy one more time, taking a poem his father has written on the day of his suicide to an Armenian priest for translation. The poem expresses the bitterness of a man who has watched his son turn away from the ways of the Old Country, a man who "loves no God but man, and especially the enemy, the Turk. The Turk . . . in his own father, in himself, and in his own son" (p. 269). Here the Turk not only symbolizes whatever threatens the ways of the family, such as alien habits adopted by the children, but in a larger context, whatever is unacceptable in another human being.

Though the priest praises the poem, Rock's response indicates his emotional void as a son. For if his father has been hurt by his son's Americanization, Rock has been equally wounded by his father's suicide: " 'I'm not going to kill myself about anything,' Rock said, 'or anybody, and I'll tell you why. I want my son to know that his father is somewhere in the world, demanding nothing of his son, offering nothing to him so that if ever his son wishes to speak to a friend, his father will be there to speak to' " (271). Rock then goes on to encourage hatred of the Turk ("Let the Turk heal himself in the hatred of the family")(273), because hatred—along with love—is the ultimate family feeling, a sign of life filling the outer spiritual void.

Rock's determination not to repeat his father's failure continues to the end. Unlike Paul Scott who travels east to die, Rock Wagram concludes his self-exploration on a more positive note: "I don't like to work for money, but I'm going to try to do it. I'm a father, and I haven't any choice any more, that's all" (300). Yet despite this promise, the ending returns to the larger Saroyan pattern, for Rock finds himself alone, on the road, clutching the token of love (a fake coin Ann Ford has given him stamped with the ironically misspelled "I lovea you"), rather than touching the reality of human intimacy.[13]

The Laughing Matter, the darkly ironic novel that completes this sequence, intensifies and makes more explicit the tensions of the previous two works, especially about the passions that split the ethnic husband from his wife. Set amid the autumn vineyards of Fresno, the story broods on the extent to which an unforgiving pride can ruin a family.

Hearing from his wife that she is pregnant with a child not his own, Evan Nazarenus responds with icy rage. But as with the earlier stories, the reader cannot fully understand Evan's anger without connecting it to a moribund heritage, which has saddled him with a burden of "pride and loneliness." Describing his father's destiny in America to his brother, Even bitterly comments:

> "What did the old man do? He comes to America, works hard, after three years sends for his wife and son. They come, another son is born, he thinks he's going to have the family at last that he's always wanted, a lot of boys, a lot of girls, all of them well, their mother well, their father well, but two years after his wife reaches America she's dead, and he doesn't want to look at another woman. He can't. He becomes a sad old man in a silly little cigar store in Paterson, New Jersey, living for his sons. *You* know what's happened to *you,* Dade. And here it is happening to me, too. What for, Dade? What'd he do wrong? What'd I do?"[14]

Evan's questions restate the concerns of the previous protagonists even more specifically. Early loss of a parent and the dissolution of family ties because of cultural assimilation have left him without an emotional anchor. His inability to embrace the unborn child denotes his own poverty of self, a self he has never learned to love. He thus answers his wife's plea that he accept the illegitimate child with: "I would love the stranger. I would love without pity . . . but where is there in my own stranger's heart the means and nature of such love? Where is it, Swan?" (165).

As in *Rock Wagram,* members of the ethnic group both defend and admonish the central character. Here, after Swan commits suicide, Dr. Altoun suggests that the instability of the marriage stemmed from her being nonethnic: "With one of *us,* it would take a great deal to end a marriage" (232). On the other hand, Evan's brother Dade supports the wife's behavior. He insists that by leaving her alone long enough to fall into adultery, Evan has reneged on his primary duty, to be at the center of his family: "The family is all there is. Fool with the family and you've finished everything" (228). As a gambler who has learned from his domestic losses, Dade reiterates the Saroyan belief that we invent truth as we go along, and the choice between pride and love is as arbitrary as the toss of a coin: "Flip for it. . . . To be kind, or to be proud. That's what it comes to" (121).

Though Evan's "call" is in the conditional—"I'll love you *if* you have an abortion"—passages of great descriptive simplicity present Saroyan's ideal of family life with allegorical dignity. In these vignettes, the narrative assumes a soothing symmetry that symbolizes the perfection neither Evan nor any real family can ever achieve. In the following example, we see the parents take their children to church, an exercise in family ritual:

> It had large stained-glass windows that Red and Eva wanted to see from the inside, and seemed to all of them in appearance most nearly what a church ought to be. It was built of wood, painted white, had a nice steeple, and when they reached it the bell was ringing. . . . A woman was playing something on the organ. The windows were beautiful pictures, one mainly in blue, one mainly in red, one mainly in green, and one mainly in yellow. The light that filled the place had all of these colors it it. The place was both dazzling and peaceful. (149)

But because such moments stand for an ideal Evan cannot sustain, they give way to their opposite in melodrama. As the novel comes to a close, the action speeds up and the complications increase to the point that Elizabeth Bowen commented in a review that "too much happens, with too great rapidity and too violently . . . accordingly one loses the sense of magnitude."[15] Swan's pregnancy and later suicide not only spoil the symmetry of Evan's family vision, but start a series of tragedies. Evan accidentally wounds his brother, who subsequently dies; Swan's alleged lover commits suicide, leaving documents that clarify the innocence of the relationship; and just as Evan finally decides to act responsibly toward his children and drives swiftly home, a tire explodes on his car and motion comes to a halt. He is trapped by matter itself: "Something began to laugh. He had no way of knowing if it was himself, his life, his father's life, his wife Swan's life, his brother's life, the smashed junk of the automobile, or the smashed junk of matter itself laughing (253). The ending thus enacts a waking nightmare for Saroyan, in which he faces the most painful issues of his life, places the faults that plague him onto the whims of chance, and makes his final escape through motion: "It was one accident after another, ending in laughter" (253).[16]

Coming to the end of this short series of autobiographical fiction, one suspects that Saroyan's personality was much more bedeviled than his oft expressed pseudophilosophy of love and brotherhood would lead us to believe. Excerpts from recent biographies by his son Aram, and Barry Gifford and Lawrence Lee merely reconfirm what Saroyan revealed through his work. Loneliness and viciousness, vented in fits of screaming and irrationality, tormented Saroyan's life in fact as well as fiction. To round out the picture, Aram Saroyan describes the clannish protectiveness of his ethnic group, bringing to mind La Piere's observations about the Armenian colony of Fresno:

> In the early days, after a blowup with my mother, he would run to the Armenians, who embraced him and sympathized with him and all but gave him the crown and scepter because it would be impossible, after all, that this wonderful man, this poet of people and light and laughter and fruit and bread and water, this profound and beautiful soul was not being taken advantage of viciously by this girl, who was not even an Armenian but Jewish. A gold digger, perhaps.[17]

What emerges from these memories is the portrait of a man who could resist closeness to others, who after the end of his marriage consigned his sexuality to the "threat-free, almost impersonal domain, of the call girl" (87) and avoided intimacy with his children. In short, Aram Saroyan spots the same irony in his father's life that lies at the heart of his work: that "one of the most loveable father figures of American letters" (118), the poet of the family, was himself inadequate to the demands of family life, especially its Armenian variant.

Regarding Saroyan's writing, this biographical perspective supports the notion that many of his excesses—his gushy sentimentality, facile worldview, smug self-confidence, and sloppy editing[18]—often masked a wariness about the value of anchoring art and relationships in disciplined thought and behavior. Genuine sentiment needs no exaggeration, but does depend on a fine emotional tuning sensitive to others. Accordingly, some critics have charged that the novel is Saroyan's least successful genre, for he had little interest in character for its own sake.[19]

Nevertheless, we know from his portrayals of Armenians elsewhere, notably stories and vignettes of his family in Fresno, that Saroyan could depict beloved family members and friends with spirit and faithfulness to their personalities. But in this fictional sequence he keeps describing the ethnic group as "dying," possibly a vague recognition of Armenia's long history of persecution; the dwindling numbers of Armenia's surrogates, the Assyrians; or the corrosive effects of assimilation into this culture. Yet beyond this minimally valid tag, there is not much that is Armenian or Assyrian or halfway "ethnic" about the characters in any of these stories, if by those terms we mean a detailed and accurate delineation of a people. They are merely props for the central character's introspective battles, bearing foreign-sounding names, sometimes suspicious of outsiders or quaint in speech, patient with whatever fate brings, but leaving us hard-pressed to identify them as Armenian, Assyrian, or whatnot.

And finally, to refute another critical defense brought to Saroyan's aid, this disregard of character does not necessarily denote an allegorical intent, just as his frequent refusal to deal with evil does not neatly transform him into an affirmative writer.[20] It is more accurate to say that his preoccupation with anger and denial simply blocked interest in persons and social forces removed from his struggles. The profile of Saroyan's career thus resembles the motions of the trapeze artist in whom he first projected his symbolic self, hurtling between the poles of a flabby acceptance of the "all" and a self-punishing denial of human closeness, occasionally achieving a fragile balance in works such as *My Heart's in the Highlands,* where trust and faith lighten the impoverished lives of an ethnic family. Throughout this dialectic, Saroyan's descriptions of family and ethnicity mirrored his fluctuating loyalties: at one extreme he honored the axiom that had insured the Armenians' survival—"Fool with the family and you've finished everything." But because of the uniquely knotted strands of his life, he cast his final lot in the orphan's world; to the end he would carry childhood images of the disaffected with him, mirrors of his fate, as this description of a schoolmate in "The Death of Children" makes so poignantly clear:

> There was Carson Sampler, a sullen-faced boy, the son of no-account Southerners who had come West in a wagon, penniless, hungry, and mean. . . . He was always alone, and for a long time I was on the verge of going up to him and speaking to him, but there was something about his loneliness and his defiance that was too noble to be touched, and I was afraid to speak to him. . . . He stopped coming to school suddenly. . . . He became in time the vague sort of identity I sometimes met in dreams. In remembering him it would seem he had never lived, that I had known him only in the secrecy of my sleep. But I could never forget the defiance of his pinched face and the loneliness that stood with him, shivering.[21]

DIANA DER HOVANESSIAN Language as History

Up to 1915 Armenian literature in the homeland had found new life through the impetus of nineteenth-century nationalism. Many gifted poets emerged from this renaissance, only to number among the first victims of mass slaughter. But though massacre pruned back the artistic growth of the Armenians, it did not destroy it. From the beginnings of Armenian life in America, as elsewhere in the diaspora, poetry expressed the spectrum of immigrant experience. Through this portable medium, passion and declamatory zeal found an outlet. With the generations, a distinctive body of Armenian-American poetry has formed. Although there is no simple way to categorize this work, it does explore some of the great themes of American ethnic experience as well as American experience at large—the role of a native language in sustaining and reinventing ethnicity, the stages of settlement that lead to full inhabitation, the role of suffering in cultural revitalization. I would like to review the work of four poets who address these issues and help develop our understanding of what it means to be Armenian-American.

Born and raised in New England, Diana Der Hovanessian has followed a respected tradition in Armenian culture as an accomplished translator of Armenian poetry. Her *Anthology of Armenian Poetry* (1978) is a landmark work, making three thousand years of Armenian experience and poetry available to an English-speaking public. Her own poetry, translated and published in the Soviet Union and Europe as well as in the United States, is marked by the translator's sensitivity to words and names as artifacts in their own right. At its best, this love of language is combined with a teasing insight into human nature; her wit sharpens her poetry and heightens its riddlelike effects.

Armenian poets often indulge their tactile love for "the sun-baked taste of Armenian words" in poems about their language. In Der Hovanessian, this sensory response sometimes appears in the literal rendering of an Armenian metaphor, as in "The Bottomless Eye," which begins:

> "Please don't give me any more doodads.
> My eye with the hole has healed."
> Aunt Berta[1]

Atchke' dzag, literally "eye with a hole," is an Armenian expression for fathomless greed. This saying aptly captures the nuances of this peasant woman's "childish greed" that stuffs trinket boxes till "the locks snap open." But once we lift the floodgate on our greed, the world no longer waits to dump its accumulations into our bulging pockets; even when we try to rid ourselves of the junk, it finds its way back. This truth can be expressed in any language, but the Armenian saying goes to the "bottom" of the matter: it is after all the eye that "multiplies the light," and drops us into the well of karma where we drown in our greed.

In "Teacher of Armenian," Der Hovanessian translates the Armenian words for colors literally to capture the experience of learning Armenian as an English speaker. Honoring the transformative gift of Mesrob's alphabet in the fifth century—which divided the Armenian from his Greek brother and made Armenian literature possible—she also reaffirms the resilience of these delicate letters, a sturdiness that will withstand the attack of neon lights and resentful students who glare at words that stand for the Armenian tricolor—red, blue, and color-of-orange. Like so many teachers of the native language who came to a deserted classroom "after a long day at the lab," "thinking this is for the last time" (96), the teacher of Armenian seems to act from instinct; the glory is not in the result, but in a word-by-word vindication. In "Teaching You Armenian," Der Hovanessian depicts the sensuality of the two major Armenian dialects, suggesting the intimate relation between the tongue as an organ of taste and a medium of language:

The Magical Pine Ring

To understand
the western dialect
you must breathe in
the heavy air
of the Mediterranean
and eat the pink flesh
of a ripe apricot
while I speak.
If the apricot
is not truly ripe
you will need two.

She then describes the fragile yet resilient beauty of the eastern dialect, whose "long pale roots"

grow so strong
that transplanted anywhere
its flowers change
the passing winds
into pauses
between Armenian songs. (80)

Both poems speak for the need to nurture the language, to give it "nursery care," though we cannot judge its future ("thinking this is for the last time"). They contrast the lush beauties of the Armenian language with the annihilation it undergoes in American society. But even a word or an expression shared between two who understand this tongue brings a peculiar satisfaction. In "Two Armenians Walking on Sunday," as two Armenians meet to celebrate the rites of a minor race—"You know / you're laughing because / you've survived"—and plough through the grass for the joy of undirected "motion," they discover one of the guardian spirits of their native culture flying through the grass like a white butterfly:

"That's one of the ghosts
of the 34 Armenian dialects
inquiring into
our quiet."

And when two Armenians
are quiet it's not
because there's nothing to say. (78–79)

Again, the fragility of the small butterfly that dances above like a phantom or an aura belies the indestructibleness of the thirty-four dialects. Even in silence, the ghosts of these dialects bless the reunion of Armenians, just as ancestral ghosts sanctify group revival. These poems argue that to be Armenian one must have a tongue capable of tasting and reproducing the sounds of Armenian, language and nationality denoted by one word.

Many of Der Hovanessian's most memorable poems playfully explore the fusion of Armenian and American. "Noblesse Oblige" in particular, with its characteristically compact syntax and etched metaphors winks at WASP condescension with a knowingness that washes over the uninitiated:

> At the second floor
> restaurant of the Eiffel Tower
> an Australian woman asked
> me for a match.
>
> How did you know
> I spoke English?
> I asked.
>
> I can always tell
> another Anglo-Saxon
> anywhere!
>
> How? I'm Armenian
> cut and dried.
> that is to say, cut
> from an Armenian vine and
> bleached in the sun like
> a good California raisin.
>
> Why, you're speaking English
> very well, she said,
> we'll let you be
> an Anglo-Saxon
> sweetie-pie. (16)

This poem delightfully undercuts typical assumptions. To be "cut from an Armenian vine" and matured under the sun of an ethnic upbringing—

like the "California raisins" Armenian farmers bring to harvest—does not announce itself to the naive eye of the majority, which chooses to see bleaching where there is actually a darkening and accenting of essential differences. Here, the ability to explain one's heritage *in English* counts for more in ethnic labeling than *what* one says—especially in the Eiffel Tower, amid a multicultural crush.

This same economy of line and wry awareness of biases that define us appears in "Roots":

> Where are your philosophical
> roots? my teacher asked.
> And I looked down
> at my shoes, one inch deep
> into the environment.
> I don't know,
> I answered. I see only
> that I am surrounded
> by daily biases. (95)

Like shoes "one inch deep into the environment," our "daily biases" protect us from the tactile realities of the earth and carry us through the world unrooted. Such cushioning severs us from an authentic relationship to the world, as well as from our "philosophical roots."

In the end, the conscious search for knowledge of these roots must yield to indirect means of finding them. In "The Past," Der Hovanessian confronts a legacy that defies an arbitrary, imposed order with its own chaotic will, "like a drawer / of cutlery / dumped in / every whichway" (68). In "How to Choose Your Past," images that elude tidy analysis cleverly reflect the paradoxical demands of "keeping the past":

> You flatter me by asking
> for an immortal poem.
> Mine tear in my hand
> like old directions
> for keeping the past:
> "This way. No, that way.
> Do it right"
> Or are mislaid
> with the secrets an old
> Egyptian gave me for
> out-formaldehyding

formaldehyde: "Preserve
only what you choose" and
"Keep it hidden a while
under pyramids until
it comes to a point."
Nothing seems to reach
that far. (25)

As the unassuming tone implies, a deliberate assault on the past defeats the purpose of channeling a legacy, just like writing poems consciously for the sake of "immortality". Carefully trying to preserve the past, we only see it shrivel because we deny its organic relation to the present ("immortal" means deathless, but what is deathless is also in a sense lifeless). "Choosing the past" requires indirection: discovering personally significant seeds in the inherited traditions, burying these in a safe spot, even mislaying them for a while, not trying to figure it all out, to allow germination. For unlike pyramids—symbols of focus, direction, and power—which come to a point through conscious labor, the secrets of the past can come to their "point" only if we let the unconscious work on the images, the anecdotes, the random "cutlery" that we choose to preserve. Here, safe from the "daily biases" that sever us from our roots, these snatches of history blossom in the elusive center of our psyche and lead us much further toward integration than would a mechanical and dogmatic embrace of "official histories" open to revision or deification.

In "Learning an Ancestral Tongue," the organic nature of language encourages us to let the mysteries of the past speak in their own time, through the soil of a fertile imagination:

My ancestors talk
to me in dangling
myths.

Each word a riddle,
each dream
heirless

On sunny days
I bury
words.

The Magical Pine Ring

They put out roots
and coil around
forgotten syntax.

Next spring a full
blown anecdote
will sprout. (79)

Again, recovering this past is not a matter of archeology, of organizing historical givens, but of demonstrating faith in its living potential. These last two poems set the fragility and age of the Armenian heritage against the symbols and images that promise renewal, whether these be the megaliths that funneled fresh water through the centuries or the memory of periodic retreats to mountain fortresses as foreign invaders plundered the countryside: when monks protected the core of their religious, literary, and scientific traditions in candlelit caves; and when architects seized necessity to experiment with new structural techniques—"Preserve only what you choose"; "Keep it hidden a while / under pyramids until / it comes to a point. / Nothing seems to reach / that far." Similarly, the dangling, fragmentary myths and unclaimed dreams that are the heritage of the Armenian-American also contain a promise. Like medieval colophons written by Armenian scribes, haunting us with their truncated pleas for audience, the words of the ancestral tongue also revalidate the axiom: the part equals the whole. If one but plants the chosen seed deeply enough, the entire cultural tree will sprout, a "full blown anecdote."

Der Hovanessian cultivates a language that proves itself a teacher of admirable resources, mirroring itself in playful poems that dangle with myth and shy away from tidy expositions. As they coil around the imagination, charming and surprising the reader with their rooted wisdom, we see that such an engagement with the native language is one of the best ways to discover the uniquely inventive and pragmatic voice of the Armenian spirit. Der Hovanessian's poetry thus refutes criticisms such as the following, which deplore the anachronistic hold of the Armenian language over the Armenians:

> Most of the difficulties the Armenians are experiencing in their efforts to adapt and survive stem from this "fixation" [on the "mythic" hold of the language]. That is why, formed in a different world and by different types of Armenians, this language is often not adapted to our times and may even hinder the efforts

> of the Armenians of the Diaspora to preserve a national identity and to create.[2]

And yet paradoxically, these poems also support this statement: in American English, they—and the poetry of Armenian-Americans in general—effectively channel an evolving Armenian identity. They bear testimony that sowed in the soil of the New World, this ancient language must also bear a transplanted meaning, helping Armenian-Americans translate and fall heir to the dreams of an often riddlelike past.

DAVID KHERDIAN Making Whole the Past

Like Diana Der Hovanessian, David Kherdian turns to his past to "gain the future." Much of his poetry traces the distinct stages of one ethnic group settling the new land. Born in Racine, Wisconsin (an early pocket of the Armenian population), in 1931, he "began writing at the age of 27, but had to put it aside to absorb and pass through the influence of William Saroyan."[1] For variety, Kherdian's background is equaled only by the range of his writing: he has worked as a door-to-door magazine salesman, shoe salesman, bartender, day laborer, and factory worker. In 1966 he founded the Giligia Press and continued as an editor until 1973. Besides publishing many collections of poetry, Kherdian has edited an anthology of poetry by Fresno poets, *Down at the Santa Fe Depot,* and an anthology of contemporary American poetry, *Traveling America with Today's Poets.* He has also written for children and younger adults; of interest are his retelling of his mother's passage from Turkey to America in *The Road from Home* and *Finding Home,* and a recently published novella, *A Song for Uncle Harry.*

For Kherdian, the images of settlement resemble the images of art itself; both come into focus through reflection and time: "It is my early life that concerns me, but it is very nearly impossible to talk about this life, except perhaps as art, because that is the dimension it most nearly approximates. . . . I find in my writing that I gain the future by reclaiming and making whole the past."[2] Because "making whole the past" requires a cyclic return and meditation on the half-hazy images of childhood, many of Kherdian's poems evoke the moods and inhabitants of Racine. Besides these cameos of forgotten Armenians who speak only through memory, he captures the nuances of love between second-generation Armenians in poems of courtship and marriage, and completes the cycle of immigration in poems that fully locate him in the here and now.

In his portraits, Kherdian illustrates how quickly we can forfeit the chance gifts of the present. In "Dear Mrs. McKinney of the Sixth Grade," his "failure of feeling" prevents him from greeting a beloved teacher glanced at a bus stop; he is left instead with a poem "in which only time and loss, not / you and I, are the subject to be held."[3] Yet only as time passes does the veiled meaning of the past emerge, as in "The Greek Popcorn Man," whose "lighted head" is masked by the urgencies of "sex-taunted" adolescence.[4] Whether we neglect the momentary chance or gain clarity from it later, it is poetry that "holds" the "meaning" of the encounter. For Kherdian, his memories of the Armenians carry the most potent charge. Of these, none are so movingly recalled as the old men. Anyone who grew up when the first immigrants were entering old age will recall the often lonely lives of these men, many of them bachelors, their working years over, cut off from the homeland, parked in park benches, department store mezzanines, or Armenian coffeehouses. In poems such as "Dtah Dtah," Kherdian identifies these men as the guardian deities of Armenian-American life, holy fools whose wisdom lay in patient anonymity:

> Seated on a metal folding chair
>   long afternoons
>   in front of the church
> An old nameless Armenian man
>   anonymous except for nationality
>   and a secret bond
>   between God and countrymen.
> Sundays he became a part of the throng
>   and shuffled quietly inside
>   always out of sight
> But all week held this mysterious vigil
>   in old clothes
>   and beatific smile.

Strange how men for whom I held
a secret pity then
were really the guardians
of a way of life
and life itself.
(*Homage to Adana*)

Silently, these men's personalities permeated the sites they claimed, until the place became one with the man. Torn from their native soil and dreaming their piece of the collective vision in anonymous corners, these men become the angels of transition between the immigrant generations and those that followed; their importance did not lie in what they said or did, but in their meditations on the "secred bond between God and countrymen." Inarticulate as they may have been, they provided a link that future generations would look to. As they sat on their metal folding chairs and benches, firm supports in the uncultivated soil of the New World, they not only maintained their ties to church and nature, but created a radiant space where change and permanence harmonized.

In other poems of witness, Kherdian shows time distancing the generations, as in "The Middle-Aged Armenian Men." Here silence foreshadows cultural disintegration as newly arrived Armenian immigrants walk and worry through equally silent streets. Frustrated by the "unruly" preoccupations of children who ignore their oratories on the native culture, they fret over the inevitable "barriers." Again, only time delivers a belated harvest as "grown children" seek out the old men who still "carry Armenia / in their fallen faces" and dive into "the rush of blood that brought / them to this moment in time" (*Homage to Adana*). Just as Der Hovanessian recognizes that "the rush of blood" can upset the hopes of ethnic parents if the patient drudgery of mediating figures such as the teacher of Armenian is absent, here too the labors of these dispirited fathers bear a belated fruit. But the image of young men driven to reclaim Armenia in the coffeehouses of America brings a wry smile: like the "fallen faces" of the old men, Armenia is itself an age-worn ideal. What these young men are tracing is much more vital: the steps of the passage that reaches from the past to "this moment in time," where the strands of their personal myths converge.

Though many of these second-generation Armenians would not face the exile and loneliness of the older generation, they met stern challenges of their own. In "S. G.," Kherdian suggests how much these children needed mature role models, men and women *not* tied like dutiful children to old-country parents. After Moe, "the damnest" and most stylish athlete the Armenian community ever had fails to make the team, he is slowly caught by old-world patterns:

> It was seeing you restless in
> the bars, driving a dump truck
> living alone with your eighty
> year old parents, that was
> harder to take than having our
> only Armenian hometown athlete
> *not* make the big time.
> They cut you once, you cut us twice.
>
> Why can't our heroes grow up?[5]

The impatience of the colloquial diction and the images of trapped energy vent frustration at watching an idol "strike out" in the major leagues. Elsewhere, in his elegy "Jack Taktakian," Kherdian shifts perspective by honoring the sacrifice of a less gifted son to his family's needs, a sacrifice seen more clearly in time. Like the old men on their folding chairs and benches, this young man seems to have taken a "lesser path." But in time his devotion becomes another "link to this new, strange land" (*I Remember Root River*).

Kherdian's family typifies the ethnic family in transit. In "To My Sister" he speaks for all who found themselves strangers to one another, "shy, reclusive, and alone," unable to find a "healing grace" by mating with the new soil; once the "living racial embrace" is broken, a family becomes "a strange thing":

> It is a private peace we have made,
> each in his own way, though we shared
> one home, in this country that would never
> be home.
>
> (*Homage to Adana*)

Isolated by their "private peace," children cannot own their cultural legacy until time helps them harvest and "recapture" it on their own terms. This harvest often comes through images of reconciliation, as in "Sparrow," where Kherdian pays his homage to the fallout of 1915; here a bitter past is borne through the dignity of contentment:

She makes her lunches
   with what we leave.
Morsels that give proportion
   to her quiet life
of decency.

She asks for little
   having once lost all.
She comes quietly to her
   life of transformed sorrow.
Sitting down to her lunch
   she has the window, its light,
and her small bowls.
   We call it sparrow's lunch
and have given her that name:

Teasing what we cannot belittle
   and must adore.[6]

The spare syntax and form mirror the mood. Like the old man who sits like an icon before the church, this woman's simple needs belie her inner wealth. "The window, its light, and her small bowls"—these are enough to hold the essentials, a truth recovered after once losing all. In "My Mother and the Americans," the simplicity of the mother's artistic insight, that is, seeing from a "peculiarly oblique angle," deftly translates one culture into another:

. . . one day,
looking out the window into
memory and the future,
she announced:
                    "These Americans raise
their children like chickens—
   Any which way."
      (*On the Death of My Father*)

As in "Sparrow," the mother is positioned close to a window, a filter of "memory and the future." But in this poem, the actual window is the Armenian expression that channels this bit of folk wisdom; drawn from a memory rich with the images of a peasant past, this saying aptly parodies an unbridled American upbringing.

Elsewhere, Kherdian cyclically explores his relationship to his father, a man who "came from Adana," "wasn't educated anywhere," "growled like a crossed lion when Armenian-angry"; he "was bear silent when not" angry, and "died in a Milwaukee hospital . . . far from any home" ("My Father," *On the Death of My Father*). This man's conflicts with his son over "painting the garden fence" and "resistance to Armenian food" originate in the son's "struggle for identity" and his silent yearnings for the old soil:

> Why have I waited until your death
> to know the earth you were turning
> was Armenia, the color of the fence
> your homage to Adana, and your other
> complaints over my own complaints
> were addressed to your homesickness
> brought on by my English.
> ("For My Father," *Homage to Adana*)

Though moments of truce appear, as when they stand together and "man to man . . . pissed against / the factory walls,"[7] only through death and poetry does Kherdian recover his father's essence. In "On the Death of My Father," he unites himself to his father and then to his ancestral source as he releases his "soil-splashed" body to the earth, "where once he played in tales that / have been handed down":

> Toss him and catch him
> in your cloudy hands.
> He'll know your touch, his
> feet, when he comes to you
> are sure to be bare.
> (*On the Death of My Father*)

Rescued from the cement of the alien city, the father is freed through ritual and poetry to mate with the earth. Likewise, the "tales that have been handed down," emblems of a "circling fading time," will link his son to the future. In "Melkon," Kherdian again links the living and the dead through a mediating symbol; here, a rug inherited from his father becomes a fitting "support" for self-discovery:

> Father, I have your rug.
> I sit on it now—not as you

did, but on a chair before
a table, and write.

The rug—like the old men of the park, like cherished customs and heirlooms, and like poetry itself—is a witness of change. As such, it acquires a new function, holding the sacred "things" of the past and becoming the space where the generations enter communion:

In my nomadic head I carry all
the things of my life,
determined by memory and love.
And on certain distant nights,
I take them one by one,
And count.
And place them on your rug.
(*I Remember Root River*)

Marriage marks a new stage in settlement. A casual report of the trip back from the license bureau, "The Subway Encounter," ends with a reference to the novelty—and perhaps the security—that an Armenian finds in marrying another Armenian in this land of thirty-one flavors. In "This Evening," Kherdian describes the subtle adjustments made even when backgrounds are similar, as his wife prepares a meal with pine nuts and exotic spices that carry the poet from the traditions of one family to another. And in "Of Husbands and Wives," he delights in ethnicity as a subversive activity, shaping the perceptions of thousands through artists who transpose the forms of their inherited physiognomy onto the pictures they create.

Moving finally to a country life, Kherdian also completes the cycle of his journey, especially in his collection *Any Day of Your Life* (1975). In these poems about "the settling of America" (the title of his anthology of American ethnic poets), he weds himself and his family to the earth, "our final comfort and friend." A pervasive contentment in recovering the family tradition, in moving beyond the "private peace" it had to be for immigrants and their children, and coming to savor the fullness of the moment—all of this is reflected in "In the Tradition." Its matter-of-fact tone speaks a calm acceptance of self, the reward of being fully present to a time and place:

My family, my wife says,
is all that is important

to me, and saying that
she turns and gives her
full attentionto the tollhouse cookies that will soon
emerge from the batter
being beaten by the mixer
that frightens the cat.

And so, the three of us are
in the kitchen, 11:15 P.M.—
a late night drink for me,
a mild fright for the cat,
and cookies for my wife.

Family enough or not, this
is who we are, where we live
and how it is done. It is
part of the formula of life,
and keeping it good and simple
in a poem helps to give pre-
eminence to life. Give thanks
to my wife.[8]

The effortless movement of the poem is its strength. Its self-confidence—"this is who we are, where we live and how it is done"—has nothing "to prove"; it does not lean on ethnic props and stands on its "good and simple" truth; like a recipe for tollhouse cookies, it offers a wholesome "formula of life," of traditions growing naturally from the needs and desires of the moment.

In "From the Window," Kherdian watches his wife walking through the yard, "returning her thoughts to the earth," bringing to mind "fruits of another summer":

the three winds of the family
with all elements in moving
conjunction, caught in a drama
only I can see . . . and we are
all atmosphere . . . I, shimmering
at the window (dazed by love),
watching Nonny kneeling on the
new sod—and Missak, suddenly

still, turns & looks beyond,
beyond grass & woods & home,
attuned to his other secret life.
(*Any Day of Your Life*)

The poem offers a final metaphor for Kherdian's writing, a window that opens onto the past, bringing to mind the fruits of other summers. The dance of the present ("the three winds of the family / with all elements in a moving conjunction") is best apprehended through reflection or its agent, the transparent medium of poetry. This window not only directs his gaze outward, but catches the shimmering vision of his wife; it is thus the meeting place of two spheres, house and yard, inner and outer. Similarly, Kherdian's poems unite his family's past with his present, his instincts with his aesthetics. Of this desire to reach the primary space of creation, beyond dualities, he writes: "What we know as growing children is instinctive and inseparable from our ecology, because we are controlled then by sun and tides, and our moods are more animal than human. . . . And it is as an artist that I am returning to what was once mine by birthright."[9]

As an emblem of a being "inseparable from" its ecology, the cat "attuned to his other secret life" embodies the wisdom buried in each of us, much like Der Hovanessian's inverted pyramid. But only if we kneel "on the new sod" of the here and now can our thoughts and flesh recover our most profound birthright, a heritage of human awareness older than our ethnic identity. Once more poetry can lead us to this end, inviting us to see the beauty "out there beyond the window. . . ."

HAROLD BOND Illuminating the Dark

Years ago, as a graduate student becoming absorbed in the literature of American ethnic minorities and beginning the recovery of my own Armenian-American self, I discovered two poems by Harold Bond. His non-Armenian name with its connotations of coherence and welding seemed a more appropriate signature than the family's original name of Bondjoukjian; the name went well with poems that led me to remembrance. The first, "The Chance," was about all of us who grew up as naive, nervous children of immigrants, plunging daily into an alien world, "weeing" in our pants because we got too wrought up in art class or because we could not bridge the distance to the nearest rest room in time. It described our desperate desire to do it right, to find our way through a world of confused and confusing colors. "Letter to an Aunt" led me even further, urging me to embrace that little girl and the parents who had gifted her with "blood and belief" as well as darkness and uncertainty. Articulating the burdens and opportunities that come with an ethnic heritage, the "Letter" helps "locate" the second generation at the edges of growth.

Bond was born in Boston in 1939 and completed his education at Northeastern University in Boston and the University of Iowa. He has worked as a production editor and copy editor; more recently, he has been an instructor for poetry workshops at the Cambridge Center for

Adult Education in Cambridge and has participated in the poets-in-the-school program in Massachusetts. His work has been widely anthologized and three volumes of his poetry have been published: *The Northern Wall* (1969); *Dancing on Water* (1970); and *The Way it Happens to You* (1979). In commenting on his literary likes and dislikes, he catalogs an eclectic list and concludes with a comment that echoes the affirmative perspective in his work:

> I can't think of a poet in this century—one I have read, of course—who hasn't written something I have admired or enjoyed. I suppose that says something about the eclecticism of tastes. What I think it also says is that I'd rather find something to like than something to dislike in a poet.[1]

Although he is the son of Armenian immigrants, Bond's poetry does not generally deal directly with his Armenian heritage. Nevertheless, one of the major themes of this work—the nature and the urgency of creation—is at the center of Armenian-American literature. First and foremost, Bond's thickly textured poems draw attention to themselves as artifacts. Through syntax that is often involuted or distorted, diction that resurrects forgotten words, symmetry in form and metrical adjustments that mirror subject matter, he demonstrates a carefully crafted technique. At their best, his lyrics, fables, and dramatic monologues give pleasure through their variety in form, mood, and subject matter. Yet it is Bond's ironic sense, his odd juxtapositions of polarities, and his willingness to undercut himself and his subjects with sly wit that are most distinctive. His work charts the growth of a hard-won affirmation, by turns brooding and playfully aware of a personal and collective past that speaks to American culture with insight.

It has been said that the Armenians' favorite color is black. Some of the reasons may emerge as we trace the psychological and aesthetic connotations of this "non-color" that haunts Bond's poetry. At times, black represents the space of creation, the imageless or shadowy backdrop that holds form and beauty, as in "The Welding Shop" where the transmutation of objects symbolizes rebirth through creation:

> Here objects are what they were not
> and everything is pliable.
> The outer world is made to fit
> only what can be viable.

(It is a hole within a hole.
There are no colors, only black
The darkness there is sometimes whole
or brilliant with the welder's spark.)

We bring the broken curios
we cannot come to dispossess.
We bring our broken whatnot whose
dominion we would reassess.

(It is a womb within a womb.
there are no images not steel.
the recreated shapes for whom
we save our lives are always real.)[2]

In the space of creation, the outer world must only fit "what can be viable," the needs of the new form brought to life by "the welder's spark." Conversely, odd snippets of matter or language that fit nowhere else and which "we cannot come to dispossess"—bound to us by necessity or affection—find dominion here, in this "hole within a hole," that inventive void where cast-off forms take on reshaped meanings. Like many of Bond's other poems, "The Welding Shop" is thus concerned with the transforming power of that supreme welder's art, poetry.

In other poems that probe the power of darkness, Bond notes the unexpected beauty of chrysanthemums sown in the night by "some fool or flower lover." The incongruity of their location next to a fire hydrant affronts a transitory human order, just as the wind serves a higher, natural order by picking "at those petals, / raining seed far and wide across the town."[3] Bond varies this theme in "Twelve by Four," where "in the swell of summer" a black man and his two sons dig through "rock, bone and clay", and where they dug,

a flower shop,
of all things, was opened, and each day now racks
of roses and chrysanthemums burst and drop,
pushed up by the sweat of those black backs.
(*The Northern Wall,* 28)

In these poems, black is identified with the primal creative urge, which works through "great travail"; elements are uprooted and cast by nature every which way to guarantee continuity of life.

Elsewhere, Bond uses a black image to signify the hardcore truth people ignore through superficiality, as in "The Stone." When a woman in black withdraws life savings from a bank to buy a stone for her husband, the teller hears her say "stove" for "stone":

> How nice, he
> tells her. And in time to have
>
> it delivered for Christmas.
> How kind. How considerate.

Left in tears, the woman finds her only consolation in the bank manager, who has

> cradled his arms around her
> like a good Santa Claus. He
> is apologizing for
>
> his employee's error. That
> being Christmas it was not
> at least in the wrong spirit.
> (*The Northern Wall,* 23–24)

The only simile in the poem, "like a good Santa Claus," emphasizes the shallow sympathy impervious to the blackness of the woman's grief. By extension, Christmas, that white and snowbound season, becomes an emblem of the blanketing that covers tangled motives under tinsel cheer. And yet, the mood of poem is not a clear black or white moroseness: the mistake "was not / at least in the wrong spirit."

In "Another Rescue" Bond suggests the multiple uses of the dark—to discover, to forget, the night can accommodate all the seasons of the heart. From under an "old stone bridge," away from bursts of "preholiday fireworks," he sees the lights of a patrol car "flood the walkway":

> Should anyone ask, I will say
> I am thinking beautiful thoughts:
>
> the calves of women or the hooves
> of mountain goats. I have come here
> to discover what troubles me,

or to forget, I am unsure which.
It is a night for all seasons.
Something is dying here.
(*The Way It Happens to You,* 61)

As the imagery implies, his descent under the bridge, away from the patrol car and fireworks, reflects the intermingling processes of the psyche, where the waters of the unconscious must retreat from the high beams of the conscious to rescue, to reintegrate. It is a place where something is always dying, even as something is always about to be born. Ironically, the poet carries "a dime and an ID," slim insurance against the unexpected arrest or the chaos that may drag him up too soon.

Even when uninterrupted, retreat is never permanent. Creation demands a periodic return to the outer light, as expressed through tiers of paradox in "The Keys":

We have undergone these small mutations,
driving home, the ceremony of fire
tempered now by the fumbling of your hands,

your impossible, womblike pocketbook
swallowing up the keys you cannot find,
the right hand nervous on the jammed car lock,

none of the old, sweet, familiar windfalls,
brassiere hooks clicking open in your hands,
garter snaps popping like champagne bottles,

your breath heavy, car windows closing where
gendarmes, tigers, madmen pocket the night
against the ceremony of our fire,

only now your distant fumbling for keys,
and home, parked, turning on the overhead,
saying, Here, light, light for you to see by.[4]

Within each tier, a shell of darkness—incarnating as night, car, pocketbook, woman—invites and sometimes swallows the keys that open into meaning. In the innermost holes burns "the ceremony of fire," lit like an ignition key starting a car. Here inhibitions are burnt in a ritual enacted in the dark, freeing the senses to catch the fleeting forms of Eros. Popping "like champagne bottles," garter snaps unlock and free effervescent spirits, making them impervious to the demons—"gendarmes, tigers, madmen"—whose fires consume the outer dark. But like any creative realm, this inner space is vulnerable to those "small mutations" that sabotage ecstasy, those subtle reminders of flux, of passion spent, of that mundane fumbling that jams the car lock and breaks one into two. Disillusionment threatens the end of the ride: house keys are misplaced and a false light shatters physical communion. Yet like a final paradox, tongue-in-cheek whimsy deflects self-pity: perhaps the key to this poem is that there is just as much love in offering a needed overheard light as in kindling an ephemeral lust.

Images of blackness also shape poems about the American scene in *The Way It Happens to You*. These poke fun at the eccentricities of American character and speech, ranging from the ironies of the illiterate "Street Preacher's Handout" whose "effectual fervent prayer" "awaileth much" (32–33); to the coldly precise and meaningless syntax of "The Perfectionist," who exhorts us to "be eclectic as the cross hairs on a tail-/ gunner's sense of his own sighting of himself" (48); to the glib panorama of suburban America in "The Glove," recovered "grease-stained behind the cash register of / the Campus Grill" (46–47). Especially zestful are the infectious, jerky rhythms of a "bug-eyed" jazz fan in "The Gold Tooth"; racing after the Newport star, the poet catches flashes of authentic gold as his car races up to Sonny Stitt from behind:

> It was Charlie Parker
> night in Newport. I thought how
> they called Sonny a poor
>
> man's Charlie Parker all those
> years. Well, Sonny clipped his wings
> in Newport. Sonny was
>
> like the wind. That night all you
> heard was his big bag of brass
> flashing like a gold tooth.
> (*The Way It Happens to You,* 20–21)

The poem moves like a "flash" and Sonny is "like the wind"—black, energetic, his gold tooth an emblem of light and soul-deep laughter and persistence, what Ralph Ellison calls the "brassy affirmation" of music in the night. With animal grace his Cadillac speeds away from the sneers of the jaded. To catch Sonny is to "catch on."

Other poems hint at the future of a neon-lit America, where posh high rises face rumbling four-lanes, and cement and reservoirs cover fertile earth. In "Letters from Birmingham," Bond sits in an all-night diner, loading his letters home with the waitress's small talk, deflecting the messianic impulses that fester in the hot, benighted city. In "This Time of Tiger," he remains in retreat until the storm has cleared. Again the protective force is identified with a black, a "tall Negress" who serves him coffee. As unknown eyes watch and "pummel" him, and the "storefront lights" leave him naked, his only comfort comes from the dark warmth of the coffee and silence itself: "I am the lamb in / this time of tiger" (*The Northern Wall,* 29). As this poem reiterates, two kinds of light cast opposing rays in Bond's work: there are the harsh, threatening "storefront lights" that represent cheap Christmas cheer as in "The Stone," or any false power that assaults and distorts; by contrast, there is the light that appears in "The Gold Tooth," identified with a self-generated and gentle illumination from within, a soul force that probes the darkness outside and informs the "ceremony of fire."

Finally, in "Our Fathers' Sons," he finds in the emptiness of a New England drought a providential force; only the drought can bring the fertility back to this town where "the waters daily recede":

> And our fathers' sons, settled in the sprawl
> beyond this valley, will return their fields to seed.
> (*The Northern Wall,* 27)

Throughout these poems the will to survive, to not let go, balances the faith that unseen forces promise harmony in the long view. If silence is Bond's "only plan," it is not the sign of passivity. Just as three thousand years of Armenian history suggest the regenerative power of self-exile, of playing the lamb in "this time of tiger," here too Bond discovers a place apart where spirit can flourish. Significantly, the sons will return the "fields to seed," as guardians of tradition, unhindered by the wounds of history.

Another piece of Bond's creative strategy stems from the allure of the occult, a recognition that unseen (black) forces that we do not control move through and shape our lives. In his droll dramatic monologue, "A Heathen's Sport," a "preposterously overgrown mountain trout" victimizes the three owners of a New England farm, resisting all natural attempts to eradicate him:

> Of course you could flood him with toxicants,
> or you could even drain the pond, a most
> foolhardy choice, what with the drought and all.
> We are, in any case, all God's creatures.
> Think, if you must, of Daniel Webster,
> years ago in the selfsame hillsides,
> taking on none but the devil himself.
> We have each of us our burden, as it is.
> (*The Way It Happens to You,* 34–35)

Like a miniature Moby Dick, this trout stands for the intractable supernatural that sustains as well as destroys. Any attempt to get rid of him spells disaster, because it means draining the area of dwindling water resources.

But for the believer, the supernatural reveals its charms with miraculous results. In "Gypsy," syntax seduces us into creative trance:

> On an afternoon, passing the Gypsy parlor,
> I was beckoned in by a crooked finger
> whose owner told me of the knowledge of my coming
> as it was revealed in a vision of her dreaming.

The poet indulges with a resultant "reconditioning of forces inside out":

> And she left me with my indulgence unbroken
> as her craft turned to art in the act of creation,
> all things in their probability being equal
> turning within themselves as fact, fool or fable.
> (*The Northern Wall,* 21)

"Fact, fool or fable"—the choice determines our approach to life and our chances of survival, as we transmute a superficial mechanical "craft" into the healing art of the believer. Practicing this wisdom, in "Dancing on Water" Bond turns the ragged dance of life into another fable, an assertion of faith in a wintry landscape. In the final stanzas, he describes the most basic choice we make, as he "balks gravity by timing":

Harold Bond

Something

is special in the way I walk, sealegs
to be sure but drunken only in what
blue waters will not buoy me up. These rags
of kneebones for my fable, can we not

call it beautiful that I move over
such fathoms in this my clumsy fashion?
We will say I am dancing on water
in my faith. Ladies, I must dance or drown.
(*Dancing on Water,* 23)

Here the decision to live or die is expressed as the choice between dancing or drowning. This poem thus completes the journey begun in "The Welding Shop." At the literal level, it confronts the treacheries of the body: "these rags of kneebones" show no respect for the conventions of movement. As the woozy rhythms suggest, to "dance or drown," to defy the gravity of bodily chaos, to answer nihilism with a clumsy dance that bravely uses the only materials available—this is the key to survival, the same axiom the daredevils of the Armenian epic knew so well.

Three poems with an Armenian subject unite these themes and point toward the ethnic sources of Bond's credo. "Postscript:Marsh" begins with a note: "The Armenian is an historical phenomenon. He should have been extinct generations ago," and continues with a catalog of group and family history overtaken by the Turk, "mounted on his black, / oversexed steed." But while the ironies of the Armenian past fade and the old grow "wrinkles over their scars," picketing the UN in memory of the dead, the life force moves a younger generation to propagate in the "group-heavy frost" of the Fresno vineyards (*Dancing on Water,* 59–61). This poem echoes one of Michael J. Arlen's observations in *Passage to Ararat,* that the only antidote to the fixation on the massacres by the older generation is the forward motions of the "impatient young men." Here, as in "Our Fathers' Sons," the culture once more escapes extinction—not through the senile protests of old men, but the "dark-haired youngbloods" who return the fields to seed, venting the same passion that drives the Turk's "black, oversexed steed."

Survival is also the subject in the widely anthologized "The Chance," another fable. Its autobiographical core is an endearing account of a child's wavering sense of ethnicity; for a little boy with a foreign accent, new to the rigors of grammar school, *every* act is chancy:

First grade. I am the skinny
one with the foreign accent. I am
so scared I think I will wee
in my pants. Miss Breen is teaching us
colors. We are cutting out
strips of paper in the fashion of
Indian feathers. We must

order them in descending hues on
a black headband. I cannot
understand Miss Breen. It is not done
the way it should be: blue with
yellow and black with white. Unless I
do something soon Miss Breen will
say I am a dumb Armenian. So

without looking I shuffle
my feathers in my hand. I paste them
over my headband. I spill
my pastepot, and I know I will wee
now because here comes Miss Breen,
only Miss Breen says, Good, Harold, good,
blue after purple and green

after blue. It happened, it happened
like a rainbow, like a swatch
of oil on water, eight feathers thieved
in perfect succession one
on the other. Miss Breen did not say
I am a dumb Armenian,
and I do not even have to wee.

(*The Northern Wall*, 9)

Here again, risky as the gesture is, the little boy decides to act—to create—even if he does so without looking, clumsily and frantically, his tense and breathless rhythms voicing his worry. As before, his project is to "thieve order," to rearrange a jumble of colors against a black headband. The reward of his courage is twofold: the teacher's praise and the miracle of creation: "It happened, it happened / like a rainbow, like a swatch / of oil on water, eight feathers thieved / in perfect succession one / on the other." At its best, school becomes another place of refuge, where the child receives his "first grade" lessons in creative survival.

At another level, this poem is a commentary on the American "experiment": in our land of many "colors," the only hope of democratic order lies in arranging our multiethnic affairs against a "black headband" that honors our nation's deepest roots in the culture of the native American and then fashioning a festive war bonnet with the feathers of other immigrant groups. This creative ideal can best be achieved, freeing us to dance our national dance, if the guardians of the national creed, the Miss Breens who administer the sanctions of our institutions and guide the energies of a diversified population, can harmonize the need for social, or classroom, order with a compassionate respect for the differing needs and gifts of individuals. Bond communicates the teacher's sympathy unobtrusively; her positive effect on the child is proportionate to her restraining her negative judgments.

Many of the above themes coalesce in "Letter to an Aunt," a poem whose universal message is rooted in Bond's ethnicity. For many reasons I find it a key work in Armenian-American literature, a powerful statement about inheritance that simply declares that we exist without apology:

> I am writing by candle from the Cape.
> An August storm has blown the power down.
> The house is in darkness;
> trees are screaming at my window.
> I hope to finish before the candles stop.
> You have seen my poems
> and find them generally black.
> I am forced to show you I can laugh.
> Yesterday at Zack's there was a drummer
> who played with reversed sticks.
> He told me he tries to make sounds,
> mostly makes noise.
> We laughed. This I think funny, you will not.
> And is, in any case, peripheral to the purpose.
> Anyone can laugh.

What I am to write you of is belief.
Today I spent the afternoon
on a seacliff under a lighthouse.
Every stalk in sight was broken by the wind.
I almost cried. This you think funny, I do not.
This is my belief. This I cannot explain.
I am also to write you of blood.
My mother told me once I am alive now
only because she was at a missionery's
when her village was bombed in the war.
This is blood. This is what I am.
I have never gone hungry
or lacked a place to sleep.
If I write black, know that, like the storm
outside, like the lack of light
inside, it has no image, form, color,
is only belief and blood and what it is.[5]

The first stanza locates the poet at the edges of a darkened America: an August storm screams through the landscape, bringing upheaval; only the candles—symbols of a fragile yet steady light from within—make vision and communication possible. The poet addresses his night letter to his aunt, a member of the older generation. Though they share a heritage, the aunt's vision is illuminated by other "lights," especially if she is an immigrant. In laughter, Bond has found an apt symbol of the division. What we think funny and why, how we express our amusement, reveals much about our private and cultural histories; it is a complex barometer of where we are detached, where we have the most perspective. On a broader scale, his observation, "You have seen my poems and find them generally black," not only apples to Bond's work, but to the mood of modern life, where affirmations of traditional ideals are rare or cheaply won, where laughter denotes hysteria or a "Santa Claus" mask for underlying doubt: at one level, anyone *can* laugh. The musician's joke, which only another artist or "creator" can appreciate, reinforces this notion: anyone can make "noises"—just reverse the sticks. What is demanding is the graceful creation of form, "sounds."

The beginning of the second stanza varies the light-and-dark imagery of the first. As we saw in "Another Rescue," Bond often retreats to the underground vigil to discover or forget. Here the lighthouse, like the candles, nurtures his vision of grass broken by the wind, an image that—for an Armenian—inevitably conjures up the nightmares of the past, fields of humanity cut down by the Turkish scythe. Yet just as wind casts seeds as well as uprooting life, so too this sacrifice may be redeemed through a rekindling of belief in the younger generation. The actual expression of this commitment demands existential choices: where, for example, are the contemporary models for healing massacre fallout? The ironic legacy of any child born to survivors only complicates the difficulty; for these children, life is the direct result of a precious chance: their parents escaped. Hence, "my mother told me once I am alive now / only because she was at a missionary's / when her village was bombed in the war." This then is "blood," the life stream that carries the fears and hopes of one generation into the next: "This is what I am."

Further, just as the widow in "The Stone" demands acknowledgment of her grief, here too the black reality of the group past demands testimony and integration—otherwise the tears will never stop. What makes this task so difficult is a twofold problem. First, it is hard to find purpose in a shadowy grief that seems to grow more remote with time. Second, the living web of the ethnic family has weakened; it no longer holds the "image, form, color" of the past. Yet the children's integration is necessary to the well-being of two generations: the parents work out their trauma by telling stories; the telling *is* the cure, giving experience a warmth and wholeness it could not have otherwise. Thus, if the parents do not communicate with their children, they are doubly blocked, for they are denied a field in which to plant the stories. The result is that they stay cut off from the validation of passing their personal myths—their blood-beliefs—into the future, much like the medieval Armenian scribes who cast their colophons into an uncertain world with no guarantee that anyone would hear.

If the children try to retreat from the blackness, they only delay their maturation: one cannot escape one's body and inbred responses to the world, those nameless fears parents pass on to us. In this respect, children of ethnics are vulnerable; more often than not, accounts of Armenian-American children focus on the intense curiosity and protectiveness of their immigrant parents, their obsessive need to safeguard offspring from new demons.

Yet what alleviates this blackness of trauma is the same blood tie that transmitted it. The mother has told the boy of her own narrow escape from death. He lives with this knowledge and finds purpose—belief—in it. But his purpose is as complex and hard to articulate as the "color" black, which light can so easily penetrate and nevertheless resists definition ("it has no image, form, color"). Conversely, just as black is the foundation for all color, this informing purpose impels any meaningful action. And for Bond, the worthiest responses to the "screaming trees" are first to communicate—he reaches out to his aunt, tries to explain who he is despite their differences in age and outlook. His gesture implies the responsibility of the older generation to the young: to accept where their children *are,* and find in this the evolution of their own identity. Second, he creates; he witnesses the void outside in history and inside the heart, and by portraying it, transforms its meaning. At this level, the "letter" guides any marginal trying to "cross the bridge" between past and present, Old Country and New World: we have to begin where we are—the margins—by exploring the poles that tear at us and by defying assimilation into a light that can annihilate. Just as the Armenians—those "classic marginals"—perpetuated a full cultural tradition through candlelit eons, the ethnic artist (*any* artist) must make the marginality count. Inspired by this "black" challenge, he will create work of lasting import.

Reweaving the Rug: Symmetry and Rebirth in the Poetry of PETER BALAKIAN

In a short article on Arshile Gorky, the Armenian-American poet Peter Balakian describes the effect of his family's past on his own work: "The 'sinew of identity' compels the imagination; our ancestors find us just as we find them"[1]. Balakian's poetry—like Gorky's visual art—offers a model of how this discovery proceeds; as he weaves the strands of history—familial, ethnic, national, and planetary—into a design that reflects deeper levels of integration, fragments not only tell their stories, but seed new life-forms. Balakian's three collections are *Father Fisheye*[2], *Sad Days of Light*[3], and *Reply from Wilderness Island*[4]. Though the emphasis of each is distinct, the "sinew" of carefully interwoven imagery unifies the poetry and carries it forward. The major themes of the poetry are prefigured in "The Return," a poem included in *Father Fisheye*. Here the silence of the water and signs of a current that drags men downstream farther than the fish suggest the danger of tracking the stream to its destination. But despite that chance, another current of belief pulls at the imagination:

> You want to believe this river
> has direction,
> that small tributaries up north
> empty into this wide span of gray water,

that there is a system
of xylem and phloem
beneath the bottom
that guides the water carefully
to a point where
gulls appear from behind black rock. (35)

Moving through these lines as their deepest current is a search for "direction," for a form that contains and propels even the smallest "tributaries" of experience in a dual cultural tradition, so that they are free to enter a new point of creation. Though the containers will change from poem to poem, they will always transform their contents to new purposes. The tough "xylem and phloem," which guide the stream to the point of transformation, function much like natural counterparts of the artistic process, which funnels the events of history and leads to their apotheosis. Amid the process nothing guarantees that it will come "to a point"; however, as this poem ends, the image of an Amish farmer nursing the growth of his beard and his tomatoes through cold April nights plants faith in a soil where patterns of order work their magic, keeping evil influences submerged:

the hex sign on his barn
rotates his wife's face
in a pattern that keeps
each season's sorcerer
beneath the corn. (36)

At the other extreme, the images of the poet's cultural past both challenge and feed the belief that life has direction. Setting forth Armenia's role in this poetry is "The History of Armenia," the first poem in *Sad Days of Light*. Despite the Armenians' preoccupation with their history, few accounts have captured the horror of their past as neatly as this piece. The poem presents a natural world in total disorder as witnessed by a woman whose mind shares that breakdown. The scene of the poem is New Jersey, but psychologically it takes place in a land where the sun has gone bad. Holes and fissures—in the earth, in the heavens, in the body—show the universal rot, and the wind blowing through the eyes of the grandmother runs with an acid that burns vision and refuses to die down. With the sky torn into shreds, even the angels are maimed, and the rivers filled with massacre debris. The final stanza presents a world where only a breath marks the shift from normality into dissolution; and time, like every other natural force, reverses on itself, moving from present to past tense:

> Grandpa is pressing
> pants, they came for him
> before the birds were up—
> he left without shoes
> or tie, without shirt
> or suspenders.
> It was quiet —
> the birds, the birds
> were still sleeping. (5)

The primary legacy of this history is dismemberment and exile, a collective memory clogged with death and images of birds unable to bear witness. For an artist, re-creating a stable, workable world from the rubbish, where life comes to a point, or at least discovering pieces that can still serve life, becomes the main task. Though Armenia appears consistently in Balakian's poetry, especially in the remaining poems in *Sad Days of Light,* in this poem Armenia's central role as a synecdoche is established: the history of Armenia *is* history, with each fragment of family and cultural experience mirroring all human experience.

"Thoreau at Nauset," a longer poem in *Reply from Wilderness Island,* amplifies Balakian's task as an artist. Set in the center of the collection, after more personal poems about his father's death, this imaginative monologue is a bracing counterpoint and commentary on the rest. Thoreau's sane, detached voice weaves the facts of human and natural history into a sturdy, yet buoyant ethos that teaches us how to bear the past. The three sections of the poem, each a meditative account of a day on Cape Cod, lead us from inland to the central darkness of what can be seen. Thoreau, never as comfortable with the ocean as with the waters of the interiors, is nevertheless an ideal observer of this landscape, registering its stark lessons on his naturalist's eye. The first day's entry presents a toughened landscape where sight is misted and life-forms adapt to the assault of wind:

> there must be sinewy stuff
> so strong in those branches
> which look like knots
> growing from knots

that with each winter's
peeling they grow stouter. (33)

Images of tough, fibrous substances appear regularly in Balakian's work. For example, the grandmother of "Granny, Making Soup" (in *Sad Days of Light*) adds the tendons of the lamb to the water of the soup and later a "little meat . . . for our own teeth" (14). Similarly, the pig's stomach in "Blood Pudding" (*Reply from Wilderness Island,* 75–77), which holds the ingredients for the pudding, is fibrous with veins. Here, the hardiness of the landscape has challenged its inhabitants—Indians and Englishmen—as much as the vegetation, daring them to toughen up or be destroyed. This strength develops by imitating the branches "which look like knots growing from knots"—that is, by feeding on tendons or meat or mealy corn, or whatever firms the spirit and secures it to the bottom, beyond wind and dissolution. Noting life patterns shared by the generations, Thoreau observes, "History strikes me as ever present" (35); history here is a soil fertilized by past suffering and ripe for plantings of the living. Reading through the flux, Thoreau's dry, matter-of fact voice identifies forces that operate by nonlinear laws:

Against the flux of events
nature brings us to each other,
plucks us from the straight line
we walked the day before. (35)

These lines are pivotal in the larger context of the poetry taken as a whole, for they reaffirm a deeper truth that intersects random events at every point, realigning pieces into a more authentic order than they might have had before. But just as developing fiber requires eating fiber, nature can bring us to one another only if we put our hands in the same soil that our ancestors turned.

In the second section, an account of the second day of the journey, neither wind nor rain keep the travelers from reading under their umbrellas, a flaunting detail thrown at the timid. But the book they read is not written by human hands; instead, it is the work of nature in a storm. This section takes place in a more primeval, wilder setting than the first, closer to the ocean—the tones of gray and silver in the sky, the beach, and waves are "more sullen" than peeling fall scrub; yet the mix and immediacy of these elements confronts Thoreau with a riddle central to Balakian's work as well:

Who can understand beauty
in its own moment?
Our careless yawning eyes
are forever looking at the firmament
for a sudden change
that will set the axis right. (36)

The simplicity of the question belies the elusiveness of an easy answer. Again, placed in a broader context, this passage echoes to imagery from previous poems; this firmament we scan for quick fixes is, after all, the same natural "umbrella" ripped apart by genocide in "The History of Armenia." And the "sudeen change" that shakes the psyche in that poem only sets the axis askew; the grandmother cannot even trust the sky not to fall completely, raining corpses and other, unnamed horrors. From this perspective, to yawn at the firmament seems a luxury open to the protected few. But Thoreau, tough-minded observer that he is, proposes that we "understand beauty in its own moment," even when it is as sullen and dreary and violent as the storm; he suggests that we take it into the body, like "the scent of narcissus / or the whippoorwill's / rising cry." Through this active engagement, we catch up with the present and with any "meaning" that events might have; this is a meaning that does not fall from the sky but rises from the moment.

The kelp that Thoreau next studies typifies an organism well suited to its circumstances. It stands for an archaic wisdom of form: a wanderer from the deep that gathers names and light, soft at the root, yet branching out with a "rubbery toughness" that can surrender to "the feline curve of the water"; in all these ways, the kelp models a way of living in the deep without being destroyed. The description of mackerel gulls, which completes the day's entry, complements that of the kelp; unlike the kelp, the birds seem "adapted / to their circumstances more by spirit / than by beak or leg":

They are among the anomalous creatures—
that inhabit the endless
funnel of wind
whirling the far edge
of what they eye can see. (38)

In "The Return," gulls burst from behind the black rock when the river reaches its destination; elsewhere, in "The New World: Spring Lake, New Jersey, 1925" (included in *Sad Days of Light*), "a garland of mackerel / gulls" crowns "the swelling tide" of the grandmother's descendants. In each instance, these birds convey courage and a spiritual joy that rises and swoops to the occasion. Although their white exuberance contrasts with the blacks and blues of rocks and ocean, the gulls lift our vision of the primary power these darker, deeper forces serve: "whirling the far edge / of what the eye can see," they live at the margins of what can be known and reassure us that the "endless funnel of wind"—or history—does not dead-end.

In the third entry, Thoreau ends his day with an ascetic supper of clam, "tough but sweet," and comes to a "Humane House," a refuge for shipwrecked sailors. His twilight moments with the "architecture of storm" usher him into prehistory: shut up against the storm, offering no way in except a door, the Humane House—or Charity House—ironically affirms its title. Kneeling by a knothole to peer into the dark room, Thoreau steps into the same mystery the gulls whirl through earlier, and his eye drifts through the hole:

> as if a lee current led
> it gently to a still center
> and there in the quiet dry
> dark I stood—
> my legs as light
> as the corn sheaves (39)

The "still center," ringed by darkness and reflected in his "pupil dilating," is a healing point; as such it is the essence of charity and humaneness; it quiets thought, and lightens and softens the body:

> and my skin could've been slit
> as a sculler slits a man-
> of-war's membrane so the poison
> will leak out. (39–40)

On the previous day, we have seen Thoreau cut into the rubbery kelp, exploring its insides and wrapping its blades about his wrists. Here, the sinister image of the breathing darkness slitting his own membrane—not tough but soft, gelatinous—creates an odd parallel that reinforces the power of what he has tapped into. In a sense, the meditation through the funnel answers his earlier question: "who can understand beauty in its own moment?" For by shifting the focus from "up there" in the firmament to "inside" the humane house of his immediate awareness, Thoreau spiritually "sets the axis right." The poem ends with him emerging from his absorption, chilled and numbed by an outer darkness, which comes cyclically no matter what:

> The sun had gone down
> when I stood up—
> the cold set,
> my chest numb as sand. (40)

The poem thus moves from the inland to the edge of the land and finally into a psychological space that includes both. In its entirety "Thoreau at Nauset" recounts a journey in which nature not only "brings us to each other," but brings us to ourselves.

"Physicians"[5] is a poignant counterpart to "Thoreau at Nauset." Though the setting, time, and personae have shifted, it explores similar regions of the soul. Emerging from the strands of previous lyrics, this introspective poem tightens the connections among earlier themes. Here the distance between the personal and the collective, the past and the present, and West and East narrows to the point where the inner eye unites fragments into larger patterns of meaning. "Physicians" takes place inside St. John the Divine, which for its patrons is much like a Humane House for shipwrecked urbanites. Though Thoreau's "architecture of storm" is stripped of ornamentation, leaving him to use a knothole to peer inside, the church is "swaddled" in the "dirty air" of urban congestion. "Cherub faces" and "imitation lapiz lazuli" substitute for knotholes, and the symbolism of the Christian myth confronts the visitor from any angle. Most significantly, the poet here sits inside, completely contained by this membrane, which barely separates the sacred from the secular, from the outer, "smogged in" darkness. As the poet makes his way through a building filled with intimate personal memories, his eye falls on "the leaded panes / of a wordless narrative"; the "cooked tones hold fast" as his eye makes its way "through refractions of the glass." Here in this supernatural glow, one can see by the power of a sustaining light that guides one toward the least frequented—and shadowy—corners of the heart. Having opened the doors to "St. Saviour's Chapel," the poet has thus entered the inward funnel of history; the path leads to the causal levels of human experience, to the still point where ancestors speak to us in the language of archetypal memories.

The rest of the poem is an extended meditation on how two men, the poet's grandfather and father, have "made the rounds" of their inner lives. Like the kelp, they are creatures of the deep; professionally they have both been physicians, but so far as they mediate between the known and unknown, also a type of priest. The grandfather is a man dispersed from his homeland by collective calamity, a fate described with an economy that matches the circumscription of his exile:

> my grandfather. His mind
> ringing with the five languages
>
> of hs exiled life.
> his German medical texts
> like small suitcases.

This man is the speaker of an earlier poem in *Sad Days of Light,* "In the Turkish Ward," a dramatic monologue which reveals the moral dilemmas of an Armenian doctor inducted into the Turkish Army during the massacres. Toward the end of the monologue he alludes to the toll of his sacrifice:

> If my daughter knew how my hands tremor,
> how a scant tendon keeps my heart from
> dropping through my bottom. (26)

In "Physicians," the spiritual weight of what he has seen is carried into another cultural tradition. His grandson comments, "In another century he'd have / followed his uncle, / the Archbishop to the steps / of San Lazaro" (an Armenian-Catholic monastery near Venice). But in the century that takes him hostage, the conventional path of priest, even when exalted into archbishop, does not begin to probe the horror of modern Armenian experience. So, as a physician, transplanted in America, he spends his life "inside another darkness," passing "light-tipped tubes" "down the gutter / of the throat." This outward searching is a projection, and when the grandson thinks of him "rummaging" "where Mozart's high G/oboe can be trapped" in "Despond," the regions in question are inside the grandfather's own psyche; these spaces crowded with images of an ordered and elegant world are betrayed by a history that shreds the innocent.

His favorite sense organ, the eye, leads him deeper into the secrets of the bodysoul:

> Eye to eye against a lens,
> where sight and tought converge,
> he followed the retina's orange
>
> spot as if it were a moon
> orbiting Pluto—

This passage vaguely echoes Thoreau's summation in "Thoreau at Nauset," where "Against the flux of events / nature brings us to each other, / plucks us from the straight line / we walked the day before." Like nature, the eye works in cyclical patterns; it reaffirms the "ever present" dynamics that shape and reshape our histories. In contrast, linear thought has spawned most of the catastrophes of this century, not least of them genocide. This type of reasoning can be catastrophic because it never looks back—to consequences, to organisms shattered by a streamlined, "progressive" view of history. Such reasoning never completes the arc that keeps the "moon orbiting Pluto" and the natural world singing through cycles, an arc that periodically returns us to the "living fossils" of our origins and from that soil enables us to create new wholes. For a human being, then, the eye coordinates memory with vision, a task much more complex than reason can fulfill. This "eye" guides the grandfather in his "night rounds"; lifting an eyelid on "a clean metal table," he is met by a field of "empty whites":

> like scattered marbles
>
> on a desert floor
> flickering in the scoured
> Turkish moonlight.

Here, the eyes of others reflect and magnify his fate; looking into them, the motions of his mind also become circular, even sacred, as they perpetually orbit the fragments of a dismembered nation. For "against the flux of events," this physician of the eye is repeatedly brought back to witnessing and offering devotions to a nation-family scattered into oblivion. Finally, his body becomes the resting place of a vision that rings his past and his future:

The piles of Armenian

corpses he tended in Adana
in his thirtieth year
he carried in the tremor
of his hand.

The first section ends with the grandfather's death—of heart failure—and the father putting on his father's "ill-fitting white coat." Significantly, the second section contains no imagery that refers to a cultural past in describing the father's journey, unlike the grandfather's; though the decisive forms of that past may live in his awareness, their effect is hidden. This shift is reflected in the two men's specialities as doctors. The older man's focus has been the eye, but his son's is the heart, an organ assaulted by torment, as described in the following stanza:

If you could loose your love to flow
down there in the eddies that swell
and shrink against the barnacled and moss-spun
bulkheads you would see the contradictions
that feed and join the oscillations
in the unstillable red sea.

If the main task of the eye is to keep our motions circular, the heart is charged with making peace among "the contradictions that feed and join" in its chambers. Hence, its muscle must be stronger than that of any other organ, and its "bulkheads" must hold firm against an "unstillable" barrage of passions, fears, and doubts. To "loose your love" into that storm is risky at best. As these passages imply, working with the heart challenges a healer's art, testing how well contradictions are tolerated and transcended; detachment and empathy have to be balanced to avoid self-destruction. The father's response is shown in a cool, "adamant" distancing, "tying his terror / in a Windsor knot." Like his father before him, he is not a stranger to the depths himself: on "certain days," he too feels "the inward suck," the "whirling vortices where bones / of men and women disappear." In "Thoreau at Nauset," Thoreau feels his skin could be "slit" by the "wide ring" of darkness he gazes into—a darkness that can neither be described nor fathomed; but the effect of this darkness has none of the aggressive pull of the force described here, where it is transformed into a limitless void that turns defenses pale and thin, shrinking the father into formalities: "Cuff's meticulous. 'Pass / the salt, salad, please.' " The toll of trying to control such a relentless force is high, and the earlier image of the heart as "that fruit of blood" is succeeded by that of a "pumping muscle" becoming "a bag of worms" as death ends the "raucous" beat. Ultimately, the father has not been able to imitate the kelp, which triumphs through a unique harmony of toughness and softness.

The poem ends with a gentler light filling the church, turning "the deep red of the shepherds' / robes to rose," very different from the numbing cold Thoreau feels at the end of his revery. This light contrasts with the presence of the two men "behind" the poet; their sinews have not withstood mortality, "uneasy with the mortal cells":

> But, hands in clotted water.
> Pits of dark.

Their legacy is persistence equal to the terror and the will to probe the unknown, strengths necessary for an artist. But they cannot sustain a vision that leads to rebirth, or at the very least help others overcome fear. That the revery takes place inside the church, where the inner life is cherished and the colors of the spirit lighten and darken with the times of the day and of the heart, adds a needed perspective to these physicians' lives. The church—and its counterparts in Balakian's work—not only makes it possible to dig or dive into the same waters as the father and grandfather, but to do so in the presence of an alternate, healing set of symbols; these symbols, especially the Virgin and the angelic spirits that overlook the steps where the poet sits, send light and glimpses of wholeness toward the "pits of dark." As the ending of the poem suggests, both poles—represented by the images of the father and grandfather behind the poet, and of rose-tinted shepherds' robes—must be acknowledged and eventually integrated before the wounded healer within each of us can live out its destiny.

"The Oriental Rug"[6] offers an image that might birth such a view. The rug is one of the richest symbols in Balakian's work, operating at many levels as an affirmative image that contains and orders strands of history into patterns. Like the Humane House, the rug is filled with mystery; but it is a mystery that speaks through a lush, sensory beauty. Like the interior of St. John the Divine, the rug is also filled with presences; but here, they have a more immediate, tactile reality; the rug as an entity exudes a consciousness of the past, which turns it into a tragic witness—as tragic as the poet's grandfather or grandmother. Also like the church, the rug promotes contemplation, but of a very heightened order; ideally, its patterns act like a mandala, holding the conflicting contents of the imagination and inducing equilibrium through their symmetry and completeness. But as depicted here, the rug has taken a beating; the designs are askew and the weave is coming undone, all of which affects the degree of order it can re-create in the imagination. The process the poet undergoes in the poem thus resembles a deepening lifelong meditation on a damaged mandala that nevertheless bears family and cultural mysteries; the spiritual and artistic potential of such contemplation is especially charged, because the destinies of the poet and the rug are linked.

The poem begins with the poet as child sleeping on "the brushed and bruised / wool of the Kashan" on the living room floor. It is a scene that might speak to many children and grandchildren of Armenian immigrants, whose earliest contact with the Old Country came through the sensory wealth of rugs and embroideries that survived transplantation. The rug is colored with vegetable dyes made of roots, berries, and dry leaves:

> The prongy soil
> of my grandparents' world:
> southeastern Turkey, once Armenia.

Like a piece of ancestral soil, it is filled with "living fossils" that fill the eye and speak to the depths of a child's imagination more vivid than anything outside its magic borders: "Armenian green. . . . Outside my house the grass / never had such color." But with time, what was once a weathered storehouse of images comes to embody the poet's historical self as an Armenian, and as it does, our sense of who the speaker is becomes more complex: whatever has happened to the rug has happened to the speaker, as suggested in the following passage:

> Six centuries of Turkish heels
> on my spine-dyed back:
> madder, genista, sumac—
> one skin color in the soil.

As that embodiment, the rug leads to a detailed exploration of Armenia's destiny. Wherever the poet's eye follows the designs, "the wool give[s] way," echoing in chilling, nerve-jangling sounds:

> I hear wind running
> through heart strings.

> I hear an untuned zither
> plucked by a peacock's accidental strut.

The wind, which in "The History of Armenia" disperses the grandmother's sanity by distorting the present, here plays the heart with equally distorting and sinister effects; the zither and peacock, eminent symbols of lightness and grace in Armenian culture, are equally "undone." And as the "warp and weft," the coordinating axes of an entire ethos, fall apart, the pull is downward into the vegetal source.

The third section sets up a contrast that highlights the tragedy of the Armenians' plight earlier in this century. We hear the sounds of a mallet beating the knots of a rug smooth. Although this action creates a higher quality rug, it is not completely positive; the blows make warp and weft "disappear," and the sounds vibrate in the speaker's awareness

> as a knelling bell
> on the sea of Marmara
> once rang toward the civilized West.

This comparison reeks with historical irony. During the latter part of the nineteenth century and into the twentieth century, the Ottoman Turks through sociopolitical ineptitude and the Armenians through political aspirations for independence looked to Europe and beyond for assistance and sympathy. But as the not-so-civilized Turks began to slaughter the Armenians in 1915, the major response of "the civilized West" was to shake their heads. Perhaps this implicit awareness, that the powerful calls of the bell will never reach their destination, accounts for the abrupt break in the following stanza; here the speaker pitches himself into the rug, into "a spinning corolla / of an unnamed flower," following the "mud-lines" until he reaches "the dark balm"

> of my far away land—
> the poppied acres
> of Adoian's hands.

The buried sense of this "far away land" in the rug guards its innermost mystery; like "the poppied acres" that Arshile Gorky re-created as an Armenian exiled in America, this land is now reached only through an imaginative journey that descends to the living source.

The fourth section traces this journey, as the speaker pries his way into a rose, undoing the "blighted cliché" that has numbed outer consciousness of its suffering and the deeper, abiding "symmetry" at its center. As he makes his way with steady thrusts into the lush, fertile space within, beyond blight, he enters another realm of the imagination. Just as Gorky's evocations of his homeland penetrate the interiors of apricots and bones as a way of discovering what he called "the inner infinity" of Armenia, the brief interlude at the core is alive with a delicate imagery that suggests a similar discovery:

> I sucked my way into the nectaries;
> felt a hummingbird's tongue
> and the chalky wing of a moth.

Each nuance and organ of the rose, one of the hardiest of flowers, is explored, as if to keep uniting with its feminine essence. But just as Gorky's inner exploration barely compensated for the outer chaos of his life as an exile, the speaker here comes

> apart as the thorn—
> (the spiky side that kept the jackal out)
> and dispersed whatever was left
> of me to the downward pulling
> of cells sobbing in the earth.

Like Armenia, the rose for its protection has grown the thron, a tough set of sanctions, behaviors, mores to guard against violation. But in the end, that thorn cannot discriminate between lovers and enemies, and destroys whatever threatens the core. Significantly, the speaker, totally identified with the fate of the rose and totally given to grief, completes the process by dispersing himself into the primary matter—the only place from which a new whole can form. In a sense, the passage provides an apt image for the first fallout of the Armenian genocide: sharp though the thorn may have been, it could not keep the jackal out, and what little was left after the carnage—torn into individual cells of life—was forced downward, into communion with the primary sources of memory, language, image.

The fifth section carries the dispersion forward; for now the speaker walks with a rug on his back, "become to [himself] a barren land." Though the "new world sun" seems to transform its dust into "fine spume," he remains

A sick herbalist
wandering in a century
mapped by nations wandering.

As such, the speaker's fate sums up the condition of many artists in the twentieth century. Displaced either physically or psychologically, they travel light, carrying the remains of a once living myth, which at one time supported *them* and fed their imagination with affirmative patterns that shaped a redemptive worldview. Now, the rug, worn though it is, is still the only "membrane" protecting the speaker; thus it functions like the flower-patterned dress of an earlier poem, "Can I Tell My Limping Aunt," in *Sad Days of Light:* though the dress and its flowers cannot restore youth or companionship to an aging woman, they at least "keep the coming air / from getting in" and promote the basic cycle of life, as the speaker counsels:

let the petals and stems,
the silky filament and the tongues
of invisible pollen—

fall inside your dress,
fall inside your skin. (51)

A similar process operates here. An herbalist collects medicinal plants; he is an archaic type of physician, who in the language of "The Return," knows what "hex sign" to use against "each season's sorcerer." Hence his knowledge and effectiveness draw more on an intuitive awareness of the natural elements than on formal training. In these times, herbalists are more needed than ever because the varieties of illness have grown in number; yet with the land—inside and outside the psyche—barren, it is hard to get supplies to cure others—or oneself, a catch-22 that holds many hostage. But the ending of "The Oriental Rug" moves toward rebirth, for though the rug is coming apart just as the speaker did in the previous section and the dyes are coming through the wool, the very disintegration releases vegetable matter that might seed a future, especially if it falls onto the "skin" of the exiled psyche. Sundered from the whole, each type of dye—safflower, Kermes, Madder root, and Tyrian purple—spurs a passionate, fertilizing remembrance that wakens the senses and the heart; this process climaxes in the ending stanza:

The Magical Pine Ring

Tyrian purple, from a mollusk membrane
lodged in Phoenician sand—
gurgle all your passion in my ear.

As this poetry demonstrates, no matter how often one dives to the bottom of that grief, the pain remains "unstillable." Whether we are aware of it or not, it passes through the generations, circling through the eyes and storming the defenses of the heart. Thus, acknowledging the full violation of that flower of history, Armenia, without coming apart at the thorn, asks for a fully cultivated sensibility, soft yet fibrous. This cultivation begins in childhood, when the sensory vehicles of a historical awareness seep into and activate "the wasp-nest like cells" of the imagination. With time and conscious contemplation, as the tributaries of a personal, cultural, and planetary identity join, a more profound sense of destiny emerges, which in turn is reflected in imaginative patterns of greater depth and inclusiveness. Only this sense of destiny makes it possible to transcend the barrenness, to bear the tragic weight of the rug, and to receive guidance from its depths. Followed to the end, the process—inseparable from the evolution of Balakian's poetry—will not only redeem the rose, but release the imagination into a world made whole.

ARSHILE GORKY The Implications of Culture

> Dreams form the bristles of the artist's brush. . . . In trying to probe beyond the ordinary and the known, I create an inner infinity. . . . Liver. Bones. Living rocks and living plants and animals. Living dreams . . . to this I owe my debt to our Armenian art. Its hybrids, its many opposites. The inventions of our folk imagination. These I attempt to capture directly, I mean the folklore and physical beauty of our homeland, in my works.[1]

During his short life, through a discipline that held firm through depression and catastrophe, Gorky probed the deepest recesses of memory. Even the naive eye, untrained in the idioms of modern art, can with sustained meditation enter the realm of nostalgia and beauty that Gorky created in his painting. Works such as *The Plow and the Song,* one of his later masterpieces, sing with color and movement. Shapes laden with multiple meanings point toward the infinities he loved to discover; lines curve in and out of pockets of earth; the whole is drenched in a sunny fertility that weds female to male; plant and animal forms merge, take root, take flight; smiling lips draw us into the interiors of creation. And at the heart of this extraordinary visual poem, a golden face blows a leaf into the center of a bony umbilical passage, analogue to a new genesis. Like a "living dream" or the breath of love, the image contains all that

Gorky sought to achieve, giving birth through the imagination to an Armenia vibrant with oppositions.

Whether the figures and scenes of this native land appear as the fleeting entities of his early work, "too fragile to bear the weight of personality,"[2] or in the pioneering abstract expressionism whose thick coats of paint, bright colors, and open forms gave substance to his "beloveds," Gorky's inspiration stayed fresh through lifelong dreams of his homeland. Referring often to these reveries; he wrote: "I dream of it always, and it is as if some ancient spirit within me moves my hand to create so far from our home the shapes of nature we loved in the gardens, the wheatfields, and orchards of our Adoian family in Khorkom" (Letters, 32). In other letters he records his tactile response to Armenia, its salty Lake Van, the lacework of the cross stones, the butter churns and plows, "all floating within one another and swept by the universe's ceaseless momentum just as life-nourishing blood when flowing through the body nudges the artery walls on the journey" (Letters, 25). The "hybrids" and "opposites" of Armenian art that enlivened his waking dreams inspired his synthesis and inventiveness. Throughout, Gorky's work refutes notions that "abstract expressionism does not 'mean' anything in the sense of referring beyond itself in any version of traditional symbolism."[3]

The journey toward the mastery expressed in *The Plow and the Song* began early, as a careful reading of Gorky's letters and work suggest. Eloquent and impassioned, these reveal a man eager to synthesize the best of his native traditions with the best of the modern, pushing the boundaries of both to encompass new meanings. Born Vosdanig Adoian in 1904, Gorky came from a family whose forebears included nobility going back to the Vartanantz wars of the fifth century and a continuous line of priests through thirty-eight generations.[4] His mother, a proud woman whose sense of the family's obligation to cultural continuity was decisive, was the daughter of a priest in charge of an ancestral monastery. The monastery, located at the foot of a ten thousand-foot mountain, was a treasure trove of Armenian history. Inscriptions carved in classical Armenian greeted visitors at each passageway; "brooding paintings" of Armenian kings and religious life stood beside wall stones bearing three thousand-year-old cuneiform inscriptions, reminding the visitor of the poles of Armenia's Christian and pagan heritage.

Five miles east of this monastery, Gorky's birthplace of Khorkom was equally saturated with legend. The three thousand-year-old canal of Shamiran (Semiramis) flowed through the town. Later in America, alluding to the effect of this canal on his spatial perspective, Gorky would describe its "aesthetic technology" and contrast it to the "soulless technology" of America. He then identified its universal appeal as channel of civilization itself: "Irrigation canals are the springs of Armenian civilization and an artist can learn much from them. Their swift lines form antiquity's high fashion. Our forebears hung them like pearl-spray necklaces around mountain throats" (Letters, 30).

Another ancient shrine lodged in his memory was the church on Akhtamar Island. Visible from a stony rise that looked onto Lake Van, the island was the scene of a beloved legend and one of the masterpieces of Armenian church architecture. Summing up the influence of this vivid childhood environment on Gorky, his nephew Karlen Mooradian writes: "His boyhood, an outdoor historical museum surrounded by nature's thick presence, had made him an early believer in the Armenian proverb, 'Van in this world, paradise in the next.' "[5]

Gorky's family story is no less emblematic. His father, a merchant and carpenter, had fled to America to avoid the 1908 Turkish draft, leaving his wife the care of four children. By 1915 Gorky had not only witnessed the terror infecting the Armenian population, but his mother's struggles to manage without her husband. Driven from Van by the Turkish onslaught, Gorky's family made the journey to Yerevan on foot, passing the plain of Ararat where the guardian mountain slept. The mother, by this time weak from starvation, had to be moved about by her children; finally, while dictating a letter to her husband, she fell dead. Gorky's sister describes the effect of this event on her brother: "For Gorky she was a goddess and she was no more. And he never forgot. Not even in America. He painted her, he drew her with all of his soul. She was the beautiful woman from Van's Vosdan."[6] Throughout his artistic career, his mother would appear in Gorky's paintings at crucial times, registering his ease or isolation in his adopted land.[7]

After their mother's death, Gorky and his sister made their way to Istanbul, and sailed for America a year later. They landed at Ellis Island in March 1920. After working at odd jobs, living with his elder sister (feeling estranged from a father who had remarried), and probably teaching himself art, Gorky arrived in New York in 1925. Here he shielded his past with a new name; as decoded by Harry Rand, "Gorky in Russian means 'the bitter one,' " and "Arshile is a variant of 'Achilles' "(3). Such a name suggested one "whose wrath kept him from battle until a new wrath impelled him to act." At the Grand Central School of art where he began to teach, Gorky continued to perfect his persona, dropping hints of his relation to Maxim Gorky (itself a pen name for Alexei Peshkov), yet berating the Americans for clinging to conservative art. As noted by many critics, such ambivalent signals reveal the central tension running through Gorky's life and art: the "need to establish a pedigree for his art" fighting against his embrace of the avant-garde (Rand, 4).

By the mid-1920s, Gorky had decided to become a full-time painter, and until 1929 he supported himself at the school and with private students. During the depression, not having enough money to buy the high-quality supplies he insisted on using, he worked at drawing and in 1935 drew murals for the WPA. About this time he also became part of a New York artists' group, American Abstract Artists. The collective challenge this group faced was like Gorky's: they wanted to distinguish themselves as American artists, yet at the same time "align themselves with modernist movements abroad." These modernists were opposed in theory and practice to the conservative Social Realism and Regionalism that enjoyed favor in the United States at a time of social instability, and Gorky's innovative use of abstraction would prove pivotal in their evolution. His contribution also exemplifies in another medium what Werner Sollors draws attention to in *Beyond Ethnicity,* when he observes that "ethnic writers, alerted to cultural clashes, may feel the need for new forms earlier or more intensely than mainstream authors."[8]

With the onset of World War II, Gorky offered to teach a course in camouflage. Though the class never materialized, it was a subject he was naturally suited to teach, combining his personal predelictions toward emotional self-protection with the dominant needs of a socially and politically volatile era. The economic and psychological hardships of the time were draining and as his wife remembers, "He did not live long enough to look back on those days with any sentimental softness" (Rand, 7). Speaking about camouflage in modern life, Gorky stated in his course announcement: "An epidemic of destruction sweeps through the world today. The mind of civilized man is set to stop it. What the enemy would destroy, however, he must first see. To confuse and paralyze this vision is the role of camouflage" (Rand, 175). Condensing the group instincts of millennia, Gorky would have appreciated the need to mask vulnerable truths behind an ingenuous facade, to misdirect the enemy without sacrificing his own purposes; "seeing" Gorky's art thus demands the same visual dexterity as those teasing pictures found in puzzle books: in both, camouflaged forms elude the unaware.

A review of the rest of Gorky's life to 1948 shows only spots free of heartache. In 1946 a fire destroyed a wealth of work, twenty-seven paintings; cancer of the colon, detected three weeks later, wasted him physically; an automobile accident just as he was beginning to return to the "sources of his art" through drawing broke his neck and numbed his right arm; and perhaps most damning to his Armenian pride, his second marriage disintegrated under the pressure. Paintings from this period reflect his personal agonizing. *The Betrothal,* executed after his cancer operation, at once pays homage to the institution of marriage and conveys an "unbearably self-mocking" awareness of his curtailed virility (Rand, 165). *The Black Monk* ("The Last Painting"), inspired by Chekov's short story of the same name, depicts the nightmarish spectre that beckoned Gorky to lay down a worn body and spirit.

Even after his suicide by hanging in 1948, misfortune plagued Gorky's "beloveds," as Rand catalogs; none of the murals survived—either dismantled, destroyed, or painted over; two of his major works, *The Orators* and *The Calendars,* were burned; and finally in 1962 "fifteen works in transit from New York to California for an exhibition were lost in an airplane crash (8). This series of catastrophes eerily reflects the relentless destruction that had swept Gorky's homeland. Yet, in both instances what has survived is impressive; in Gorky's case, it testifies to a powerful and prolific personality, forging an original aesthetic out of his yearning for a past drenched in myth.

To balance the demands of an American identity without abandoning the past, Gorky wove dreamlike images of Armenia through his art, veiling his content through a rich yet economical iconography. His recurring concerns appear early in his art; in one famous sequence of drawings and paintings, he—like other homeless immigrants—contemplates a photograph of himself and his mother, taken when he was eight. He uses his exploration of modern painting technique to deepen his meditation on the past, dissecting the picture "into constituent parts" and then varying these. Again, what is striking about this work is the calm and careful placement of the two figures. The mother, self-contained in her beauty, gazes into an indeterminate future; her rounded eyes, huge with a meaning that cannot be read, draw us into their orbit. Her son, presenting her with a flower, separated by more than physical space, becomes a figure in exile; his gaze, an emblem of silent longing and homage.

Although he has been accused of imitating Picasso and other major modern artists, Gorky drew even more lavishly from the traditions of Armenian art. He often defended the contributions of this "small and humble people" against the "mis-used technology and commercial philistinism" he found in America. In the following passage from a letter to his nephew he describes the hidden yet intensely felt sources of Armenian art:

> The great art of our people lies hidden in ruins and amid the daily life of remote villages. Our great art has been created by an

> innocent people who were never accustomed and never had through the sad ages any opportunity to tell the world about their achievements. We are a race of artists. . . . Armenia has not only been at the crossroads of the world, but has built them with its own sinews. (Letters, 42)

Deeply sensitive to the Armenian past, Gorky was a great admirer of the thirteenth-century monk Toros Roslin, an artist who drew from diverse traditions—Oriental, Western, Byzantine—and infused the whole with his inventiveness and humanism. Roslin's faithfulness to the particulars of Armenian life broke through the stiff posturings of the Byzantines and gave the Armenians a truthful self-image. In admiration, Gorky wrote in 1944: "Toros Roslin is the Renaissance. What electricity the man contains. For me, he is the greatest artist the world produced before the modern age and his use of dimension is exceeded solely by cubism. Masterful dimensionality, unsurpassed. I bow before our Toros" (Letters, 33). Later, describing childhood memories of Armenian art, he again praised the innovations of the medieval miniaturists "with their beautiful Armenian faces, subtle colors, their tender lines and the calligraphy." Significantly, what excited Gorky most in Roslin's work was its "plasticity" and mastery of color, major concerns of modern Western art. And what frustrated him most was the fact that no one in the West had heard of an artist who had "accomplished a sensitivity centuries before [the Byzantines and Italians]," and who held the key that would unlock some of the major issues in European and American art (Letters, 34).

Frustration with the aesthetic ignorance of westerners would continue through Gorky's life and make him chafe at inaccurate pigeonholes. The following passage from a letter to his sister shows his Armenian self-respect torn by his desire to achieve worldwide fame:

> Vartoosh dear, do you realize how the critics ramble, the mask that hides their vacuum? . . . Mother's Armenian eyes they call Picasso's, Armenian melancholy they term Byzantine and Russian. And if I correct them and say "No, dear sirs, you are in error for these are Armenian eyes." Then they look at you strangely and say that such corrections are merely exaggerations of "small-nation chauvinism." . . . I resent their chauvinistic accusations when I attempt to explain my ideas. (Letters, 29)

Nevertheless, Gorky's attraction to Roslin before much was in print on him not only demonstrates his acute eye, but suggests his affinities with the earlier artist; chief among these are the curiosity and the inclusiveness of Gorky's art. His whimsical forms echo the gaiety and vividness of the miniatures; uninhibited pagan shapes crowd the space with kinetic color. A careful look at the fantastic forms that fill Roslin's illustrations, the *gentani* that crawl through and around the margins of his pages, charming us with visions of unknown worlds, brings to mind equally fanciful forms in Gorky's art. According to some commentators, Gorky's "cubism" also derived from the Armenian legacy, inspired by the rich motifs found on carpets in the Van and Ararat area and reflected in the work of Sarkis Pidzak, the last of the great Cilician miniaturists. Gorky was familiar with both the work of Pidzak and the motifs of these carpets before he left his native land.[9]

In other respects, too, Gorky drew upon the "authentic colors" and shapes of his native Armenia. As he wrote to his sister: "Painting on *Gurrick* eggs was my introduction to the use of color. Nature in Armenia was an inexhaustible paint tube. And brushes once dipped in it can dance to their own songs" (Letters, 32). He then testifies to his well-known enthusiasm for Armenian story and song:

> Dearest ones, perhaps it is because I recall so well the silver songs of the story-teller and the evening recitations of our Adoians that I need Armenian song and poetry for inspiration when I paint. They are nature's tastiest addictions. Singing Toumanian's poems is a necessary part of my conduct when painting. He has eyes like the sea and men sink in his gaze.

Together, these passages form the basis of Gorky's aesthetic. In search of the "tactile release" that would free color and line to dance on their own, Gorky used the model of the storyteller, whose sing-song formulas assume a life of their own through age-old repetition and an inner resonance that comes from complete familiarity with each strand of a story. An important component of Gorky's method of composition was thus his repeated rendering of an image until he had mastered it. Only after driving the image deep into his hand and psyche did he "loosen his painting's focus" (Rand, 72). As a result, what often appear to be abstract forms are the transformed images of Khorkom—his father's garden, the Tree of the Cross to which villagers attached pennants, the rock that enhanced fertility. Though his examination of his Armenian heritage was not a fact Gorky wished known by the public (suggested by his altering the spellings and names of the garden and village—Sosi to the Russian-sounding Sochi; Khorkom to Xhorkom,

Rand, 75–76), his preparations and execution were deliberate and thorough: "He imbued with meaning every nuance of a composition before he began painting and then like a storyteller repeating without change an ageless tale, he would let the painting unfold on the canvas" (Rand, 135–36). Practicing his lines much like a musician practices his scales, until the notes reach flawless pitch, Gorky perfected his facility of line and fed the spirit of the stories he loved so well into his painting, sinking all into the gaze of his artist's eye.

As Gorky's art evolved and he gained more confidence as the Armenian head of a household, longing was balanced by a comic lightness and sense of security that comes through in paintings such as *The Calendars* (1946). One of Gorky's masterpieces, the work playfully depicts a family evening before the fire. Each figure is identified through "vibrant and highly naturalistic color." Rand's decoding of this painting shows the evolution of each form and its eventual abstraction. Displaying one of the hallmarks of his style, Gorky uses color "both to obviate a form's identity and, alternately, to obscure it, a technique he perfected, using color first to identify a shape for himself and then to confuse the viewer with a repetition of the same shade in an illogical but formally pleasing location" (Rand, 125).

This painting also illustrates Gorky's sensitivity to the tiny details that communicate personality and mood, much as Roslin's miniatures do. Laden with such complex associations, these paintings entered into intimate relationship with their creator, a view poignantly supported by Gorky's statements to his sister and brother-in-law. After scoring "the cleverists," those who chase money or undermine the forward movement of modern art, he specifies his objection to the surrealists: "To its adherents the tradition of art and its quality mean little. They are drunk with psychiatric spontaneity and inexplicable dreams." He then aligns himself with many of the characters—real and fictional—encountered in this study:

> [The surrealists'] ideas are quite strange and somewhat flippant, almost playful. Really they are not as earnest about painting as I should like artists to be. Art must always remain earnest. Perhaps it is because I am an Armenian and they are not. Art must be serious, no sarcasm, comedy. One does not laugh at a loved one. (Letters, 39)

This passage clearly echoes one of the strong moods of the Armenian sensibility; it brings to mind the Armenian intellectuals of Shiragian's childhood solemnly reading *The Times,* Juno's father mocking Americans' love of baseball, Bond's sense of humor refined through his dark vision of his family past, and even Barav shaking her head at the cyclic abduction of the feminine. Here too, Armenian laughter is filtered by loss, a loss trivialized through a "flippant" attitude toward redeeming work. Though Gorky's art can project humor, it is never glib. In dismissing the surrealists (a blanket term that covered many sins for Gorky) for their rejection of tradition, he upholds the "quality" that emanates only through discipline. He states his aesthetic most simply when he writes that "great art derives from complexity, from the clash of many new and opposing ideas" (Letters, 24). This concern with the clash of "new ideas" gave intellectual substance to his experimentation that no amount of innovation for its own sake could ever achieve.

Widening his distance from the surrealists, Gorky drew his dreams not from "inexplicable" fermentations of the unconscious, but the increasingly dim memories of a highly sensuous past, which could only be transcribed through conscious effort. Similarly his "spontaneity" was not mechanical, but flowed naturally from his artistic meditations. Most significantly, in equating surrealism with "academic art under disguise," Gorky uncovers the pseudooriginality of much modern and postmodernist art. For in denying the necessary role of tradition as the channel of universal images, conventions, and attitudes, the surrealists severed the tie that makes originality possible: the dynamic tension between the collective psyche and the private, resolved in the artist's unified vision. Gorky's belief that "art must always remain earnest" not only reminds us of a view Armenians have expressed elsewhere in this study, but is a statement about creativity in general. Steeped in eons of Armenian history, Gorky understood that "earnest" art—religious and secular—had kept Armenia whole; but what made such a continuity of tradition possible was the "serious" application of artists, who distilled and embellished, simultaneously deepening and broadening the tradition. To use Bond's imagery, creation may proceed from chaos, but by definition it cannot imitate it—black must turn into the colors of creation.

Though Gorky's paintings were in a sense surrogates for people, they also expressed his love of his tradition by extending it: "From our Armenian experience will I create new forms to ignite minds and massage hearts" (Letters, 33); "Having a tradition enables you to tackle new problems with authority, with solid footing" (Letters, 33). What Gorky understood is that "originality" depends on an unbroken tie to one's "origins," that the new can never appear "spontaneously" in a creative vacuum. As Rand notes, "The pitfalls are numerous when audacity becomes the criterion of excellence. It has been a long time since an artist was judged on how many *conventions* he successfully assimilated into his art" (Rand, 45–46). Countering a trend that shed the previously accepted trappings of art, Gorky's contribution lay elsewhere, in his ability to sift through to what was of genuine value no matter what or when its origin. This ability to build a bridge between the aesthetic traditions of the past and major problems that haunted American painting in the 1930s and 1940s validated the soundness of Gorky's "method." But just as important as his technical contribution was his insistence on addressing "great topics" through his art: "love of man, love of nature, love of beauty, love of progress in the well-being of man,"[10] topics that cannot be labeled "modernist" but are always modern.

Gorky's modernity is perhaps most fully expressed through his views of abstraction. In 1947, a year before his death, he wrote: "Abstraction is the key factor of the creative imagination of man" (Letters, 39). In this lengthy letter he explains that abstractions enable us to break through the limits of nature; but in pioneering the new, we once more reach the limits of the finite. Gorky implies that life finds its vital center at the margins of our experience. Hence, "new infinities must be created so that art can progress" (Letters, 39). He further states that the "probing vehicle of abstraction" is "the emancipator of the mind," enabling the imagination to push beyond what it can understand and control, leading the artist into ever new frontiers of feeling and expression. Finally, in a passage whose diction and references to the past reveal his inspiration, he writes:

> Complexity results from the wounds inflicted upon the finite by man's search for the infinite. The bleeding of these wounds generates man's perlexity only when he does not comprehend them and they remain infinities for him. It is precisely for this reason that I feel that such bleeding is in a partial sense the creation of many windows looking upon an equal number of infinities. Mis-used technology, for example, results from the finite stagnation of its controllers, the hemorrhaging without any end in sight because inspiration to probe infinity is absent. Only when man has enough abstraction to comprehend what he sees through the many windows will the bleeding cease. (Letters, 40)

This passage is of major import in understanding the context of Gorky's art as he—an Armenian immigrant—understood it. Without ever mentioning the name of his native land or enumerating the wounds that were the legacy of all who came from there, he speaks in terms that help us locate his relationship to the sufferings he believed he had to bear and transcend. By making essential the experience of the whole, abstraction becomes the vehicle of insight and brings perspective to the senseless bleeding that generates such perplexity. One can only "abstract" very specific meanings from his statement. Take for example the infinite bleeding of millions killed in genocide, a staple event of our century, and the windows such events create on infinity—in this case the infinity of evil. Such events have no purpose unless they push us to comprehend the possibilities—good and evil—that roam through human consciousness. Thus, tragedy too, by portraying the "sorrows and losses" helps "define humanity" and "communicate the new pulse of consciousness"; it introduces the infinite into the finite. The bleeding wounds of the past remain incomprehensible for the stagnant mind, but for those who probe the pain by creating new forms—"windows"—insight results. Here Gorky echoes Armenian-American writers reviewed previously: Kherdian's windows, Bond's communiques from the dark, Der Hovanessian's microcosmic seed-words are each in some way synonymous with Gorky's vibrant "infinities." He ends the letter by defining the term:

> Infinity is beyond space. The beautiful apricot of Armenia is finite in size. But if its interior is probed, if it is explored, infinities are reached. . . . Man's mind probing the finite Armenian apricot unearths its infinite properties, its infinite secrets. . . . There is an abundance of abstractions in the Armenian experience and civilization. (Letters, 40)

As he continues by listing some of the symbols of Armenian civilization—"Akhtamar, Charahan Surp Nishan, Vart Badrik, Varaka Vank, the Rock of Van," their pivotal role in his art becomes clearer. Gorky recognized a basic truth about culture, particularly Armenian culture, namely that its creative resources are limitless. Whatever values or expressions of human experience one wants to find in the Armenian past are available if one is rooted in the culture and the lessons of group experience. It is not surprising then that Gorky adhered to the view of the art theoretician, John Graham, who wrote: "The only legitimate abstract painting is the painting based on and depending from *reality* and not abstraction" [reality here implying Gorky's "finite"]; and "the true attraction of any art is its symbolic language. . . . Culture is the knowledge of the implications of symbols" ["infinities"].[11] Reaffirming the role of culture as a carrier of this symbolic language, Gorky wrote,

"Tangible Armenia is replete with inner infinities and so too are intangible memories of Armenia, the intellectual ideas sired by it." For in supplying "infinities," symbols, of a bleeding past and its transcendence, Armenian culture has gifted the artist with the tools of survival.

Gorky's choice of the apricot as the emblem and gateway to an inner cosmos also suggests his appreciation of the existential opportunities that the small and organic offer, opportunities that Armenian poets and artists have traditionally celebrated. Just as Gorky complained of the misunderstandings artists from "small" nations were heir to, he also found creative salvation in those symbols of the culture so little known by the world at large. Much like his forebears, he eluded extinction by discovering an "inner infinity," and found in the apricot another one of those "Armenian secrets" compact with the nutrients essential to survival, sensuous, portable, evocative. Like the other cultural images he revered, each resonant with the spiritual vibrations of a universe tucked away from public scrutiny, the apricot was a "complete living unit" that gave Gorky a model for what he strived after as an artist; it was a natural counterpart to the miniatures of the great medieval illuminators who had revealed so much about the life of the Armenians through intensive exploration on a small scale.

Yet at the same time that Gorky was true to the spirit of Armenian survival, his "discovery" of the inner infinity of the object echoed the goals of other contemporary European artists who were also seeking a new "spirit in matter." Thus Paul Klee said: "The object expands beyond the bounds of its appearance by our knowledge that the thing is more than its exterior presents to our eyes."[12] Validating Gorky's ability to translate this vision, surrealist leader André Breton, whom Gorky met in the mid-1940s, gave the most prized of accolades: he judged that Gorky was "the first painter to whom the secret has been completely revealed."[13] This revealed "secret"—which moved him beyond the surrealist camp—was the key that united Gorky's modernity with his Armenian fate: responding to the blows of history, Gorky saw the task of art as not to entertain nor even to advance civilization, his protests notwithstanding. Instead, art was the "bottom line" which supported sanity itself, a ritualized way of life that gave order to the day. The "etiquette and decorum" he brought to his painting are perhaps the best illustration of this seriousness. Many who came to visit him in his studio have attested to the impeccable cleanliness of his work space, his love and respect for the finest drawing materials, and his capacity for long days of hard work. His love of Armenian song, poetry, and dance added zest and clarity to his task.

Gorky's serious intent is balanced by the seriousness of his diction. Sensitive to the sufferings of Armenian history where the absurd round of creation and destruction had ground away at the generations, Gorky turned to the images of war and suffering to describe his "three ideas,"—*Makrutyun, Danjank,* and *Hasnutyun*. At one level, these are a general description of the creative process and a literal description of his painting process; but in another sense, it is as if these stages allude to a microcosmic history of the Armenians. The static simplicity and "cleanliness" of the first stage yields to the turmoil of *Danjank:*

> The juice of the artist must be brought to the pain of boiling, tension and confusion. *Danjank* is painful but required. It activates the mind and thought. Vartoosh dear, the innate pureness of the simple can contain only so much food and then no more. The boundlessness of thought, feeling and passion. The artillery of deeper memories. Yes beloved, even the tears of our people, all of these form the materials from which the new path is built. The new path beyond the old boundaries which must be traveled before the creator can hope to find himself. (Letters, 37–38)

Like Gorky's own life, the greater part of the history of Armenia has been spent in the throes of *Danjank;* here, assaulted by "the artillery of deeper memories," "thought, feeling and passion" have had to discover new cavities of the spirit to hold and release the pain. Lit by this awareness, it is no surprise that so much of Gorky's space—especially in his later works—is filled with openings, recesses, secret passageways that lead beyond the boundaries of the known and deliver the creator and the viewer to the mythic world where fruition, *Hasnutyun,* is glimpsed.

The guide into this world of the infinite and abstract is Gorky's line, one of the signatures of his art and of his paradoxical relation to modernity. The lines of his native Van still excited him in America, emerging "like great speaking figures" from a passionate landscape; he found "principles in this for the artist. Curved lines define passion and straight lines structure" (Letters, 32). Released to tell their story, these lines wing through his work and everywhere come to an elegant point. Admired by many, this line does more than add to the pleasing surface of the paintings. Commenting on this element, Ethel Schwabacher writes, "Gorky's line was full of 'intention' and 'intellect' rather than the effortlessness which appears to have no emphasis, no insistence, nothing aggressive about it, and to exist eternally in a world of being."[14] In his letters, Gorky often referred to the importance of the line as a carrier of cultural vitality. Writing to his nephew Karlen, he advised the following:

> You must forget about shading and try to develop a beautiful, clear, and sensitive line—this is drawing—line is all important . . . the history of our Armenian people has shown us the secret of creativity. The secret is to throw yourself into the water of life again and again, not to hang back, no reservations, risk everything, but above all strike out boldly with all you have. (Letters, 42)

Once more, these passages suggest how intimately Gorky's reading of Armenian history and culture guided his theories and practice of art; throughout, when he speaks of the primacy of the "beautiful, clear, and sensitive line," the pioneering vehicle of consciousness, he is referring to much more than aesthetics. The ending assertions evoke the mood and imagery of *David of Sassoun,* where "bold little streams" strike out with all that they have, where a people make the best use possible of lunatic heroes who risk everything for the sake of autonomy. As Gorky threw himself back at the canvas again and again, striking out like a modern daredevil, these lines led the viewer away from the known into a world where passion and structure were free to mingle. Later in this letter, Gorky's diction and tone further identify the psychological impetus behind his style:

> The artist should be skeptical but never cynical. Tragedy is not the same as cynicism. There *is* hope and beauty, but portraying the tragedy of certain realities, sorrows and losses is necessary to define humanity. And this can hopefully communicate the new pulse of consciousness, of awareness, uncork the essence common to all men but forced into dormancy by societal deficiencies though restless for expression nevertheless. (Letters, 43)

This "new pulse of consciousness," the vibrancy of a tradition defined by tragedy, the conviction absent from the two-dimensional "cartoonist"—these ideas are carried by Gorky's line. Elsewhere, discussing the last stage of creation—"Hasnutyun" (fruition)—he discovers "mastery over complex things" at "that point where economy of line and color express intricacy. When the dancer dances without being there. When nature sings in her silence" (Letters, 38). And as Gorky's drawings repeatedly ask, what is more complex than a point that moves, yet what more simply rendered?

Critics sometimes gauge the success of Gorky's strategy by citing the tragic end of his life. Among these commentators, Nora Nercessian in "The Defeat of Arshile Gorky" argues that ultimately Gorky's life and spirit proved inadequate to the demands of his aesthetic, that "throughout his career [Gorky] sought the one solution which could best endure his absolute commitment to progress."[15] She then notes that Gorky maintained his notions of progress from a "defensive position," castigating any segments of society that "hindered his claims over universal progress." Although these observations have a validity, they oversimplify the nature of his final actions. Gorky's optimistic faith in reason was influenced by his experience of Armenian history. The man who had watched his mother starve in his arms after both had been forced to flee an edenic homeland was the same person who would later affirm that he responded to life as a "man from Van" and that to be "an Armenian in America is a strange thing indeed" (Letters, 30). If Gorky had repeatedly placed his faith in art as the "rational coordinator of history," it was as much from an instinctual response to the chaos of his personal and collective past as from a desire to affirm the detached role of art. His insistence throughout his letters that "there can be no anarchy in art" (Letters, 23) is uttered in the voice of one who has absorbed more than his share of social disruption and is fighting to establish at least one safe space in a land perceived as hostile. The end of this letter elaborates on the impulses that compelled him to find new levels of order: "Anarchy results from pure cynicism. This is, a disbelief in the intellectual capacity of man's mind to master complexities through his organizational and perceptive abilities and skills. Unrelenting spontaneity is chaos. . . . Great art insists upon consciousness" (Letters, 23).

Gorky's legacy as an Armenian was three millennia of abandonment to the unrelenting upheavals of warrior nations and a resiliency that often managed to overcome the odds. If he searched for a refuge from the state of siege that was his communal past in the organized world of the rational, it was a desire he shared with thousands of countrymen who had taken refuge in other orderly realms of the spirit—religious, mythological, and ideological—as chaos swept over the land. What is noteworthy about this passage, though, is not only Gorky's insistence on reason but his assertion that "great art insists upon consciousness." Nine years later in January 1948 in the last letter he wrote to his sister and brother-in-law, Gorky said much the same thing: "Technique . . . must be wedded to the aesthetic intellect, otherwise life becomes mere existence rather than fertile experience."[16] This strongly held belief in the role and the powers of the conscious mind places Gorky in the company of the century's foremost psychoanalysts. These scientists of the mind have repeatedly cautioned that for all its wealth of imagery, the unconscious is not the sole determiner of human evolution. The importance of consciousness is summed up by C. G. Jung's student, Aniela Jaffé: "Consciousness alone is competent to determine the meaning of the images and to recognize their significance for man here and now. . . . Only in an *interplay* of consciousness and the unconscious can the unconscious prove its value."[17]

Gorky never ceased to respect this interplay. As the creator of art fertile with "hybrids and opposites," he was to the end conscious of the pain of his life and his alienation from the ways of a society he did not feel sympathetic with. He ended the last letter to his sister with a poignant comment that implies how vulnerable he remained to his earlier losses: "man longs, needs to communicate with his own in the security of the shared language of comfort." It was this willed awareness of tragedy that brought him to the limit of his strength. Final paintings such as *The Limit* (1947) are in marginal territories where the known and the unknown confront each other in what Melvin Lader describes as "a precarious balance between the tension-ridden forms, the primary color accents, and the more sedate milky white and blue of the expansive color fields."[18] Or the more horrific images of the unconscious rise to "suppress" the waking world, as in *The Last Painting* (1948). Conceivably what Gorky feared more than death was abandonment to physical and emotional chaos; again following the lead of a cultural tradition that used retreat to its advantage when the odds against victory were too great, Gorky chose to withdraw from the battle. With dignity, his last known words, spoken to his friend Saul Schary, convey this attempt to exercise deliberate and conscious choice over the givens of life: "My life is over. I'm not going to live anymore."[19]

Coming full circle, we are left with the same paradox that opened this discussion: Gorky's desire to establish a pedigree for his art balanced by his embrace of the avant-garde, especially "American art's attachment . . . to the specifics of observation." This opposition is resolved in practice whenever Gorky's mastery of his native art suggested solutions to technical problems when they appeared.[20] Though Gorky considered himself an Armenian in exile, following his mother's charge to continue the ancestral line of artists, he did so by grafting himself onto a new stock. In the process, he helped the American "tree" bear fruit that was genuinely new, and not merely novel. Though not the only artist of his time to use "secret signs," "his solution to the problem was both the earliest and most elegant means of reconciling personal need and public accessibility."[21]

Leaving Gorky, one carries away an image that goes back thousands of years, the vision of Meherr Junior entombed in his rock on the plain of Van, awaiting the promised release. In a sense, Gorky's art expresses this liberation, a feat that—ironically—was best accomplished in America, a land of oppositions and contradictions ripe for synthesis. Tilling the specifics of his Armenian heritage, Gorky evaded nihilism; instead of abandoning the symbols of his past, he probed until their transformed shapes expressed the oldest of axioms: "the roots of man are the paradise."

EPILOGUE

They weave past my window
in tidy pairs, Afghan
with Afghan, Jew with Jew,
come to this college town

laden with parables,
who caravaned westward
from older miracles
wisely to the New World.

Cummerbund at midriff
and skullcap in order
they shuffle to class, laugh,
jangle at each other

in secret tongues blasted
by the Midwestern wind.
What parables are said,
divining like a wand

daily past my window?
What bag of tricks only
possessed by Afghan, Jew,
Turk or Greek sidles by

couched in some secret tongue?
Each new day I open
wide by window waiting
for miracles to happen.[1]

As "The Bag of Tricks" by Harold Bond summarizes, America is a caravan of "older miracles," a Noah's ark of ethnicity. Each fertile pair, "laden with parables," has brought its miracles to the New World where planted in the spacious fields of our soil they will sprout and recharge the American Word. Sensitive to the winds that attack diversity, the poet cautions against expecting an easy harvest. We need "divining wands," stores of sympathy and insight, to deciper the secret tongues; we need to open wide the windows of our imaginations, allowing the voices of freedom to speak at what Ralph Ellison calls the "lower frequencies" of our common humanity; and finally, we need to journey through the bazaar of multiplicity and rummage through each bag of tricks. For the miracles can occur only when all the sideling magicians are given space to conjure their portion of the national spirit, not out of our short-term utilitarian needs but our faith that their "secret tongues" glorify "the word Democratic, the word En-Masse." In this display, it will be seen that some of our more invisible ethnic groups carry the most potent magic.

As epitomized by young Meherr, the Armenians, unable to expand and extend their territorial rights after a certain point, discovered their infinity through an intensive approach to experience. Within their rock, they transmuted their experience into aesthetic and spiritual gold, until the time came to seed their parables in new soil. Up to the recent past, America faced a contrasting situation: our nation's history is the triumph of extension from sea to shining sea, an expansive freeway of possibility. But just as geographical limitations can lead to insularity, the negative by-product of extension without direction can be a gratuitous motion that skims the surface of the present, robbing us all of our moment. As a mediating backdrop, the college town in this poem, a symbol of the national whole and its unifying pledge, can draw inspiration from and impart energy to these "tidy pairs." As America makes the transition into cultural maturity and its people take the nation's vows as their own, a creative interchange in which we listen and divine one another's stores of practical wisdom will not only guarantee group survival, but give birth to the miracle of a New World: two *can* go where one cannot.

NOTES

INTRODUCTION

1. Karlen Mooradian, ed., "Letters of Arshile Gorky," *Ararat* 12 (autumn 1971), p. 32. Copyright © 1971 by Karlen Mooradian.

2. Personal interview with Avedis Bedrosian, June 6, 1981.

3. Sam Keen, "Stories We Live By," *Psychology Today* (December 1988), p. 44.

4. Kevork Emin, "Ararat," trans. Diana Der Hovanessian, *Ararat* 13 (summer 1972), p. 5. Reprinted with the permission of *Ararat,* a quarterly journal of arts and letters.

5. Vahakn Tatvian, "Rocks," trans. Diana Der Hovanessian, *Christian Science Monitor* (October 4, 1976), p. 32.

6. Kevork Emin, "Small," trans. Diana Der Hovanessian, *Ararat* 13 (summer 1972), p. 5. Reprinted with the permission of *Ararat,* a quarterly journal of arts and letters.

7. David Marshall Lang, *Armenia: Cradle of Civilization,* 3d ed. (London: George Allen & Unwin, 1980), p. 73.

8. Boris Piotrovsky, *Urartu,* trans. James Hogarth (London: The Cresset Press, 1969), pp. 71–72.

9. Ibid., p. 139.

10. Vahan Kurkjian, *A History of Armenia* (New York: Armenian General Benevolent Union, 1958), p. 49.

11. Xenophon, *The March of the Ten Thousand,* trans. H. G. Dakyns (London: MacMillan and Co., 1901), p. 96.

12. Kurkjian, *A History of Armenia,* p. 118.

13. In "Crucifixion without 'the Cross,' " Leonardo P. Alishan argues that as interpreted by the historian Yeghishé, "Vardan and his followers actually *desire* to rise above

history through this death which is understood, the martyr's death." The consequences of this peculiar form of transcendance have plagued Armenians ever since. See *Armenian Review* 38, no. 1 (1985), p. 28.

14. Elisaeus, *History of Vartan,* trans. C. F. Neumann (London: The Oriental Translation Fund, 1830), p. 20.

15. Kurkjian, *A History of Armenia,* p. 145.

16. Elisaeus, *A History of Vartan,* pp. 52–53.

17. Ibid., pp. 60–61.

18. Piotrovsky, *Urartu,* p. 47.

19. Kurkjian, *A History of Armenia,* pp. 206–7.

20. Ibid., p. 209.

21. Avedis K. Sanjian, ed., Introduction, *Colophons of Armenian Manuscripts, 1301–1480* (Cambridge, Mass.: Harvard Univ. Press, 1969), p. 21.

22. Ibid., p. 107.

23. Kurkjian, *A History of Armenia,* p. 286.

24. Ibid., p. 33.

25. R. W. Thomson, trans., *History of the Armenians* by Agathangelos (Albany: State University of New York Press, 1970), p. xiii.

26. Ibid., p. xiv.

27. Kurkjian, *A History of Armenia,* p. 368.

28. Sirarpie Der Nersessian, *Armenia and the Byzantine Empire* (Cambridge, Mass.: Harvard Univ. Press, 1945), p. 53.

29. Sanjian, Introduction, p. 2.

30. Ibid., p. 3.

31. Eghishé Charents, "I Love the Sun-Baked Taste of Armenian Words," trans. Diana Der Hovanessian, *Translation* IV (spring-summer 1977), pp. 62–63.

32. Siamanto, "The Glory of Invention," trans. Diana Der Hovanessian, *Ararat* 17 (autumn 1976), p. 10. Reprinted with the permission of *Ararat,* a quarterly journal of arts and letters.

33. Ibid.

34. Krikor Naregatsi, "Book of Lamentations," 55c, in *Anthology of Armenian Poetry,* trans. and ed. Diana Der Hovanessian and Marzbed Margossian (New York: Columbia Univ. Press, 1975) pp. 59–60.

35. Ibid., 93a, p. 63.

36. Mooradian, "Letters," p. 26.

37. See Der Nersessian, *Armenia and the Byzantine Empire,* p. 78.

38. Kurkjian, *A History of Armenia,* p. 430.

39. Der Nersessian, *Armenia and the Byzantine Empire,* p. 135.

40. Sirarpie Der Nersessian, *Armenian Art* (London: Thames and Hudson, n.d.), p. 240.

41. Der Nersessian, *Armenia and the Byzantine Empire,* p. 123.

42. Ibid., pp. 130–31.

43. Ibid.

44. Mooradian, "Letters," p. 33. As a sidenote to this discussion, to read a detailed history of Armenia is to be startled at how often Armenians have adapted to foreign conditions and moved with authority behind the scenes. One example is that several of the great Byzantine emperors were Armenian by descent. Regarding one of these monarchs, a Byzantine historian writes, "As to his immediate origin it is well known; he came from the country of the Armenians, whence, according to some, his obstinacy and his bad disposi-

tion" (Der Nersessian, *Armenia and the Byzantine Empire,* p. 19). Beginning with the reign of Basil (867–886), a family of Armenian descent occupied the Byzantine throne for more than two centuries. Even some of the usurpers were Armenian. These Armenian monarchs did not help the plight of their ancestral land. But because of their great military leadership and courage, they and the Armenian generals who served them gave the Byzantine Empire much of its luster.

45. Keen, "Stories," p. 47.

46. See Christopher J. Walker, *Armenia: The Survival of a Nation* (New York: St. Martin's Press, 1980). p. 90.

47. In Wayne S. Vucinich, *The Ottoman Empire: Its Record and Legacy* (Princeton, N.J.: D. Van Nostrand Company, Inc., 1965), pp. 166–67.

48. Walker, *Armenia,* p. 237.

49. Kurkjian, *A History of Armenia,* p. 298.

50. Barouyr Sevag, "The Analysis of Yearning (Garod)," trans. Diana Der Hovanessian, *Colorado Quarterly* 15 (summer 1976), p. 31.

51. Keen, "Stories," p. 47.

52. See Sevag, "The Analysis of Yearning," p. 31.

53. Leon Surmelian, trans., *Daredevils of Sassoun* (Denver: Alan Swallow, 1964), p. 278. Subsequent references to this work appear in the text.

54. See Daniel Varoujan, "The Red Soil," in *Anthology of Armenian Poetry,* p. 153.

55. See Kourken Mahari, "Comments on a Book," in *Anthology of Armenian Poetry,* p. 223.

56. Kevork Emin, "Small," *Ararat* 13 (summer 1972), p. 5. Reprinted with the permission of *Ararat,* a quarterly journal of arts and letters.

57. Maxine Hong Kingston, *The Woman Warrior* (New York: Vintage Books, 1976), p. 239.

TRANSPLANTATION

1. Leon Srabian Herald, "Portable in Me," in *Armenian North American Poets,* ed. Lorne Shirinian (St. Jean, Quebec: Manna, 1974), p. 69.

2. James Baloian, "Arriving in the New World," in *The Ararat Papers* (New York: Ararat Press, 1979), p. 18. Copyright © 1979 by James C. Baloian. The poem first appeared in the *Grapevine* issue of *Blackjack Magazine*.

3. Virginia Tatarian, "Photograph of Five Ancestors," in *Speaking for Ourselves,* ed. Lilian Faderman and Barbara Bradshaw, 2d ed. (Glenview, Ill.: Scott, Foresman and Company, 1975), p. 613.

4. Jack Danielian, "Armenian Culture Identity: Problems of Western Definition," in *Recent Studies in Modern Armenian History* (Cambridge, Mass.: Armenian Heritage Press, 1972), p. 131. That this "different existential reality" continued to have a profound effect on the lived worldviews of each of our ethnic groups is made clear by Michael Novak in *The Rise of the Unmeltable Ethnics.* In particular, Novak devotes one fascinating section ("Pain Is or Is Not Pain") to the sharply contrasting attitudes toward suffering and death held by native Americans, Jews, Italians, and the Irish. He finds these differ-

ences, along with other responses to the world conditioned by our ethnicity to be morally decisive

> particularly if one looks to the *meaning* and *internal effect* of action rather than to its external, pragmatic effect. Naturally enough, the American bias is to attend to the latter. We are so different that if we waited until we all agreed upon a rationale, style, and meaning for action, we would never get started. So we usually skip the personal (communal), internal relations and concentrate on pragmatic cooperation. What we lose is a sense of who we really are and what gives meaning to our lives. We spend so much time and energy in the boiler room of pragmatic activity that we do not enjoy the cruise.

See Novak, *The Rise of the Unmeltable Ethnics* (New York: MacMillan, 1971), p. 45.

5. Arra S. Avakian, *The Armenians in America* (Minneapolis: Lerner, 1977), pp. 39–40.

6. Ibid., p. 42.

7. Ibid., p. 43.

8. Oscar Handlin, *The Uprooted,* 2d ed. enlarged (Boston: Little, Brown and Company, 1973), p. 55.

9. Ibid., pp. 55–56.

10. Robert Mirak, *Torn between Two Lands: Armenians in America, 1890 to World War I* (Cambridge, Mass.: Harvard Univ. Press, 1983), pp. 40–41.

11. *Harvard Encyclopedia of American Ethnic Groups* (Cambridge, Mass.: Harvard Univ. Press, 1980), p. 139.

12. Handlin, *The Uprooted,* p. 52.

13. Personal narrative of Avedis Bedrosian.

14. Raffi Arzoomanian, "Ellis Island 101," *Ararat* 10 (spring 1969), p. 11. Reprinted with the permission of *Ararat,* a quarterly journal of arts and letters.

15. Nona Balakian, "Writers on the American Scene," *Ararat* 18 (winter 1977), p. 24. Reprinted with the permission of *Ararat,* a quarterly journal of arts and letters.

16. Laura Kalpakian, "The Land of Lucky Strike," *Ararat* 20 (spring 1979), p. 19. Reprinted with the permission of *Ararat,* a quarterly journal of arts and letters.

17. George Mardikian, *Song of America* (New York: McGraw-Hill, 1956), p. 46.

18. *Harvard Encyclopedia of American Ethnic Groups,* p. 141.

19. Personal narrative of Avedis Bedrosian.

20. Mirak, *Torn between Two Lands,* pp. 87–88.

21. Ibid., p. 90.

22. Ibid., pp. 93–94.

23. Ibid., p. 105.

24. Mardikian, *Song of America,* p. 73.

25. Ibid., pp. 92–93.

26. Ibid., p. 139.

27. Ibid., p. 137.

28. Mirak, *Torn between Two Lands,* pp. 115–16.

29. Quoted by Mirak, *Torn between Two Lands,* pp. 117.

30. Personal narrative of Avedis Bedrosian.

31. Mirak, *Torn between Two Lands,* p. 119.

32. A. I. Bezzerides, *Thieves' Market* (New York: Charles Scribner's Sons, 1949), p. 166.

33. Richard Tracy La Piere, "The American Colony in Fresno County, California: A Study in Social Psychology," Ph.D. diss. Standford Univ., 1930, p. 329.

34. Ibid., p. 346.

35. Ibid., p. 408.

36. *Harvard Encyclopedia of American Ethnic Groups,* p. 139.

37. John Barsamian, "Ashod's Boarding House," *Ararat* 21 (spring 1980), p. 20. Reprinted with the permission of *Ararat,* a quarterly journal of arts and letters.

38. Marjorie Housepian, *A Houseful of Love* (New York: Random House, 1954), p. 124.

39. Mirak, *Torn between Two Lands,* p. 241.

40. *Harvard Encyclopedia of American Ethnic Groups,* p. 146.

41. Ibid.

42. Sonia Shiragian, "A Visit to Armenia," *The New Yorker* (April 27, 1963), p. 45.

43. Mirak, *Torn between Two Lands,* p. 183.

44. Quoted by Mirak, *Torn between Two Lands,* p. 191.

45. Ibid., p. 189.

46. Ibid., pp. 249–50.

47. Ibid., pp. 173–74.

48. Bedros Norehad, "The Press: Maybe That's What's Wrong with Them," *Ararat* 18 (winter 1977), p. 92. Reprinted with the permission of *Ararat,* a quarterly journal of arts and letters.

49. Mirak, *Torn between Two Lands,* p. 249. Partisan newspapers probably did more than any other force in the community to prepare for Archbishop Tourian's assassination, having sustained an extended attack on him for weeks before the tragedy.

50. Mardikian, *Song of America,* pp. 146–47.

51. Norehad, "The Press," p. 94.

52. Ibid.

53. Personal narrative of Avedis Bedrosian.

54. Mirak, *Torn between Two Lands,* p. 172.

55. Ibid., p. 140.

56. A. I. Bezzerides, "Dreamers," in *Three Worlds* (Boston: Hairenik Press, 1939), pp. 238–39.

57. Ibid., p. 239.

58. Shiragian, "A Visit to Armenia," p. 48.

59. Ibid., p. 46.

60. Mirak, *Torn between Two Lands,* p. 169.

61. Ibid., p. 170.

62. William Saroyan, "My Cousin Dikran," in *My Name Is Aram* (New York: Harcourt, Brace and Company, 1937), pp. 99–100.

63. Personal narrative of Avedis Bedrosian.

64. Ibid.

65. *Harvard Encyclopedia of American Ethnic Groups,* p. 142.

66. Ibid. Armenians now have the highest proportion of Ph.D.'s of any ethnic group.

67. Personal narrative of Ossana Kinossian.

68. Advice given me as I left for college.

69. Marjorie Housepian, "The Myth of the Melting Pot," *Ararat* 18 (winter 1977), p. 8. Reprinted with the permission of *Ararat,* a quarterly journal of arts and letters.

70. La Piere, "The Armenian Colony," pp. 81–82.

71. Raffi Arzoomanian, *The Moths,* in *Four Plays* (New York: Ararat Press, 1980), p. 187.

72. La Piere, "The Armenian Colony," p. 192.

73. Ibid., p. 193.

74. H. H. Kelikian, "Crossroads in Wasteland," *Ararat* 16 (summer 1975), p. 11. Reprinted with the permission of *Ararat,* a quarterly journal of arts and letters.

75. Ibid., p. 15.

76. Mardikian, *Song of Armenia,* p. 71.

77. Hapet Kharibian, "Home in Exile," *Ararat* 13 (autumn 1972), p. 6. Reprinted with the permission of *Ararat,* a quarterly journal of arts and letters.

78. La Piere, "The Armenian Colony," p. 251.

79. Ibid., p. 254.

80. Shahan Shahnour, *Retreat without Song,* ed. and trans. Mischa Kudian (London: Mashtots Press, 1982), p. 88.

81. M. Vartan Malcolm, *The Armenians in America* (Boston, 1919), p. 127.

82. Mardikian, *Song of Armenia,* p. 85.

83. La Piere, "The Armenian Colony," p. 239.

84. Ibid., p. 242.

85. Arlene Voski Avakian, "Armenian-American Women: The First Word. . . ." Working Paper for the Women and Ethnicity Project, Brown University, March 1983, p. 24.

86. Edward Dorian, "The Silk Tie," *Ararat* 4 (winter 1963), p. 21. Reprinted with the permission of *Ararat,* a quarterly journal of arts and letters.

87. Helene Pilibosian, "With the Bait of Bread," in *Carvings from an Heirloom: Oral History Poems* (Watertown, Mass.: Ohan Press, 1983), p. 49. Originally published in *Ararat* quarterly.

88. La Piere, "The Armenian Colony," p. 256–57.

89. Karl J. Kalfaian, "Juno in the Pine Ring," *Ararat* 16 (winter 1975), p. 2. Reprinted with the permission of *Ararat,* a quarterly journal of arts and letters.

90. Danielian, "Armenian Culture Identity," p. 192.

91. Michael M. J. Fischer, "Ethnicity and the Post-Modern Arts of Memory," in *Writing Culture,* ed. James Clifford and George E. Marcus (Berkeley: Univ. of California Press, 1986), p. 196.

92. Antranig Antreassian, "The Cup of Bitterness," in *The Cup of Bitterness and Other Stories,* trans. Jack Antreassian (New York: Ashod Press, 1979), p. 116.

93. Isha Upanishad, *The Upanishads,* trans. Swami Prabhavananda and Frederick Manchester (New York: New American Library, 1957), p. 28.

94. Leo Hamalian, "Unmaking It in America," *Ararat* 18 (winter 1977), p. 66. Reprinted with the permission of *Ararat,* a quarterly journal of arts and letters.

95. Ibid., p. 67.

96. See Walter Benjamin's essay, "The Storyteller: Reflections on the Works of Nikolai Leskov," in *Illuminations,* ed. Hannah Arendt (New York: Harcourt, Brace & World, 1968), pp. 83–110.

97. James Baloian, "Destiny," in *The Ararat Papers,* p. 25.

98. Personal narrative of Avedis Bedrosian.

99. Quoted by Mirak, *Torn between Two Lands,* p. 279.

100. Laura Kalpakian, "Reunion," *Ararat* 11 (spring 1980), p. 29. Reprinted with the permission of *Ararat,* a quarterly journal of arts and letters.

101. Michael Krekorian, "Avedis," in *Corridor: Fictions by Michael Krekorian* (New York: Ashod Press, 1989), p. 63.

102. Personal narrative of Avedis Bedrosian.

103. Leo Hamalian, "The Armenian in Fiction," in *Burn after Reading* (New York: Ararat Press, 1978), p. 57.

104. Ibid., pp. 87–93.

105. Housepian, *A Houseful of Love,* p. 126.

106. Ibid., pp. 201–2.

107. Leon Surmelian, "The American Writer of Armenian Birth," *Ararat* 15 (spring 1964), pp. 52–53. Reprinted with the permission of *Ararat,* a quarterly journal of arts and letters.

108. Harry Barba, "The Armenian Cowboy," *Ararat* 15 (autumn 1964), p. 24. Reprinted with the permission of *Ararat,* a quarterly journal of arts and letters.

109. Ibid., p. 30.

110. Shiragian, p. 44.

111. Leon Surmelian, "The Sombrero," *Ararat* 11 (spring 1980), p. 31. Reprinted with the permission of *Ararat,* a quarterly journal of arts and letters.

THE REVOLT FROM THE PAST

1. Robert Beverley, *The History and Present State of Virginia,* ed. Louis B. Wright (Chapel Hill: The University of North Carolina Press, 1974), p. 213.

2. William Bradford, "Of Plymouth Plantation," in *The American Puritans: Their Prose and Poetry,* ed. Perry Miller (Garden City, N.Y.: Anchor Books, 1956), p. 17.

3. Solomon Stoddard, "Concerning Ancestors," in Miller, ed., *The American Puritans,* p. 223.

4. Novak, *The Rise of the Unmeltable Ethnics,* p. 112.

5. Henry David Thoreau, *Walden,* ed. J. Lyndon Shanley (Princeton, N.J.: Princeton University Press, 1971), p. 98.

6. Henry David Thoreau, *A Week on the Concord and Merrimack Rivers,* ed. Carl J. Hovde (Princeton, N.J.: Princeton University Press, 1980), p. 55.

7. On the one hand, Hawthorne avoided too close a contact with the aboriginal forest and felt unequal to doing imaginative justice to his environment: "The page of life that was spread out before me seemed dull and commonplace, only because I had not fathomed its deeper import. A better book than I shall ever write was there; leaf after leaf presenting itself to me, just as it was written out by the reality of the flitting hours, and vanishing as fast as written, only because my brain wanted the insight and my hand the cunning to transcribe it." See "The Custom House" introduction to *The Scarlet Letter* (New York: Washington Square Press, Inc., 1966), p. 38. Yet Hawthorne did value the historical resonance of Salem where his family roots were. Earlier in "The Custom House," he writes of his affection for the town: "The settlement is probably assignable to the deep and aged roots which my family has struck into the soil . . . the mere sensuous sympathy of dust for dust. Few of my countrymen can know what it is; nor, as frequent transplantation is perhaps better for the stock, need they consider it desirable to know" (7). But through "transplantation is perhaps better for the stock," on balance Hawthorne's succeeding comments belie this sentiment:

> This long connection of a family with one spot, as its place of birth and burial, creates a kindred between the human being and the locality, quite independent of any charm in the scenery or moral circumstances that surround him. It is not love, but instinct. . . . It is no matter that the place is joyless for him; that he is weary of the old wooden houses, the mud and dust, the dead level of site and sentiment, the chill east wind the chillest of social atmospheres,—all these, and whatever faults besides he may see or imagine, are nothing to the purpose. The spell survives, and just as powerfully as if the natal spot were an earthly paradise. So it has been in my case. (9–10)

8. Herman Melville, *Moby Dick; or, The Whale,* ed. Charles Feidelson, Jr. (New York: The Bobbs-Merrill Company, Inc., 1964). p. 533. Subsequent references to this edition appear in the text.

9. Frank Norris, *McTeague* (Port Washington, N.Y.: Kennikat Press, Inc., 1967), p. 373.

10. Walter Benjamin, "The Storyteller," in *Illuminations* (New York: Harcourt, Brace and World, Inc., 1968), p. 96. This quotation is Benjamin's translation of a passage from a short story by Nikolai Leskov called "The Alexandrite."

11. W. H. Auden, from *In Time of War,* in *Chief Modern Poets of England and America,* vol. 1, ed. Gerald Dewitt Saunders, John Herbert Nelson, and M. L. Rosenthal, 4th ed. (New York: The Macmillan Company, 1962), p. 357.

12. T. S. Eliot, "Tradition and the Individual Talent," in *The Sacred Wood* (London: Methuen and Co., Ltd., 1960), p. 49. Ethnic writers, carrying and extending the traditions of their group, often come to the same conclusion as Eliot. Ralph Ellison thus says much the same thing in his discussion of black music in America: "Perhaps in the swift change of American society in which the meanings of one's origin are so quickly lost, one of the chief values of music lies in its power to give us an orientation in time. In doing so, it gives significance to all those indefinable aspects of experience which nevertheless help to make us what we are." See Ellison's "Living with Music," in *Shadow and Act* (New York: Vintage Books, 1972), p. 198.

13. Daniel Hoffman, "The American Hero: His Masquerade," in *Theories of American Literature,* ed. Donald M. Kartiganer and Malcolm A. Griffith (New York: The MacMillan Company, 1972), p. 230. As Hoffman argues, an American epic literature will only emerge when Americans recognize that "Prometheus chained to the rock is not only myth but reality, while the image of Davy Crockett striding over the hills, exempt from sacrifice for the price of sunlight in his pocket is our nation's self-defeating dream."

14. Norman Mailer, "The White Negro," in Kartiganer and Griffith, eds., *Theories of American Literature,* p. 287.

15. Ibid., p. 288.

16. Gary Snyder, "O Waters," in *Turtle Island* (New York: New Directions, 1974), p. 73. Copyright © 1974 by Gary Snyder. Reprinted by permission of New Directions Publishing Corp.

17. "Mother Earth: Her Whales," in Snyder, *Turtle Island,* pp. 47–49.

18. Walt Whitman, "Song of Myself," in *American Poetry and Poetics,* ed. Daniel G. Hoffman (New York: Anchor Books, 1962), p. 158.

19. Gordon D. Morgan, *America without Ethnicity* (Port Washington, N.Y.: Kennikat Press, 1981), p. 124.

20. See Arthur Mann, *The One and the Many* (Chicago: Univ. of Chicago Press, 1979).

21. Thomas Sowell, *Ethnic America* (New York: Basic Books, Inc., 1981), p. 285.

22. Wayne C. Miller, "Cultural Consciousness in a Multi-Cultural Society: The Uses of Literature," *MELUS Journal* 8 no. 3 (1981), p. 30.

23. Gordon, p. 124.

24. Marcus Klein, *Foreigners: The Making of American Literature* 1900–1940 (Chicago: Univ. of Chicago Press, 1981), p. 226.

25. Ibid., p. 288.

26. Werner Sollors, *Beyond Ethnicity: Consent and Descent in American Culture* (New York: Oxford Univ. Press, 1986), p. 31.

27. Ibid., p. 244.

28. Ibid.

29. Fischer, "Ethnicity and the Post-Modern Arts of Memory," in Clifford and Marcus, eds., *Writing Culture,* p. 196.

30. Ibid.

31. Ibid.

32. Edward Minasian, "The Armenian Immigrant Tide," in *Recent Studies in Modern Armenian History* (Cambridge, Mass.: Armenian Heritage Press, 1972), p. 110.

33. Vahé Oshagan, "The Theme of the Armenian Genocide in Diaspora Prose," *Armenian Review* 38, no. 1 (1985), pp. 52–53.

34. Harry Keyishian, "Between Worlds" *Ararat* 15 (summer 1964), p. 28. Reprinted with the permission of *Ararat,* a quarterly journal of arts and letters.

35. William Saroyan, *Here Comes, There Goes, You Know Who* (New York: Simon and Schuster, 1961), pp. 68–69.

36. Harold Bond, "The Welding Shop," in *The Northern Wall* (Boston: Northeastern University Press, 1969), p. 25.

37. Sollors, *Beyond Ethnicity,* p. 249.

38. Christopher Lasch, *The Culture of Narcissism* (New York: Norton, 1978), pp. 89–90.

39. Perhaps the most notable area that needs attention is the experience of Armenian-American women. Most of the writers who deal with Armenian-American experience are men, and though there are many sensitive portraits of women in their work, nowhere is there a sustained depiction of the unique challenges and traumas women of this ethnic group have had to face since the beginning of their history.

EMMANUEL VARANDYAN

1. Nona Balakian, "Writers on the American Scene," *Ararat* 18 (winter 1977), p. 21. Reprinted with the permission of *Ararat,* a quarterly journal of arts and letters.

2. See Vahé Oshagan, "The Literature of the Persian Armenians," *Ararat* 39 (summer 1979), pp. 28–36. Reprinted with the permission of *Ararat,* a quarterly journal of arts and letters.

3. Emmanuel Varandyan, *The Well of Ararat* (Garden City, N.Y.: Doubleday, Doran, and Co., 1938), p. 48. Subsequent references to this work appear in the text.

4. Balakian, "Writers on the American Scene," p. 21.

5. Maxwell Geismar, rev. of *The Well of Ararat, Booklist* (Jan. 9, 1938), p. 8.

6. Alfred Kazin, "A Tale of Persia," rev. of *The Well of Ararat, The New York Times Book Review* (Jan. 9, 1938), p. 7.

7. Courtlandt Canby, "Persian Wedding," rev. of *The Well of Ararat, The Saturday Review,* (Jan. 15, 1938), p. 7.

8. Balakian, "Writers on the American Scene," p. 22.

9. Emmanuel Varandyan, "Ahssadhur: The Gift of God," *Ararat* 1 (spring 1960), p. 8. Reprinted with the permission of *Ararat,* a quarterly journal of arts and letters. Subsequent references to this work appear in the text.

PETER SOURIAN

1. Balakian, "Writers on the American Scene," p. 20.

2. Peter Sourian, *Miri* (New York: Pantheon, 1957), p. 78. Subsequent references to this work appear in the text.

3. Nona Balakian, "Search for the Elusive Truth," rev. of *The Best and Worst of Times* by Peter Sourian, *Ararat* 2 (summer 1961), p. 58. Reprinted with the permission of *Ararat,* a quarterly journal of arts and letters.

4. Peter Sourian, *The Gate* (New York: Harcourt, Brace and World, 1965), p. 89. Subsequent references to this work appear in the text.

5. Lasch, *The Culture of Narcissism,* p. 88.

PETER NAJARIAN

1. Mark Malkasian, "Armenians in the United States: A Culture of Cowardliness," *The Armenian Mirror-Spectator* (September 1, 1984), p. 3.

2. Oshagan, "The Theme of the Armenian Genocide," p. 59.

3. Peter Najarian, *Voyages* (New York: Pantheon, 1971), p. 39. Subsequent references to this work appear in the text.

4. Peter Najarian, *Daughters of Memory* (n.p.: City Miner Books, 1986), p. 117. Subsequent references to this work appear in the text.

MICHAEL J. ARLEN

1. Michael J. Arlen, *The View from Highway 1* (New York: Farrar, Straus & Giroux, 1974), p. 9.

2. Michael J. Arlen, *Exiles* (New York: Farrar, Straus and Giroux, 1970), pp. 72–73. Subsequent references to this work appear in the text.

3. See Robert H. Hewsenian, "Short Day's Journey into Night," *Ararat,* no. 18 (1964), p. 48. Reprinted with the permission of *Ararat,* a quarterly journal of arts and letters.

4. Michael J. Arlen, *Passage to Ararat* (New York: Farrar, Straus and Giroux, 1975), p. 59. Subsequent references to this work appear in the text.

5. Peter Prescott, cited in *Contemporary Authors,* New Revision Series, 13 (Detroit: Gale Research Co., 1984), p. 26.

6. In arguing that there is more than one way to view the role of the massacres in Armenian life today, I am guided by Viktor Frankl's views in *Man's Search for Meaning* (New York: Simon and Schuster, 1962). A serious lack in studies of the Armenian massacres concerns the diversity of emotions and attitudes that survivors have experienced since 1915.

RICHARD HAGOPIAN

1. Richard Hagopian, *Faraway the Spring* (New York: Scribner, 1959), p. 201. Subsequent references to this work appear in the text.

2. Richard Hagopian, *Wine for the Living* (New York: Scribner, 1956), p. 61. Subsequent references to this work appear in the text.

3. Harry Keyishian, "Between Worlds," p. 31.

WILLIAM SAROYAN

1. William Saroyan, *Obituaries* (Berkeley, Calif.: Creative Arts Book Company, 1979), p. 330.

2. William Saroyan, "Antranik of Armenia," in *The Saroyan Special* (New York: Harcourt, Brace and Co., 1948), p. 83.

3. William Saroyan, *Rock Wagram* (Garden City, N.Y.: Doubleday and Company, 1951), p. 183. Subsequent references to this work appear in the text.

4. William Saroyan, *Here Comes, There Goes, You Know Who* (New York: Simon and Schuster, 1961), p. 3. Subsequent references to this work appear in the text.

5. William Saroyan, *My Name Is Aram* (New York: Harcourt, Brace and Co., 1940), pp. 203–4.

6. William Saroyan, "The Armenian and the Armenian," in *The Saroyan Special,* p. 128.

7. La Piere, "The Armenian Colony," p. 339.

8. William Saroyan, *The Time of Your Life* (New York: Harcourt, Brace and Co., 1939), p. 112.

9. The third mousetrap was the army.

10. William Saroyan, *The Assyrian,* in *The Assyrian and Other Stories* (New York: Harcourt, Brace and Company, 1950), p. 35. Subsequent references to this work appear in the text.

11. The character of Curti Urumiya is probably based on the Armenian multimillionaire, Calouste Gulbenkian, who also lived in Portugal.

12. According to Gifford and Lee in *Saroyan: A Biography,* Saroyan's mother did not take to his wife with the warmth he describes in *Rock Wagram.*

13. Rock's token reminds us of the shiny copper penny the hero of "The Daring Young Man on the Flying Trapeze" clutches before slipping into death. The penny with its clearly legible "In God We Trust" stands for the same duality that challenges Rock, the tension between hope and the disbelief that only a gamble on life can release.

14. William Saroyan, *The Laughing Matter* (Garden City, N.Y.: Doubleday, 1953), p. 73. Subsequent references to this work appear in the text.

15. Elizabeth Bowen, "In Spite of Words," *New Republic* 128 (March 9, 1953), p. 19.

16. Howard Floan, in *William Saroyan* (New York: Twayne, 1966), p. 44, comments that although Saroyan's subject and style are often naturalistic, his characters' immunity to environmental forces sets him apart from the mainstream of naturalism. But in *The Laughing Matter,* even this barrier falls as a malevolent chance catches up with Evan.

17. Aram Saroyan, "Daddy Dearest," *California* (July 1982), p. 87. Subsequent references to this article appear in the text. Aram Saroyan's biography of his father has subsequently been published as *Last Rites: The Death of William Saroyan* by William Morrow & Company.

18. John Brooks in a review of *Rock Wagram* spoke for many when he wrote, "[Saroyan's ruminations] are full of painfully obvious statements tediously and insistently repeated, full of self-contradiction and cancelings-out, full of the beery adoption of meaningless words as temporary pets—full in short of sloppy writing." *The Saturday Review* (March 24, 1951), p. 13.

19. This weakness in characterization was one Saroyan was aware of. Floan recounts an anecdote in which a friend brought Saroyan's social myopia to the author's attention, to which he replied: "I have been at work trying to correct this unfortunate condition, but I haven't made it. . . . I can't excuse it, I can't find an explanation for it, I know I do nothing rude deliberately" (*William Saroyan,* p. 150).

20. For example, Floan concludes his study by stating, "Instead of a literature of denial or of anger, [Saroyan's] is one of affirmation" (p. 155). But based on these three pieces of longer fiction, such an assertion has to be qualified.

21. William Saroyan, "The Death of Children," in *The Saroyan Special,* p. 73.

DIANA DER HOVANESSIAN

1. Diana Der Hovanessian, "The Bottonless Eye," in *How to Choose Your Past* (New York: Ararat Press, 1978), p. 5. Copyright Diana Der Hovanessian. Subsequent references to this work appear in the text.

2. Oshagan, "The Literature of the Persian Armenians," *Ararat* 20 (summer 1979), p. 36 (Supplement), footnote 12. Reprinted with the permission of *Ararat,* a quarterly journal of arts and letters.

Notes

DAVID KHERDIAN

1. David Kherdian, *Down at the Santa Fe Depot* (Fresno, Calif.: The Giligia Press, 1970), p. 68.

2. Ibid.

3. David Kherdian, "Dear Mrs. McKinney of the Sixth Grade," in *I Remember Root River* (Woodstock, N.Y.: The Overlook Press, 1978), pt. 2.

4. David Kherdian, "The Greek Popcorn Man," in *Homage to Adana* (Mount Horeb, Wis.: Perishable Press, 1970). Subsequent references to this work appear in the text.

5. David Kherdian, "S. G.," in *I Remember Root River,* pt. 2.

6. David Kherdian, "Sparrow," in *On the Death of My Father and Other Poems* (Fresno, Calif.: Giligia Press, 1970), pt. 1.

7. David Kherdian, "a poem for my father," in *Looking over Hills* (Lyme Center, N.H.: Giligia Press, 1972).

8. David Kherdian, "In the Tradition," in *Any Day of Your Life* (Woodstock, N.Y.: The Overlook Press, 1975). Subsequent references to this work appear in the text.

9. Kherdian, *Down at the Santa Fe Depot,* p. 69.

HAROLD BOND

1. *Contemporary Authors,* New Revision Series, 11 (Detroit: Gale Research Co., 1984), p. 79.

2. Harold Bond, "The Welding Shop," in *The Northern Wall* (Boston: Northeastern University Press, 1969), p. 25. Copyright © 1969 by Harold Bond. Reprinted with the permission of the author. Subsequent references to this work appear in the text.

3. Harold Bond, "Some Fool or Flower Lover," in *The Way It Happens to You* (New York: Ararat Press, 1979), p. 49. Copyright © 1979 by Harold Bond. Reprinted with the permission of the author. Subsequent references to this work appear in the text.

4. Harold Bond, "The Keys," in *Dancing on Water* (West Branch, Iowa: The Cummington Press, 1970), p. 31. Copyright © 1970 by Harold Bond. Reprinted with the permission of the author. Subsequent references to this work appear in the text.

5. Harold Bond, "Letter to an Aunt," in *Speaking for Ourselves: American Ethnic Writing,* ed. Lillian Faderman and Barbara Bradshaw (Glenview, Ill.: Scott, Foresman and Co., 1969, 1975), p. 618. Reprinted with the permission of Scott, Foresman and Co.

PETER BALAKIAN

1. Peter Balakian, "Arshile Gorky's Embroidered Apron," *The Agni Review* 26 (1988), p. 126.

2. Peter Balakian, *Father Fisheye* (New York: Sheep Meadow Press, 1979). Copyright Peter Balakian.

3. Peter Balakian, *Sad Days of Light* (New York: Sheep Meadow Press, 1983). Copyright Peter Balakian.

4. Peter Balakian, *Reply from Wilderness Island* (New York: Sheep Press). Copyright Peter Balakian.

5. Peter Balakian, "Physicians" (unpublished poem, 1990). Copyright 1990 Peter Balakian.

6. Peter Balakian, "The Oriental Rug," *Poetry* 2 (1985), pp. 78–85. Copyright Peter Balakian.

ARSHILE GORKY

1. Karlen Mooradian, ed., "The Letters of Arshile Gorky," p. 29. Subsequent references appear in the text.

2. Harry Rand, *Arshile Gorky: The Implications of Symbols* (Montclair, N.J.: Allanheid, Osmun and Co., 1980), pp. 3–4. Subsequent references to this work appear in the text.

3. See J. Hillis Miller, *The Poets of Reality* (New York: Atheneum, 1974), p. 9.

4. Karlen Mooradian, "The Man from Van," *Ararat* 11 (fall 1971), p. 7. Reprinted with the permission of *Ararat,* a quarterly journal of arts and letters.

5. Ibid., p. 2.

6. Vartoosh Mooradian, interview with Karlen Mooradian, *Ararat* 11 (fall 1971). Reprinted with the permission of *Ararat,* a quarterly journal of arts and letters.

7. Rand argues that the retreating feminine figure in the Connecticut landscape of *Waterfall* signals Gorky's growing ease in the countryside of his adopted land (*Arshile Gorky,* p. 96).

8. Sollors, *Beyond Ethnicity,* p. 247.

9. Karlen Mooradian, *Arshile Gorky Adoian* (Chicago: Gilgamesh Press, Ltd., 1978). pp. 184–85.

10. Arshile Gorky, "Toward a Philosophy of Art," trans. Karlen Mooradian, in *Arshile Gorky: Drawings to Paintings,* p. 36.

11. Cited by Rand, *Arshile Gorky,* p. 111.

12. Quoted by Aniela Jaffé in "Symbolism in the Visual Arts," in *Man and His Symbols,* ed. Carl G. Jung (New York: Dell Publishing, 1968), p. 292.

13. Quoted by Melvin P. Lader, *Arshile Gorky* (New York: Abbeville Press, 1985), p. 82.

14. Ethel Schwabacher, "Further Thoughts on Gorky," in Mooradian, trans., *Arshile Gorky: Drawings to Paintings* (exhibition catalog), p. 89.

15. Nora Nercessian, "The Defeat of Arshile Gorky," *Armenian Review* 36, no. 1 (1983), p. 97.

16. Karlen Mooradian, *The Many Worlds of Arshile Gorky* (Chicago: Gilgamesh Press, 1980), p. 313.

17. Jaffé, "Symbolism in the Visual Arts," p. 297.

18. Lader, *Arshile Gorky,* p. 98.

19. Mooradian, *The Many Worlds of Arshile Gorky,* p. 207.

20. As a result, when Rand cites the "concrete" cubism of Max Weber and Gorky's "uncelebrated" friendship with him, it is hard to say how formative Weber's and American art's "literalness" were on Gorky, for this same quality pervades Armenian art. See Rand, *Arshile Gorky,* p. 135.

21. As a side note, Rand observes that Jackson Pollock, whose work represents the "other early achievement of Abstract Expressionism," may well have shifted the direction of his art after viewing an exhibition of Gorky's last paintings: "Soon after seeing the Gorky show Pollock returned to painting the figure, and from 1951 until the time of his death five years later, it may be argued he never abandoned it" (Rand, *Arshile Gorky,* p. 217).

EPILOGUE

1. Harold Bond, "The Bag of Tricks," in *The Northern Wall,* p. 22.

BIBLIOGRAPHY

Anthology of Armenian Poetry. Trans. and ed. Diana Der Hovanessian and Marzbed Margossian. New York: Columbia University Press, 1978.

Antreassian, Antranig. *The Cup of Bitterness and Other Stories*. Trans. Jack Antreassian. New York: Ashod Press, 1979.

Ararat: A Decade of Armenian-American Writing. Ed. Jack Antreassian. New York: Press of the Armenian General Benevolent Union, 1969.

Arlen, Michael J. *Exiles*. New York: Farrar, Straus & Giroux, 1970.

———. *Passage to Ararat*. New York: Farrar, Straus & Girox, 1975.

———. *The View from Highway 1*. New York: Farrar, Straus & Giroux, 1974.

Armenian-American Poets: A Bilingual Anthology. Comp. and trans. Garig Basmadjian. Detroit: Alex Manoogian Cultural Fund of the AGBU, 1976.

Arzoomanian, Raffi. *Ellis Island 101*. *Ararat,* no. 38 (1969), pp. 10–13.

———. *The Moths*. In *Four Plays*. New York: Ararat Press, 1980.

Avakian, Arlene Voski. "Armenian-American Women: The First World . . ." Working Paper for Women and Ethnicity Project, Brown University, March 1983.

Avakian, Arra S. *The Armenians in America*. Minneapolis: Lerner Publications Company, 1977.

Balakian, Nona. "Writers on the American Scene." *Ararat,* no. 69 (1977), pp. 15–25.

Balakian, Peter. "Arshile Gorky's Embroidered Apron." *The Agni Review* 26 (1988), pp. 123–26.

———. *Father Fisheye*. New York: The Sheep Meadow Press, 1979.

———. "The Oriental Rug." *Poetry* 2 (1985), pp. 78–85.

———. "Physicians." Unpublished poem, 1989.

———. *Reply from Wilderness Island*. New York: The Sheep Meadow Press, 1988.

———. *Sad Days of Light*. New York: The Sheep Meadow Press, 1983.

Bibliography

Baloian, James. "Arriving in the New World" and "Destiny." In *The Ararat Papers*. New York: Ararat Press, 1979.

Barba, Harry. "The Armenian Cowboy." *Ararat,* no. 19 (1964), pp. 22–30.

Barsamian, John. "Ashod's Boarding House." *Ararat,* no. 82 (1980), pp. 14–22.

Bedrosian, Avedis. Personal interviews. December 1980 to August 1985.

Benjamin, Walter, "The Storyteller." In *Illuminations*. New York: Harcourt, Brace and World, Inc., 1968.

Beverley, Robert. *The History and Present State of Virginia*. Ed. Louis B. Wright. Chapel Hill, N.C.: The University of North Carolina Press, 1974.

Bezzerides, A. I. "Dreamers." In *Three Worlds*. Boston: Hairenik Press, 1939, pp. 237–41.

———. *Thieves' Market*. New York: Charles Scribner's Sons, 1949.

Bond, Harold. *Dancing on Water*. West Branch, Iowa: The Cummington Press, 1970.

———. *The Northern Wall*. Boston: Northeastern University Press, 1969.

———. *The Way It Happens to You*. New York: Ararat Press, 1979.

Bowen, Elizabeth. "In Spite of Words." Rev. of *The Laughing Matter,* by William Saroyan. *New Republic* (March 9, 1953), p. 19.

Bradford, William. "Of Plymouth Plantation." In *The American Puritans: Their Prose and Poetry*. Ed. Perry Miller. Garden City, N.Y.: Anchor Books, 1956.

Brooks, John. Rev. of *Rock Wagram,* by William Saroyan. The Saturday Review (March 24, 1951), p. 13.

Canby, Courtlandt. "Persian Wedding." Rev. of *The Well of Ararat,* by Emmanuel Varandyan. *The Saturday Review* (Jan. 15, 1938), p. 7.

Danielian, Jack. "Armenian Cultural Identity: Problems in Western Definition." In *Recent Studies in Modern Armenian History*. National Association for Armenian Studies and Research, Inc. Cambridge, Mass.: Armenian Heritage, 1972.

Der Hovanessian, Diana. *How to Choose Your Past*. New York: Ararat Press, 1978.

Der Nersessian, Sirarpie. *Armenia and the Byzantine Empire*. Cambridge, Mass.: Harvard Univ. Press, 1945.

———. *The Armenians*. New York: Praeger Publishers, 1970.

Dorian, Edward. "The Silk Tie." *Ararat,* no. 13 (winter 1963), pp. 18–24.

Eliot, T. S. "Tradition and the Individual Talent." In *The Sacred Wood*. London: Methuen and Co., Ltd., 1960.

Elisaeus. *History of Vartan*. Trans. C. F. Neumann. London: The Oriental Translation Fund, 1830.

Fischer, Michael M. J. "Ethnicity and the Post-Modern Arts of Memory." In *Writing Culture*. Ed. James Clifford and George E. Marcus. Berkeley: University of California Press, 1986, pp. 194–233.

Floan, Howard. *William Saroyan*. New York: Twayne, 1966.

Geismar, Maxwell. Rev. of *The Well of Ararat,* by Emmanuel Varandyan. *Booklist* (Jan. 9, 1938), p. 8.

Gifford, Barry, and Lawrence Lee. *Saroyan: A Biography*. New York: Harper & Row, 1984.

Hagopian, Richard. *The Dove Brings Peace*. New York: Farrar & Rinehart, Inc., 1944.

———. *Faraway the Spring*. New York: Scribner, 1952.

———. *Wine for the Living*. New York: Scribner, 1956.

Hamalian, Leo. "The Armenian in Fiction." In *Burn after Reading*. New York: AGBU, 1978, pp. 50–70.

———. "Unmaking It in America." *Ararat,* no. 69 (winter 1977), pp. 66–67.

Bibliography

Handlin, Oscar. *The Uprooted*. Boston: Little, Brown and Company, 1973.

Harvard Encyclopedia of American Ethnic Groups. Cambridge, Mass.: Harvard University Press, 1980.

Hawthorne, Nathaniel. *The Scarlet Letter*. New York: Washington Press Inc., 1966.

Hewsenian, Robert H. "Short Day's Journey into Night." *Ararat,* no. 18 (spring 1964), pp. 45–48.

Hoffman, Daniel, "The American Hero: His Masquerade." In *Theories of American Literature*. Ed. Donald M. Kartiganer and Malcolm A. Griffith. New York: MacMillan, 1972, pp. 196–232.

Housepian, Marjorie. *A Houseful of Love*. New York: Random House, 1957.

"Isha Upanishad." In *The Upanishads*. Trans. Swami Prabhavananda and Frederick Manchester. New York: New American Library, 1957.

Jaffé, Aniela. "Symbolism in the Visual Arts." *Man and His Symbols*. Ed. Carl G. Jung. New York: Dell Publishing, 1968, pp. 255–322.

Kalfaian, Karl J. "Juno in the Pine Ring." *Ararat,* no. 61 (winter 1975), pp. 2–11.

Kalpakian, Laura. "The Land of Lucky Strike." *Ararat,* no. 78 (spring 1979), 12–19.

———. "The Reunion." *Ararat,* no. 82 (spring 1980), pp. 26–29.

Kazin, Alfred. "A Tale of Persia." Rev. of *The Well of Ararat,* by Emmanuel Varandyan. *The New York Times Book Review* (Jan. 9, 1938), p. 7.

Keen, Sam. "Stories We Live By." *Psychology Today* (December 1988), pp. 44–47.

Kelikian, H. H. "Crossroads in Wasteland." *Ararat,* no. 63 (summer 1975), pp. 10–15.

Keyishian, Harry. "Between Worlds." *Ararat,* no. 19 (summer 1964), pp. 27–31.

Kharibian, Hapet. "Home in Exile." *Ararat,* no. 13 (autumn 1972), pp. 3–8.

Kherdian, David. *Any Day of Your Life*. Woodstock, N.Y.: The Overlook Press, 1975.

———, ed. *Down at the Santa Fe Depot*. Fresno, Calif.: The Giligia Press, 1970.

———. *Homage to Adana*. Mount Horeb, Wis.: Perishable Press, 1970.

———. *I Remember Root River*. Woodstock, N.Y.: The Overlook Press, 1978.

———. *The Nonny Poems*. New York: MacMillan, 1974.

———. *On the Death of My Father*. Fresno, Calif.: Giligia Press, 1968.

Kingston, Maxine Hong. *The Woman Warrior*. New York: Vintage Books, 1977.

Klein, Marcus. *Foreigners: The Making of American Literature 1900–1940*. Chicago: University of Chicago Press, 1981.

Krekorian, Michael. "Avedis." *Corridor: Fictions by Michael Krekorian*. New York: Ashod Press, 1989.

Kurkjian, Vahan M. *A History of Armenia*. New York: Press of the Armenian General Benevolent Union, 1958.

Lader, Melvin P. *Arshile Gorky*. New York: Abbeville Press, 1985.

Lang, David Marshall. *Armenia: Cradle of Civilization*. 3d. ed. London: George Allen & Unwin.

La Piere, Richard Tracy. "The Armenian Colony in Fresno County, California." Ph.D. Diss. Stanford, 1930.

Lasch, Christopher. *The Culture of Narcissism*. New York: Norton: 1978.

Mailer, Norman. "The White Negro." In *Theories of American Literature*. Ed. Donald M. Kartiganer and Malcolm A. Griffith. New York: MacMillan, 1972, pp. 274–94.

Malcolm, M. Vartan. *The Armenians in America*. Boston, 1919.

Mann, Arthur. *The One and the Many: Reflections on the American Identity*. Chicago: University of Chicago Press, 1979.

———, ed. *Immigrants in Americaxn Life*. Boston: Houghton Mifflin Company, 1974.

Mardikian, George. *Song of America*. New York: McGraw Hill, 1956.

Melville, Herman. *Moby Dick; or, The Whale*. Ed. Charles Feidelson, Jr. New York: The Bobbs-Merrill Company, 1964.

Miller, J. Hillis. *Poets of Reality*. New York: Atheneum, 1974.

Miller, Wayne C. "Cultural Consciousness in a Multi-Cultural Society: The Uses of Literature." *MELUS Journal* 8, no. 3 (1981), pp. 29–44.

Minasian, Edward. "The Armenian Immigrant Tide." In *Recent Studies in Modern Armenian History*. Cambridge, Mass.: Armenian Heritage Press, 1972.

Mirak, Robert. *Torn between Two Lands: Armenians in America, 1890 to World War I*. Cambridge, Mass.: Harvard Univ. Press, 1983.

Mooradian, Karlen. *Arshile Gorky Adoian*. Chicago: Gilgamesh Press Ltd., 1978.

———, ed. "The Letters of Arshile Gorky." *Ararat*, no. 48 (autumn 1971), pp. 19–43.

———. *The Many Worlds of Arshile Gorky*. Chicago: Gilgamesh Press, 1980.

Mooradian, Vartoosh. Personal interview with Karlen Mooradian. *Ararat*, no. 48 (autumn 1971), pp. 10–19.

Morgan, Gordon D. *America without Ethnicity*. Port Washington, N.Y.: Kennikat Press, 1981.

Najarian, Peter. *Daughters of Memory*, n.p.: City Miner Books, 1986.

———. *Voyages*. New York: Pantheon Books, 1971.

Nercessian, Nora. "The Defeat of Arshile Gorky." *Armenian Review* 36, no. 1 (1983), pp. 89–99.

Norehad, Bedros. "The Press: Maybe That's What's Wrong with Them." *Ararat*, no. 69 (winter 1977), pp. 92–97.

Norris, Frank. *McTeague*. Port Washington, N.Y.: Kennikat Press, 1967.

Novak, Michael. *The Rise of the Unmeltable Ethnics*. New York: Macmillan, 1972.

Oshagan, Vahé. "The Literature of the Persian Armenians." In *Ararat*, no. 39 (summer 1979), pp. 28–36.

———. "The Theme of the Armenian Genocide in Diaspora Prose." In *Armenian Review* 38, no. 1 (1985), pp. 50–60.

Pilibosian, Helene. "With the Bait of Bread." In *Carvings from an Heirloom: Oral History Poems*. Watertown, Mass.: Ohan Press, 1983, p. 49.

Piotrovsky, Boris B. *Urartu*. Trans. James Hogarth. London: The Cresset Press, 1969.

Rand, Harry. *Arshile Gorky: The Implications of Symbols*. Montclair, N.J.: Allanheid, Osmun & Co., 1980.

Sanjian, Avedis K., ed. *Colophons of Armenian Manuscripts, 1301–1480*. Cambridge, Mass.: Harvard Univ. Press, 1969.

Saroyan, Aram. "Daddy Dearest." *California* (July 1982), pp. 84–87, 118–20.

Saroyan, William. *The Assyrian*. In *The Assyrian and Other Stories*. New York: Harcourt, Brace and Company, 1950.

———. *Here Comes, There Goes, You Know Who*. New York: Simon and Schuster, 1961.

———. *The Laughing Matter*. Garden City, N.Y.: Doubleday, 1953.

———. *My Name Is Aram*. New York: Harcourt, Brace and Company, 1940.

———. *Obituaries*. Berkeley, Calif.: Creative Arts Book Company, 1979.

———. *Rock Wagram*. Garden City, N.Y.: Doubleday & Company, 1951.

———. *The Saroyan Special*. New York: Harcourt, Brace and Company, 1948.

———. *The Time of Your Life*. New York: Harcourt, Brace and Company, 1939.

Schwabacher, Ethel. "Further Thoughts on Gorky." *Arshile Gorky: Drawings to Paintings*. Exhibition catalog, pp. 87–90.

Shahnour, Shahan. *Retreat without Song*. Ed. and trans. Mischa Kudian. London: Mashtots Press, 1982.

Shiragian, Sonia. "A Visit to Armenia." *The New Yorker* (April 21, 1963), pp. 44–48.

Snyder, Gary. *Turtle Island*. New York: New Directions, 1974.

Sollors, Werner. *Beyond Ethnicity: Consent and Descent in American Culture*. New York: Oxford Univ. Press, 1986.

Sourian, Peter. *The Gate*. New York: Harcourt, Brace and World, 1965.

———. *Miri*. New York: Pantheon, 1957.

Sowell, Thomas. *Ethnic America: A History*. New York: Basic Books, Inc., 1981.

Surmelian, Leon, trans. *Daredevils of Sassoun: The Armenian National Epic*. Denver: Alan Swallow: 1964.

———. "The Sombrero." *Ararat,* no. 82 (spring 1980), pp. 30–33.

Tatarian, Virginia. "Photograph of Five Ancestors." In *Speaking for Ourselves*. Ed. Lillian Faderman and Barbara Bradshaw. Glenview, Ill.: Scott, Foresman and Company, 1975, p. 613.

Terzian, James P. "The Return of Johnny Calendar." *Ararat*. no. 10 (spring 1962), pp. 2–13.

Thomson, R. W., trans. *History of the Armenians*. By Agathangelos. Albany: State University of New York Press, 1970.

Thoreau, Henry David. *Walden*. Ed. J. Lyndon Shanley. Princeton, N.J.: Princeton Univ. Press, 1971.

———. *A Week on the Concord and Merrimack Rivers*. Ed. Carl J. Hovde. Princeton, N.J.: Princeton Univ. Press, 1980.

Varandyan, Emmanuel. "Ahssadur: The Gift of God." *Ararat,* no. 1 (spring 1960), pp. 6–10.

———. *The Well of Ararat*. Garden City, N.Y.: Doubleday, Doran & Company, 1938.

Vucinich, Wayne S. *The Ottoman Empire: Its Record and Legacy*. Princeton, N.J.: D. Van Nostrand Inc., 1965.

Whitman, Walt. "Song of Myself." In *American Poetry and Poetics*. Ed. Daniel G. Hoffman. New York: Anchor Books, 1962.

Xenophon. *The March of the Ten Thousand*. Trans. H. G. Dakyns. London: MacMillan and Company, 1901.

INDEX

Index